THE VANISHED POMPS OF YESTERDAY

Some Ran

B

LORD FREDERIC HAMILTON

Author of "Here, There and Everywhere," "The Days Before Yesterday," etc., etc.

A New and Revised Edition

NEW YORK

GEORGE H. DORAN COMPANY

PRINTED IN THE UNITED STATES OF AMERICA

THE VANISHED POMPS OF YESTERDAY

TO

EMILY LADY AMPTHILL

MY FIRST CHEFESSE

WITH EVER-GRATEFUL RECOLLECTIONS

OF HER KINDNESS

FOREWORD

TO THE SECOND EDITION

The account of the boating accident at Potsdam on page 73, differs in several particulars from the story as given in the original edition. These alterations have been made at the special request of the lady concerned, who tells me that my recollections of her story were at fault as regards several important details. There are also a few verbal alterations in the present edition.

CONTENTS

CHAPTER I

CHAPTER II

CHAPTER III

CHAPTER VI

CHAPTER VII

CHAPTER VIII

THE VANISHED POMPS OF YESTERDAY

"Lo, all our Pomp of Yesterday
Is one with Ninevah and Tyre!"

—RUDYARD KIPLING

THE VANISHED POMPS OF YESTERDAY

CHAPTER I

Special Mission to Rome—Berlin in process of transformation—Causes of Prussian militarism—Lord and Lady Ampthill—Berlin Society—Music-lovers—Evenings with Wagner—Aristocratic Waitresses—Rubinstein's rag-time—Liszt's opinions—Bismarck—Bismarck's classification of nationalities—Bismarck's sons—Gustav Richter—The Austrian diplomat—The old Emperor—His defective articulation—Other Royalties—Beauty of Berlin Palace—Description of interior—The Luxembourg—" Napoleon III "—Three Court beauties—The pugnacious Pages—" Making the Circle "—Conversational difficulties—An ecclesiastical gourmet—The Maharajah's mother.

THE tremendous series of events which has changed the face of Europe since 1914 is so vast in its future possibilities, that certain minor consequences of the great upheaval have received but scant notice.

Amongst these minor consequences must be included the disappearance of the Courts of the three Empires of Eastern Europe, Russia, Germany, and Austria, with all their glitter and pageantry, their pomp and brilliant *mise-en-scène*. I will hazard no opinion as to whether the world is the better for their loss or not; I cannot, though, help experiencing a feeling of regret that this prosaic, drab-coloured twentieth century should have definitely lost so strong an element of the picturesque, and should have permanently severed a link which bound it to the traditions of the mediæval days of chivalry and romance, with their glowing colour, their splendid spectacular displays, and the feeling of continuity with a vanished past which they inspired.

A tweed suit and a bowler hat are doubtless more practical for everyday wear than a doublet and trunk-hose. They are, however, possibly less picturesque.

Since, owing to various circumstances, I happen from my very early days to have seen more of this brave show than has fallen to the lot of most people, some extracts from my diaries, and a few personal reminiscences of the three great Courts of Eastern Europe, may prove of interest.

Up to my twentieth year I was familiar only with our own Court. I was then sent to Rome with a Special Mission. As King Victor Emmanuel had but recently died, there were naturally no Court entertainments.

The Quirinal is a fine palace with great stately rooms, but it struck me then, no doubt erroneously, that the Italian Court did not yet seem quite at home in their new surroundings, and that there was a subtle feeling in the air of a lack of continuity somewhere. In the "'seventies" the House of Savoy had only been established for a very few years in their new capital. The conditions in Rome had changed radically, and somehow one felt conscious of this.

Some ten months later, the ordeal of a competitive examination being successfully surmounted, I was sent to Berlin as Attaché, at the age of twenty.

The Berlin of the " 'seventies " was still in a state of transition. The well-built, prim, dull and somewhat provincial *Residenz* was endeavouring with feverish energy to transform itself into a World-City, a *Welt-Stadt*. The people were still flushed and intoxicated with victory after victory. In the seven years between 1864 and 1871 Prussia had waged three successful campaigns. The first, in conjunction with Austria, against unhappy little Denmark in 1864; then followed, in 1866, the " Seven Weeks' War," in which Austria was speedily brought to her knees by the crushing defeat of Königgrätz, or Sadowa, as it is variously called, by which Prussia not only wrested the hegemony of the German Confederation from her hundred-year-old rival, but definitely excluded Austria from the Confederation itself. The Hohenzollerns had at length supplanted the proud House of Hapsburg. Prussia had further virtually conquered France in the first six weeks of the 1870 campaign, and on the conclusion of peace found herself the richer by Alsace, half of Lorraine, and the gigantic war indemnity wrung from France. As a climax the King of Prussia had, with the consent of the feudatory princes, been proclaimed German Emperor at Versailles on January 18, 1871, for Bismarck, with all his diplomacy, was unable to persuade the feudatory kings and princes to acquiesce in the title of Emperor *of* Germany for the Prussian King.

The new Emperor was nominally only *primus inter pares;* he was not to be over-lord. Theoretically the crown of Charlemagne was merely revived, but the result was that henceforth Prussia would dominate Germany. This was a sufficient rise for the little State which had started so modestly in the sandy Mark of Brandenburg (the "sand-box," as South Germans contemptuously termed it) in the fifteenth century. To understand the mentality of Prussians, one must realise that Prussia is the only country *that always made war pay.* She had risen with marvellous rapidity from her humble beginnings entirely by the power of the sword. Every campaign had increased her territory, her wealth, and her influence, and the entire energies of the Hohenzollern dynasty had been centred on increasing the might of her army. The Teutonic Knights had wrested East Prussia from the Wends by the Power of the sword only. They had converted the Wends to Christianity by annihilating them, and the Prussians inherited the traditions of the Teutonic Knights. Napoleon, it is true, had crushed Prussia at Jena, but the latter half of the nineteenth century was one uninterrupted triumphal progress for her. No wonder then that every Prussian looked upon warfare as a business proposition, and an exceedingly paying one at that. Everything about them had been carefully arranged to foster the same idea. All the monuments in the Berlin streets were to military heroes. The marble groups on the Schloss-Brücke represented episodes in the life of a warrior. The very songs taught the children in the schools were all militarist in tone: "The Good Comrade," "The Soldier," "The Young Recruit," "The Prayer during Battle," all familiar to every German child. When William II, ex-Emperor, found the stately "White Hall" of the Palace insufficiently gorgeous to accord with his megalomania, he called in the architect Ihne, and gave directions for a new frieze round the hall representing "victorious warfare fostering art, science, trade and industry." I imagine that William in his Dutch retreat at Amerongen may occasionally reflect on the consequences of warfare when it is *not* victorious. Trained in such an atmosphere from their childhood, drinking in militarism with their earliest breath, can it be wondered at that Prussians worshipped brute-force, and brute-force alone?

Such a nation of heroes must clearly have a capital worthy of them, a capital second to none, a capital eclipsing Paris and Vienna. Berliners had always been jealous of Vienna, the traditional "Kaiser-Stadt." Now Berlin was also a "Kaiser-Stadt," and by the magnificence of its buildings must throw its older rival completely into the shade. Paris, too, was the acknowledged centre of European art, literature, and fashion. Why? The French had proved themselves a nation of decadents, utterly unable to cope with German might. The sceptre of Paris should be transferred to Berlin. So building and renovation began at a feverish rate.

The open drains which formerly ran down every street in Berlin, screaming aloud to Heaven during the summer months, were abolished, and an admirable system of main drainage inaugurated. The appalling rough cobble-stones, which made it painful even to cross a Berlin street, were torn up and hastily replaced with asphalte. A French colleague of mine used to pretend that the cobble-stones had been designedly chosen as pavement. Berliners were somewhat touchy about the very sparse traffic in their wide streets. Now one solitary *droschke,* rumbling heavily over these cobble-stones, produced such a deafening din that the foreigner was deluded into thinking that the Berlin traffic rivalled that of London or Paris in its density.

Berlin is of too recent growth to have any elements of the picturesque about it. It stands on perfectly flat ground, and its long, straight streets are terribly wearisome to the eye. Miles and miles of ornate stucco are apt to become monotonous, even if decorated with porcelain plaques, glass mosaics, and other incongruous details dear to the garish soul of the Berliner. In their rage for modernity, the Municipality destroyed the one architectural feature of the town. Some remaining eighteenth century houses had a local peculiarity. The front doors were on the first floor, and were approached by two steeply inclined planes, locally known as *die*

Rampe. A carriage (with, I imagine, infinite discomfort to the horses) could just struggle up one of these *Rampe,* deposit its load, and crawl down again to the street-level. These inclined planes were nearly all swept away. The *Rampe* may have been inconvenient, but they were individual, local and picturesque.

I arrived at the age of twenty at this Berlin in active process of ultra-modernising itself, and in one respect I was most fortunate.

The then British Ambassador, one of the very ablest men the English Diplomatic Service has ever possessed, and his wife, Lady Ampthill, occupied a quite exceptional position. Lord Ampthill was a really close and trusted friend of Bismarck, who had great faith in his prescience and in his ability to gauge the probable trend of events, and he was also immensely liked by the old Emperor William, who had implicit confidence in him. Under a light and debonair manner the Ambassador concealed a tremendous reserve of dignity. He was a man, too, of quick decisions and great strength of character. Lady Ampthill was a woman of exceptional charm and quick intelligence, with the social gift developed to its highest point in her. Both the Ambassador and his wife spoke French, German, and Italian as easily and as correctly as they did English. The Ambassador was the *doyen,* or senior member, of the Diplomatic Body, and Lady Ampthill was the most intimate friend of the Crown Princess, afterwards the Empress Frederick.

From these varied circumstances, and also from sheer force of character, Lady Ampthill had become the unchallenged social arbitress of Berlin, a position never before conceded to any foreigner. As the French phrase runs, "*Elle faisait la pluie et le beau temps à Berlin.*"

To a boy of twenty life is very pleasant, and the novel surroundings and new faces amused me. People were most kind to me, but I soon made the discovery that many others had made before me, that at the end of two years one knows Prussians no better than one did at the end of the first fortnight; that there was some indefinable, intangible barrier between them and the foreigner that nothing could surmount. It was not long, too, before I became conscious of the under-current of intense hostility to my own country prevailing amongst the "Court Party," or what would now be termed the "Junker" Party. These people looked upon Russia as their ideal of a Monarchy. The Emperor of Russia was an acknowledged autocrat; the British Sovereign a constitutional monarch, or, if the term be preferred, more or less a figure-head. Tempering their admiration of Russia was a barely-concealed dread of the potential resources of that mighty Empire, whose military power was at that period absurdly overestimated. England did not claim to be a military State, and in the "'seventies" the vital importance of sea-power was not yet understood. British statesmen, too, had an unfortunate habit of indulging in sloppy sentimentalities in their speeches, and the convinced believers in "Practical Politics" (*Real Politik*) had a profound contempt (I guard myself from saying an unfounded one) for sloppiness as well as for sentimentality.

The Berliners of the "'seventies" had not acquired what the French term *l'art de vivre*. Prussia, during her rapid evolution from an insignificant sandy little principality into the leading military State of Europe, had to practise the most rigid economy. From the Royal Family downwards, everyone had perforce to live with the greatest frugality, and the traces of this remained. The "art of living" as practised in France, England, and even in Austria during the seventeenth and eighteenth centuries was impossible in Prussia under the straitened conditions prevailing there, and it is not an art to be learnt in a day. The small dinner-party, the gathering together of a few congenial friends, was unknown in Berlin. Local magnates gave occasionally great dinner-parties of thirty guests or so, at the grotesque hour of 5 p.m. It seemed almost immoral to array oneself in a white tie and swallow-tail coat at four in the afternoon. The dinners on these occasions were all sent in from the big restaurants, and there was no display of plate, and never a single flower. As a German friend (probably a fervent believer in "Practical Politics") said to me, "The best ornament of a dinner-table is also good food"; nor did the conversation atone by its brilliancy for the lack of the dainty trimmings which the taste of Western Europe expects on these occasions. A never-failing topic of conversation was to guess the particular restaurant which had furnished the banquet. One connoisseur would pretend to detect "Hiller" in the soup; another was convinced that the fish could only have been dressed by "Poppenberg." As soon as we had swallowed our coffee, we were expected to make our bows and take our leave without any post-prandial conversation whatever, and at 7 p.m. too!

Thirty people were gathered together to eat, *weiter nichts,* and, to do them justice, most of them fulfilled admirably the object with which they had been invited. The houses, too, were so ugly. No *objets d'art,* no personal belongings whatever, and no flowers. The rooms might have been in an hotel, and the occupant of the rooms might have arrived overnight with one small modest suit-case as his, or her, sole baggage. There was no individuality whatever about the ordinary Berlin house, or *appartement.*

I can never remember having heard literature discussed in any form whatever at Berlin. For some reason the novelist has never taken root in Germany. The number of good German novelists could be counted on the fingers of both hands, and no one seemed interested in literary topics. It was otherwise with music. Every German is a genuine music-lover, and the greatest music-lover of them all was Baroness von Schleinitz, wife of the Minister of the Royal Household. Hers was a charming house, the stately eighteenth century *Haus-Ministerium*, with its ornate rococo *Fest-Saal*. In that somewhat over-decorated hall every great musician in Europe must have played at some time or other. Baron von Schleinitz was, I think, the handsomest old man I have ever seen, with delightful old-world manners. It was a privilege to be asked to Madame de Schleinitz's musical evenings. She seldom asked more than forty people, and the most rigid silence was insisted upon; still every noted musician passing through Berlin went to her house as a matter of course. At the time of my arrival from England, Madame de Schleinitz had struck up a great alliance with Wagner, and gave two musical evenings a week as a sort of propaganda, in order to familiarise Berlin amateurs with the music of the "Ring." At that time the stupendous Tetralogy had only been given at Bayreuth and in Munich; indeed I am not sure that it had then been performed in its entirety in the Bavarian capital.

In the *Fest-Saal*, with its involved and tortured rococo curves, two grand pianos were placed side by side, a point Wagner insisted upon, and here the Master played us his gigantic work. The way Wagner managed to make the piano suggest brass, strings, or wood-wind at will was really wonderful. I think that we were all a little puzzled by the music of the "Ring"; possibly our ears had not then been sufficiently trained to grasp the amazing beauty of such a subtle web of harmonies. His playing finished, a small, very plainly-appointed supper-table was placed in the middle of the *Fest-Saal,* at which Wagner seated himself alone in state.

Then the long-wished-for moment began for his feminine adorers. The great ladies of Berlin would allow no one to wait on the Master but themselves, and the bearers of the oldest and proudest names in Prussia bustled about with prodigious fussing, carrying plates of sauerkraut, liver sausage, black puddings, and herring-salad, colliding with each other, but in spite of that managing to heap the supper-table with more Teutonic delicacies than even Wagner's very ample appetite could assimilate.

I fear that not one of these great ladies would have found it easy to obtain a permanent engagement as waitress in a restaurant, for their skill in handling dishes and plates was hardly commensurate with their zeal. In justice it must be added that the professional waitress would not be encumbered with the long and heavy train of evening dresses in the "'seventies." These great ladies, anxious to display their intimate knowledge of the Master's tastes, bickered considerably amongst themselves. "Surely, dear Countess, you know by now that the Master never touches white bread."

"Dearest Princess, Limburger cheese is the only sort the Master cares for. You had better take that Gruyère cheese away"; whilst an extremely attractive little Countess, the bearer of a great German name, would trip vaguely about, announcing to the world that "The Master thinks that he could eat two more black puddings. Where do you imagine that I could find them?"

Meanwhile from another quarter one would hear an eager "Dearest Princess, could you manage to get some raw ham? The Master thinks that he would like some, or else some raw smoked goose-breast." *"Aber, allerliebste Gräfin, wissen Sie nicht dass der Meister trinkt nur dunkles Bier?"* would come as a pathetic protest from some slighted worshipper who had been herself reproved for ignorance of the Master's gastronomic tastes.

It must regretfully be confessed that these tastes were rather gross. Meanwhile Wagner, dressed in a frock-coat and trousers of shiny black cloth, his head covered with his invariable black velvet skull-cap, would munch steadily away, taking no notice whatever of those around him.

The rest of us stood at a respectful distance, watching with a certain awe this marvellous weaver of harmonies assimilating copious nourishment. For us it was a sort of Barmecide's feast, for beyond the sight of Wagner at supper, we had no refreshments of any sort offered to us.

Soon afterwards Rubinstein, on his way to St. Petersburg, played at Madame de Schleinitz's house. Having learnt that Wagner always made a point of having two grand pianos side by side when he played, Rubinstein also insisted on having two. To my mind, Rubinstein absolutely ruined the effect of all his own compositions by the tremendous pace at which he played them. It was as though he were longing to be through with the whole thing. His "Melody in F," familiar to every school-girl, he took at such a pace that I really believe the virulent germ which forty years afterwards was to develop into Rag-time, and to conquer the whole world with its maddening syncopated strains, came into being that very night, and was evoked by Rubinstein himself out of his own long-suffering "Melody in F."

Our Ambassador, himself an excellent musician, was an almost lifelong friend of Liszt. Wagner's wife, by the way, was Liszt's daughter, and had been previously married to Hans von Bulow, the pianist. Liszt, when passing through Berlin, always dined at our Embassy and played to us afterwards. I remember well Lord Ampthill asking Liszt where he placed Rubinstein as a pianist. "Rubinstein is, without any question whatever, the first pianist in the world," answered Liszt without hesitation. "But you are forgetting yourself, Abbé," suggested the Ambassador. "Ich," said Liszt, striking his chest, "Ich bin der einzige Pianist der Welt" ("I; I am the only pianist in the world"). There was a superb arrogance about this perfectly justifiable assertion which pleased me enormously at the time, and pleases me still after the lapse of so many years.

Bismarck was a frequent visitor at our Embassy, and was fond of dropping in informally in the evening. Apart from his liking for our Ambassador, he had a great belief in his judgment and discretion. Lady Ampthill, too, was one of the few women Bismarck respected and really liked. I think he had a great admiration for her intellectual powers and quick sense of intuition.

It is perhaps superfluous to state that no man living now occupies the position Bismarck filled in the "'seventies." The maker of Modern Germany was the unchallenged dictator of Europe. He was always very civil to the junior members of the Embassy. I think it pleased him that we all spoke German fluently, for the acknowledged supremacy of the French language as a means of communication between educated persons of different nationalities was always a very sore point with him. It must be remembered that Prussia herself had only comparatively recently been released from the thraldom of the French language. Frederick the Great always addressed his *entourage* in French. After 1870-71, Bismarck ordered the German Foreign Office to reply in the German language to all communications from the French Embassy. He followed the same procedure with the Russian Embassy; whereupon the Russian Ambassador countered with a long despatch written in Russian to the Wilhelmstrasse. He received no reply to this, and mentioned that fact to Bismarck about a fortnight later. "Ah!" said Bismarck reflectively, "now that your Excellency mentions it, I think we did receive a despatch in some unknown tongue. I ordered it to be put carefully away until we could procure the services of an expert to decipher it. I hope to be able to find such an expert in the course of the next three or four months, and can only trust that the matter was not a very pressing one."

The Ambassador took the hint, and that was the last note in Russian that reached the Wilhelmstrasse.

We ourselves always wrote in English, receiving replies in German, written in the third person, in the curiously cumbrous Prussian official style.

Bismarck was very fond of enlarging on his favourite theory of the male and female European nations. The Germans themselves, the three Scandinavian peoples, the Dutch, the English proper, the Scotch, the Hungarians and the Turks, he declared to be essentially male races. The Russians, the Poles, the Bohemians, and indeed every Slavonic people, and all Celts, he maintained, just as emphatically, to be female races. A female race he ungallantly defined as one given to immense verbosity, to fickleness, and to lack of tenacity. He conceded to these feminine races some of the advantages of their sex, and acknowledged that they had great powers of attraction and charm, when they chose to exert them, and also a fluency of speech denied to the more virile nations. He maintained stoutly that it was quite useless to expect efficiency in any form from one of the female races, and he was full of contempt for the Celt and the Slav. He contended that the most interesting nations were the epicene ones, partaking, that is, of the characteristics of both sexes, and he instanced France and Italy, intensely virile in the North, absolutely female in the South; maintaining that the Northern French had saved their country times out of number from the follies of the "Méridionaux." He attributed the efficiency of the Frenchmen of the North to the fact that they had so large a proportion of Frankish and Norman blood in their veins, the Franks being a Germanic tribe, and the Normans, as their name implied, Northmen of Scandinavian, therefore also of Teutonic, origin. He declared that the fair-haired Piedmontese were the driving power of Italy, and that they owed their initiative to their descent from the Germanic hordes who invaded Italy under Alaric in the fifth century. Bismarck stoutly maintained that efficiency, wherever it was found, was due to Teutonic blood; a statement with which I will not quarrel.

As the inventor of "Practical Politics" (*Real-Politik*), Bismarck had a supreme contempt for fluent talkers and for words, saying that only fools could imagine that facts could be talked away. He cynically added that words were sometimes useful for "papering over structural cracks" when they had to be concealed for a time.

With his intensely overbearing disposition, Bismarck could not brook the smallest contradiction, or any criticism whatever. I have often watched him in the Reichstag—then housed in a very modest building—whilst being attacked, especially by Liebknecht the Socialist. He made no effort to conceal his anger, and would stab the blotting-pad before him viciously with a metal paper-cutter, his face purple with rage.

Bismarck himself was a very clear and forcible speaker, with a happy knack of coining felicitous phrases.

His eldest son, Herbert Bismarck, inherited all his father's arrogance and intensely overweening disposition, without one spark of his father's genius. He was not a popular man.

The second son, William, universally known as "Bill," was a genial, fair-headed giant of a man, as generally popular as his elder brother was the reverse. Bill Bismarck (the juxtaposition of these two names always struck me as being comically incongruous) drank so much beer that his hands were always wet and clammy. He told me himself that he always had three bottles of beer placed by his bedside lest he should be thirsty in the night. He did not live long.

Moltke, the silent, clean-shaved, spare old man with the sphinx-like face, who had himself worked out every detail of the Franco-Prussian War long before it materialised, was an occasional visitor at our Embassy, as was Gustav Richter, the fashionable Jewish artist. Richter's paintings, though now sneered at as *Chocolade-Malerei* (chocolate-box painting), had an enormous vogue in the "'seventies," and were reproduced by the hundred thousand. His picture of Queen Louise of Prussia, engravings of which are scattered all over the world, is only a fancy portrait, as Queen Louise had died before Richter was born. He had Rauch's beautiful effigy of the Queen in the mausoleum at Charlottenburg to guide him, but the actual model was, I believe, a member of the *corps de ballet* at the Opera. Madame Richter was the daughter of Mendelssohn the composer, and there was much speculation in Berlin as to the wonderful artistic temperament the children of such a union would inherit. As a matter of fact, I fancy that none of the young Richters showed any artistic gifts whatever.

Our Embassy was a very fine building. The German railway magnate Strousberg had erected it as his own residence, but as he most tactfully went bankrupt just as the house was completed, the British Government was able to buy it at a very low figure indeed, and to convert it into an Embassy. Though a little ornate, it was admirably adapted for this purpose, having nine reception rooms, including a huge ball-room, all communicating with each other, on the ground floor. The "Chancery," as the offices of an Embassy are termed, was in another building on the Pariser Platz. This was done to avoid the constant stream of people on business, of applicants of various sorts, including "D. B. S.'s" (Distressed British Subjects), continually passing through the Embassy. Immediately opposite our "Chancery," in the same building, and only separated from it by a *porte-cochère,* was the Chancery of the Austro-Hungarian Embassy.

Count W——, the Councillor of the Austrian Embassy, was very deaf, and had entirely lost the power of regulating his voice. He habitually shouted in a quarter-deck voice, audible several hundred yards away.

I was at work in the Chancery one day when I heard a stupendous din arising from the Austrian Chancery. "The Imperial Chancellor told me," thundered this megaphone voice in stentorian German tones, every word of which must have been distinctly heard in the street, "that under no circumstances whatever would Germany consent to this arrangement. If the proposal is pressed, Germany will resist it to the utmost, if necessary by force of arms. The Chancellor, in giving me this information," went on the strident voice, "impressed upon me how absolutely secret the matter must be kept. I need hardly inform your Excellency that this telegram is confidential to the highest degree."

"What is that appalling noise in the Austrian Chancery?" I asked our white-headed old Chancery servant.

"That is Count W—— dictating a cypher telegram to Vienna," answered the old man with a twinkle in his shrewd eyes.

This little episode has always seemed to me curiously typical of Austro-Hungarian methods.

The central figure of Berlin was of course the old Emperor William. This splendid-looking old man may not have been an intellectual giant, but he certainly looked an Emperor, every inch of him. There was something, too, very taking in his kindly old face and genial manner. The Crown Princess, afterwards the Empress Frederick, being a British Princess, we were what is known in diplomatic parlance as "une ambassade de famille." The entire staff of the Embassy was asked to dine at the Palace on the birthdays both of Queen Victoria and of the Crown Princess. These dinners took place at the unholy hour of 5 p.m., in full uniform, at the Emperor's ugly palace on the Linden, the Old Schloss being only used for more formal entertainments. On these occasions the sole table decoration consisted, quaintly enough, of rows of gigantic silver dish-covers, each surmounted by the Prussian eagle, with nothing under them, running down the middle of the table. The old Emperor had been but indifferently handled by his dentist. It had become necessary to supplement Nature's handiwork by art, but so unskilfully had these, what are euphemistically termed, additions to the Emperor's mouth been contrived, that his articulation was very defective. It was almost impossible to hear what he said, or indeed to make out in what language he was addressing you. When the Emperor "made the circle," one strained one's ears to the utmost to obtain a glimmering of what he was saying. If one detected an unmistakably Teutonic guttural, one drew a bow at a venture, and murmured *"Zu Befehl Majestät,"* trusting that it might fit in. Should one catch, on the other hand, a slight suspicion of a nasal "n," one imagined that the language must be French, and interpolated a tentative "*Parfaitement, Sire,*" trusting blindly to a kind Providence. Still the impression remains of a kindly and very dignified old gentleman, filling his part admirably. The Empress Augusta, who had been beautiful in her youth, could not resign herself to growing old gracefully. She would have made a most charming old lady, but though well over seventy then, she was ill-advised enough to attempt to rejuvenate herself with a chestnut wig and an elaborate make-up, with deplorable results. The Empress, in addition, was afflicted with a slight palsy of the head.

The really magnificent figure was the Crown Prince, afterwards the Emperor Frederick. Immensely tall, with a full golden beard, he looked in his white Cuirassier uniform the living embodiment of a German legendary hero; a Lohengrin in real life.

Princess Frederick Charles of Prussia was a strikingly handsome woman too, though unfortunately nearly stone deaf.

Though the palace on the Linden may have been commonplace and ugly, the Old Schloss has to my mind the finest interior in Europe. It may lack the endless, bare, gigantic halls of the Winter Palace in Petrograd, and it may contain fewer rooms than the great rambling Hofburg in Vienna, but I maintain that, with the possible exception of the Palace in Madrid, no building in Europe can compare internally with the Old Schloss in Berlin. I think the effect the Berlin palace produces on the stranger is due to the series of rooms which must be traversed before the State apartments proper are reached. These rooms, of moderate dimensions, are very richly decorated. Their painted ceilings, encased in richly-gilt "coffered" work in high relief, have a Venetian effect, recalling some of the rooms in the Doge's Palace in the sea-girt city of the Adriatic. Their silk-hung walls, their pictures, and the splendid pieces of old furniture they contain, redeem these rooms from the soulless, impersonal look most palaces wear. They recall the rooms in some of the finer English or French country-houses, although no private house would have them in the same number. The rooms that dwell in my memory out of the dozen or so that formed the *enfilade* are, first, the "Drap d'Or Kammer," with its droll hybrid appellation, the walls of which were hung, as its name implies, with cloth of gold; then the "Red Eagle Room," with its furniture and mirrors of carved wood, covered with thin plates of beaten silver, producing an indescribably rich effect, and the "Red Velvet" room. This latter had its walls hung with red velvet bordered by broad bands of silver lace, and contained some splendid old gilt furniture.

The Throne room was one of the most sumptuous in the world. It had an arched painted ceiling, from which depended some beautiful old chandeliers of cut rock crystal, and the walls, which framed great panels of Gobelin tapestry of the best period, were highly decorated, in florid rococo style, with pilasters and carved groups representing the four quarters of the world. The whole of the wall surface was gilded; carvings, mouldings, and pilasters forming one unbroken sheet of gold. We were always told that the musicians' gallery was of solid silver, and that it formed part of Frederick the Great's war-chest. As a matter of fact, Frederick had himself melted the original gallery down and converted it into cash for one of his campaigns. By his orders, a facsimile gallery was carved of wood heavily silvered over. The effect produced, however, was the same, as we were hardly in a position to scrutinise the hall-mark. The room contained four semi-circular buffets, rising in diminishing tiers, loaded with the finest specimens the Prussian Crown possessed of old German silver-gilt drinking-cups of Nuremberg and Augsburg workmanship of the sixteenth and seventeenth centuries.

When the Throne room was lighted up at night the glowing colours of the Gobelin tapestry and the sheen of the great expanses of gold and silver produced an effect of immense splendour. With the possible exception of the Salle des Fêtes in the Luxembourg Palace in Paris, it was certainly the finest Throne room in Europe.

The first time I saw the Luxembourg hall was as a child of seven, under the Second Empire, when I was absolutely awe-struck by its magnificence. It then contained Napoleon the Third's throne, and was known as the "Salle du Trône." A relation pointed out to me that the covering and curtains of the throne, instead of being of the stereotyped crimson velvet, were of purple velvet, all spangled with the golden bees of the Bonapartes. The Luxembourg hall had then in the four corners of the coved ceiling an ornament very dear to the meretricious but effective taste of the Second Empire. Four immense globes of sky-blue enamel supported four huge gilt Napoleonic eagles with outspread wings. To the crude taste of a child the purple velvet of the throne, powdered with golden bees, and the gilt eagles on their turquoise globes, appeared splendidly sumptuous. Of course after 1870 all traces of throne and eagles were removed, as well as the countless "N. III's" with which the walls were plentifully besprinkled.

What an astute move of Louis Napoleon's it was to term himself the "Third," counting the poor little "Aiglon," the King of Rome, as the second of the line, and thus giving a look of continuity and stability to a brand-new dynasty! Some people say that the assumption of this title was due to an accident, arising out of a printer's error. After his *coup d'état,* Louis Napoleon issued a proclamation to the French people, ending "Vive Napoleon ! ! !" The printer, mistaking the three notes of exclamation for the numeral III, set up "Vive Napoleon III." The proclamation appeared in this form, and Louis Napoleon, at once recognising the advantages of it, adhered to the style.

Whether this is true or not I cannot say. I was then too young to be able to judge for myself, but older people have told me that the mushroom Court of the Tuileries eclipsed all others in Europe in splendour. The *parvenu* dynasty needed all the aid it could derive from gorgeous ceremonial pomp to maintain its position successfully.

To return to Berlin, beyond the Throne room lay the fine picture gallery, nearly 200 feet long. At Court entertainments all the German officers gathered in this picture gallery and made a living hedge, between the ranks of which the guests passed on their way to the famous "White Hall." These long ranks of men in their resplendent *Hofballanzug* were really a magnificent sight, and whoever first devised this most effective bit of stage-management deserves great credit.

The White Hall as I knew it was a splendidly dignified room. As its name implies, it was entirely white, the mouldings all being silvered instead of gilt. Both Germans and Russians are fond of substituting silvering for gilding. Personally I think it most effective, but as the French with their impeccable good taste never employ silvering, there must be some sound artistic reason against its use.

It must be reluctantly confessed that the show of feminine beauty at Berlin was hardly on a level with the perfect *mise-en-scène*. There were three or four very beautiful women. Countess Karolyi, the Austrian Ambassadress, herself a Hungarian, was a tall, graceful blonde with beautiful hair; she was full of infinite attraction. Princess William Radziwill, a Russian, was, I think, the loveliest human being I have ever seen; she was, however, much dreaded on account of her mordant tongue. Princess Carolath-Beuthen, a Prussian, had first seen the light some years earlier than these two ladies. She was still a very beautiful woman, and eventually married as her second husband Count Herbert Bismarck, the Iron Chancellor's eldest son.

There was, unfortunately, a very wide gap between the looks of these "stars" and those of the rest of the company.

The interior of the Berlin Schloss put Buckingham Palace completely in the shade. The London palace was unfortunately decorated in the "'fifties," during the *époque de mauvais goût,* as the French comprehensively term the whole period between 1820 and 1880, and it bears the date written on every unfortunate detail of its decoration. It is beyond any question whatever the product of the "period of bad taste." I missed, though, in Berlin the wealth of flowers which turns Buckingham Palace into a garden on Court Ball nights. Civilians too in London have to appear at Court in knee-breeches and stockings; in Berlin trousers were worn, thus destroying the *habillé* look. As regards the display of jewels and the beauty of the women at the two Courts, Berlin was simply nowhere. German uniforms were of every colour of the rainbow; with us there is an undue predominance of scarlet, so that the kaleidoscopic effect of Berlin was never attained in London, added to which too much scarlet and gold tends to kill the effect of the ladies' dresses.

At the Prussian Court on these State occasions an immense number of pages made their appearance. I myself had been a Court page in my youth, but whereas in England little boys were always chosen for this part, in Berlin the tallest and biggest lads were selected from the Cadet School at Lichterfelde. A great lanky gawk six feet high, with an incipient moustache, does not show up to advantage in lace ruffles, with his thin spindle-shanks encased in silk stockings; a page's trappings being only suitable for little boys. I remember well the day when I and my fellow-novice were summoned to try on our new page's uniforms. Our white satin knee-breeches and gold-embroidered white satin waistcoats left us quite cold, but we were both enchanted with the little pages' swords, in their white-enamelled scabbards, which the tailor had brought with him. We had neither of us ever possessed a real sword of our own before, and the steel blades were of the most inviting sharpness. We agreed that the opportunity was too good a one to be lost, so we determined to slip out into the garden in our new finery and there engage in a deadly duel. It was further agreed to thrust really hard with the keen little blades, "just to see what would happen." Fortunately for us, we had been overheard. We reached the garden, and, having found a conveniently secluded spot, had just commenced to make those vague flourishes with our unaccustomed weapons which our experience, derived from pictures, led us to believe formed the orthodox preliminaries to a duel, when the combat was sternly interrupted. Otherwise there would probably have been vacancies for one if not two fresh Pages of Honour before nightfall. What a pity there were no "movies" in those days! What a splendid film could have been made of two small boys, arrayed in all the bravery of silk stockings, white satin breeches, and lace ruffles, their red tunics heavy with bullion embroidery, engaged in a furious duel in a big garden. When the news of our escapade reached the ears of the highest quarters, preemptory orders were issued to have the steel blades removed from our swords and replaced with innocuous pieces of shaped wood. It was very ignominious; still the little swords made a brave show, and no one by looking at them could guess that the white scabbards shielded nothing more deadly than an inoffensive piece of oak. A page's sword, by the way, is not worn at the left side in the ordinary manner, but is passed through two slits in the tunic, and is carried in the small of the back, so that the boy can keep his hands entirely free.

The "White Hall" has a splendid inlaid parquet floor, with a crowned Prussian eagle in the centre of it. This eagle was a source of immense pride to the palace attendants, who kept it in a high state of polish. As a result the eagle was as slippery as ice, and woe betide the unfortunate dancer who set his foot on it. He was almost certain to fall; and to fall down at a Berlin State ball was an unpardonable offence. If a German officer, the delinquent had his name struck off the list of those invited for a whole year. If a member of the Corps Diplomatique, he received strong hints to avoid dancing again. Certainly the diplomats were sumptuously entertained at supper at the Berlin Palace; whether the general public fared as well I do not know.

Urbain, the old Emperor William's French chef, who was responsible for these admirable suppers, had published several cookery books in French, on the title-page of which he described himself as "Urbain, premier officier de bouche de S.M. l'Empereur d'Allemagne." This quaint-sounding title was historically quite correct, it being the official appellation of the head cooks of the old French kings. A feature of the Berlin State balls was the stirrup-cup of hot punch given to departing guests. Knowing people hurried to the grand staircase at the conclusion of the entertainment; here servants proffered trays of this delectable compound. It was concocted, I believe, of equal parts of arrack and rum, with various other unknown ingredients. In the same way, at Buckingham Palace in Queen Victoria's time, wise persons always asked for hock cup. This was compounded of very old hock and curious liqueurs, from a hundred-year-old recipe. A truly admirable beverage! Now, alas! since Queen Victoria's day, only a memory.

The Princesses of the House of Prussia had one ordeal to face should they become betrothed to a member of the Royal Family of any other country. They took leave formally of the diplomats at the Palace, " making the circle " by themselves. I have always understood that Prussian princesses were trained for this from their childhood by being placed in the centre of a circle of twenty chairs, and being made to address some non-committal remark to each chair in turn, in German, French, and English. I remember well Princess Louise Margaret of Prussia, afterwards our own Duchess of Connaught, who was to become so extraordinarily popular not only in England but in India and Canada as well, making her farewell at Berlin on her betrothal. She " made the circle " of some forty people, addressing a remark or two to each, entirely alone, save for two of the great long, gawky Prussian pages in attendance on her, looking in their red tunics for all the world like London-grown geraniums—all stalk and no leaves. It is a terribly trying ordeal for a girl of eighteen, and the Duchess once told me that she nearly fainted from sheer nervousness at the time, although she did not show it in the least.

If I may be permitted a somewhat lengthy digression, I would say that it is at times extremely difficult to find topics of conversation. Years afterwards, when I was stationed at our Lisbon Legation, the Papal Nuncio was very tenacious of his dignity. In Catholic countries the Nuncio is *ex officio* head of the Diplomatic Body, and the Nuncio at Lisbon expected every diplomat to call on him at least six times a year. On his reception days the Nuncio always arrayed himself in his purple robes and a lace cotta, with his great pectoral emerald cross over it. He then seated himself in state in a huge carved chair, with a young priest as aide-de-camp, standing motionless behind him. It was always my ill-fortune to find the Nuncio alone. Now what possible topic of conversation could I, a Protestant, find with which to fill the necessary ten minutes with an Italian Archbishop *in partibus*. We could not well discuss the latest fashions in copes, or any impending changes in the College of Cardinals. Most providentally, I learnt that this admirable ecclesiastic, so far from despising the pleasures of the table, made them his principal interest in life. I know no more of the intricacies of the Italian *cuisine* than Melchizedek knew about frying sausages, but I had a friend, the wife of an Italian colleague, deeply versed in the mysteries of Tuscan cooking. This kindly lady wrote me out in French some of the choicest recipes in her extensive *répertoire,* and I learnt them all off by heart. After that I was the Nuncio's most welcome visitor. We argued hotly over the respective merits of *risotto alla Milanese* and *risotto al Salto.* We discussed *gnocchi, pasta asciutta,* and novel methods of preparing *minestra,* I trust without undue partisan heat, until the excellent prelate's eyes gleamed and his mouth began to water. Donna Maria, my Italian friend, proved an inexhaustible mine of recipes. She always produced new ones, which I memorised, and occasionally wrote out for the Nuncio, sometimes, with all the valour of ignorance, adding a fancy ingredient or two on my own account. On one occasion, after I had detailed the constituent parts of an extraordinarily succulent composition of rice, cheese, oil, mushrooms, chestnuts, and tomatoes, the Nuncio nearly burst into tears with emotion, and I feel convinced that, heretic though I might be, he was fully intending to give me his Apostolic benediction, had not the watchful young priest checked him. I felt rewarded for my trouble when my chief, the British Minister, informed me that the Nuncio considered me the most intelligent young man he knew. He added further that he enjoyed my visits, as my conversation was so interesting.

The other occasion on which I experienced great conversational difficulties was in Northern India at the house of a most popular and sporting Maharajah. His mother, the old Maharani, having just completed her seventy-first year, had emerged from the seclusion of the zenana, where she had spent fifty-five years of her life, or, in Eastern parlance, had "come from behind the curtain." We paid short ceremonial visits at intervals to the old lady, who sat amid piles of cushions, a little brown, shrivelled, mummy-like figure, so swathed in brocades and gold tissue as to be almost invisible. The Maharajah was most anxious that I should talk to his mother, but what possible subject of conversation could I find with an old lady who had spent fifty-five years in the pillared (and somewhat uncleanly) seclusions of the zenana? Added to which the Maharani knew no Urdu, but only spoke Bengali, a language of which I am ignorant. This entailed the services of an interpreter, always an embarrassing appendage. On occasions of this sort Morier's delightful book *Hadji Baba* is invaluable, for the author gives literal English translations of all the most flowery Persian compliments. Had the Maharani been a Mohammedan, I could have addressed her as "Oh moon-faced ravisher of hearts! I trust that you are reposing under the canopy of a sound brain!" Being a Hindoo, however, she would not be familiar with Persian forms of politeness. A few remarks on lawn tennis, or the increasing price of polo ponies, would obviously fail to interest her. You could not well discuss fashions with an old lady who had found one single garment sufficient for her needs all her days, and any questions as to details of her life in the zenana, or that of the other inmates of that retreat, would have been indecorous in the highest degree. Nothing then remained but to remark that the Maharajah was looking remarkably well, but that he had unquestionably put on a great deal of weight since I had last seen him. I received the startling reply from the interpreter (delivered in the clipped, staccato tones most natives of India assume when they speak English), "Her Highness says that, thanks to God, and to his mother's cooking, her son's belly is increasing indeed to vast size."

Bearing in mind these later conversational difficulties, I cannot but admire the ease with which Royal personages, from long practice, manage to address appropriate and varied remarks to perhaps forty people of different nationalities, whilst "making the circle."

CHAPTER II

Easy-going Austria—Vienna—Charm of town—A little piece of history—International families—Family pride—" Schlussel-Geld "—Excellence of Vienna restaurants—The origin of " *Croissants* "—Good looks of Viennese women—Strauss's operettas—A ball in an old Vienna house—Court entertainments—The Empress Elisabeth—Delightful environs of Vienna—The Berlin Congress of 1878—Lord Beaconsfield —M. de Blowitz—Treaty telegraphed to London—Environs of Berlin—Potsdam and its lakes—The bow-oar of the Embassy " four "—Narrow escape of ex-Kaiser—The Potsdam palaces—Transfer to Petrograd—Glamour of Russia —An evening with the Crown Prince at Potsdam.

OUR Embassy at Vienna was greatly overworked at this time, owing to the illness of two of the staff, and some fresh developments of the perennial " Eastern Question." I was accordingly " lent " to the Vienna Embassy for as long as was necessary, and left at once for the Austrian capital.

At the frontier station of Tetschen the transition from cast-iron, dictatorial, overbearing Prussian efficiency to the good-natured, easy-going, slipshod methods of the " ramshackle Empire " was immediately apparent.

The change from Berlin to Vienna was refreshing. The straight, monotonous, well-kept streets of the Northern capital lacked life and animation. It was a very fine frame enclosing no picture. The Vienna streets were as gay as those of Paris, and one was conscious of being in a city with centuries of traditions. The Inner Town of Vienna with its narrow winding streets is extraordinarily picturesque. The demolisher has not been given the free hand he has been allowed in Paris, and the fine *baroque* houses still remaining give an air of great distinction to this part of the town, with its many highly-decorative, if somewhat florid, fountains and columns. One was no longer in the "pushful" atmosphere of Prussia. These cheery, easy-going Viennese loved music and dancing, eating and drinking, laughter and fun. They were quite content to drift lazily down the stream of life, with as much enjoyment and as little trouble as possible. They might be a decadent race, but they were essentially *gemüthliche Leute.* The untranslatable epithet *gemüthlich* implies something at once "comfortable," "sociable," "cosy," and "pleasant."

The Austrian aristocracy were most charming people. They had all intermarried for centuries, and if they did not trouble their intellect much, there may have been physical difficulties connected with the process for which they were not responsible. The degree of warmth of their reception of foreigners was largely dependent upon whether he, or she, could show the indispensable *sechzehn Ahnen* (the "sixteen quarterings"). Once satisfied (or the reverse) as to this point, to which they attach immense importance, the situation became easier. As the whole of these people were interrelated, they were all on Christian names terms, and the various "Mitzis," "Kitzis," "Fritzis," and other characteristically Austrian abbreviations were a little difficult to place at times.

It was impossible not to realise that the whole nation was living on the traditions of their splendid past. It must be remembered that in the sixteenth century the Hapsburgs ruled the whole of Europe with the exception of France, England, Russia, and the Scandinavian countries. For centuries after Charlemagne assumed the Imperial Crown there had been only one Emperor in Europe, the "Holy Roman Emperor," the "Heiliger Römischer Kaiser," the fiction being, of course, that he was the descendant of the Cæsars. The word "Kaiser" is only the German variant of Cæsar. France and England had always consistently refused to acknowledge the overlordship of the Emperor, but the prestige of the title in German-speaking lands was immense, though the Holy Roman Empire itself was a mere simulacrum of power. In theory the Emperor was elected; in practice the title came to be a hereditary appanage of the proud Hapsburgs. It was, I think, Talleyrand who said "L'Autrice a la fâcheuse habitude d'être toujours battue," and this was absolutely true. Austria was defeated with unfailing regularity in almost every campaign, and the Hapsburgs saw their immense dominions gradually slipping from their grasp. It was on May 14, 1804, that Napoleon was crowned Emperor of the French in Paris, and Francis II, the last of the Holy Roman Emperors, was fully aware that Napoleon's next move would be to supplant him and get himself elected as "Roman Emperor." This Napoleon would have been able to achieve, as he had bribed the Electors of Bavaria, Württemberg, and Saxony by creating them kings. For once a Hapsburg acted with promptitude. On August 11, 1804, Francis proclaimed himself hereditary Emperor of Austria, and two years later he abolished the title of Holy Roman Emperor. The Empire, after a thousand years of existence, flickered out ingloriously in 1806. The pride of the Hapsburgs had received a hundred years previously a rude shock. Peter the Great, after consolidating Russia, abolished the title of Tsar of Muscovy, and proclaimed himself Emperor of All the Russias; purposely using the same term "Imperator" as that employed by the Roman Emperor, and thus putting himself on an equality with him.

I know by experience that it is impossible to din into the heads of those unfamiliar with Russia that since Peter the Great's time there has never been a Tsar. The words "Tsar," "Tsarina," "Cesarevitch," beloved of journalists, exist only in their imagination; they are never heard in Russia. The Russians termed their Emperor "Gosudar Imperator," using either or both of the words. Empress is "Imperatritza"; Heir Apparent "Nadslyédnik." If you mentioned the words "Tsar" or "Tsarina" to any ordinary Russian peasant, I doubt if he would understand you, but I am well aware that it is no use repeating this; the other idea is too firmly ingrained. The Hapsburgs had yet another bitter pill to swallow. Down to the middle of the nineteenth century the ancient prestige of the title Kaiser and the glamour attached to it were maintained throughout the Germanic Confederation, but in 1871 a second brand-new Kaiser arose on the banks of the Spree, and the Hapsburgs were shorn of their long monopoly.

Franz Josef of Austria must have rued the day when Sigismund sold the sandy Mark of Brandenburg to Frederick Count of Hohenzollern in 1415, and regretted the acquiescence in 1701 of his direct ancestor, the Emperor Leopold I, in the Elector of Brandenburg's request that he might assume the title of King of Prussia. The Hohenzollerns were ever a grasping race. I think that it was Louis XIV of France who, whilst officially recognising the new King of Prussia, refused to speak of him as such, and always alluded to him as "Monsieur le Marquis de Brandenbourg."

No wonder that the feeling of bitterness against Prussia amongst the upper classes of Austria was very acute in the "'seventies." The events of 1866 were still too recent to have been forgotten. In my time the great Austrian ladies affected the broadest Vienna popular dialect, probably to emphasise the fact that they were not Prussians. Thus the sentence "ein Glas Wasser, bitte," became, written in phonetic English, "a' Glawss Vawsser beet." I myself was much rallied on my pedantic North-

German pronunciation, and had in self-defence to adopt unfamiliar Austrian equivalents for many words.

The curious international families which seemed to abound in Vienna always puzzled me. Thus the Princes d'Aremberg are Belgians, but there was one Prince d'Aremberg in the Austrian service, whilst his brother was in the Prussian Diplomatic Service, the remainder of the family being Belgians. There were, in the same way, many German-speaking Pourtalès in Berlin in the German service, and more French-speaking ones in Paris in the French service. The Duc de Croy was both a Belgian and an Austrian subject. The Croys are one of the oldest families in Europe, and are *ebenbürtig* ("born on an equality") with all the German Royalties. They therefore show no signs of respect to Archdukes and Archduchesses when they meet them. Although I cannot vouch personally for them, never having myself seen them, I am told that there are two pictures in the Croy Palace at Brussels which reach the apogee of family pride. The first depicts Noah embarking on his ark. Although presumably anxious about the comfort of the extensive live-stock he has on board, Noah finds time to give a few parting instructions to his sons. On what is technically called a "bladder" issuing from his mouth are the words, "And whatever you do, don't forget to bring with you the family papers of the Croys." ("Et surtout ayez soin de ne pas oublier les papiers de la Maison de Croy!") The other picture represents the Madonna and Child, with the then Duke of Croy kneeling in adoration before them. Out of the Virgin Mary's mouth comes a "bladder" with the words "But please put on your hat, dear cousin." ("Mais couvrez vous donc, cher cousin.")

The whole of Viennese life is regulated by one exceedingly tiresome custom. After 10 or 10.15 p.m. the hall porter (known in Vienna as the "House-master") of every house in the city has the right of levying a small toll of threepence on each person entering or leaving the house. The whole life of the Vienna *bourgeois* is spent in trying to escape this tax, known as "Schlüssel-Geld." The theatres commence accordingly at 6 p.m. or 6.30, which entails dining about 5 p.m. A typical Viennese middle-class family will hurry out in the middle of the last act and scurry home breathlessly, as the fatal hour approaches. Arrived safely in their flat, in the last stages of exhaustion, they say triumphantly to each other, "We have missed the end of the play, and we are rather out of breath, but never mind, we have escaped the 'Schlüssel-Geld,' and as we are four, that makes a whole shilling saved!"

An equally irritating custom is the one that ordains that in restaurants three waiters must be tipped in certain fixed proportions. The "Piccolo," who brings the wine and bread, receives one quarter of the tip; the "Speiseträger," who brings the actual food, gets one half; the "Zahlkellner," who brings the bill, gets one quarter. All these must be given separately, so not only does it entail a hideous amount of mental arithmetic, but it also necessitates the perpetual carrying about of pocketfuls of small change.

The Vienna restaurants were quite excellent, with a local *cuisine* of extraordinary succulence, and more extraordinary names. A universal Austrian custom, not only in restaurants but in private houses as well, is to serve a glass of the delicious light Vienna beer with the soup. Even at State dinners at the Hof-Burg, a glass of beer was always offered with the soup. The red wine, Voslauer, grown in the immediate vicinity of the city, is so good, and has such a distinctive flavour, that I wonder it has never been exported. The restaurants naturally suggest the matchless Viennese orchestras. They were a source of never-ending delight to me. The distinction they manage to give to quite commonplace little airs is extraordinary. The popular songs, "Wiener-Couplets," melodious, airy nothings, little light soap-bubbles of tunes, are one of the distinctive features of Vienna. Played by an Austrian band as only an Austrian band can play them, with astonishing vim and fire, and supremely dainty execution, these little fragile melodies are quite charming and irresistibly attractive. We live in a progressive age. In the place of these Austrian bands with their finished execution and consummately musicianly feeling, the twentieth century has invented the Jazz band with its ear-splitting, chaotic din.

There is a place in Vienna known as the Heiden-Schuss, or "Shooting of the heathens." The origin of this is quite interesting.

In 1683 the Turks invaded Hungary, and, completely overrunning the country, reached Vienna, to which they laid siege, for the second time in its history. Incidentally, they nearly succeeded in capturing it. During the siege, bakers' apprentices were at work one night in underground bakehouses, preparing the bread for next day's consumption. The lads heard a rhythmic "thump, thump, thump," and were much puzzled by it. Two of the apprentices, more intelligent than the rest, guessed that the Turks were driving a mine, and ran off to the Commandant of Vienna with their news. They saw the principal engineer officer and told him of their discovery. He accompanied them back to the underground bakehouse, and at once determined that the boys were right. Having got the direction from the sound, the Austrians drove a second tunnel, and exploded a powerful countermine. Great numbers of Turks were killed, and the siege was temporarily raised. On September 12 of the same year (1683) John Sobieski, King of Poland, utterly routed the Turks, drove them back into their own country, and Vienna was saved. As a reward for the intelligence shown by the baker-boys, they were granted the privilege of making and selling a rich kind of roll (into the composition of which butter entered largely) in the shape of the Turkish emblem, the crescent. These rolls became enormously popular amongst the Viennese, who called them *Kipfeln*. When Marie Antoinette married Louis XVI of France, she missed her Kipfel, and sent to Vienna for an Austrian baker to teach his Paris *confrères* the art of making them. These rolls, which retained their original shape, became as popular in Paris as they had been in Vienna, and were known as *Croissants,* and that is the reason why one of the rolls which are brought you with your morning coffee in Paris will be baked in the form of a crescent.

The extraordinary number of good-looking women, of all classes to be seen in the streets of Vienna was most striking, especially after Berlin, where a lower standard of feminine beauty prevailed. Particularly noticeable were the admirable figures with which most Austrian women are endowed. In the far-off "'seventies" ladies did not huddle themselves into a shapeless mass of abbreviated oddments of material—they dressed, and their clothes fitted them; and a woman on whom Nature (or Art) had bestowed a good figure was able to display her gifts to the world. In the same way, Fashion did not compel a pretty girl to smother up her features in unbecoming tangles of tortured hair. The usual fault of Austrian faces is their breadth across the cheekbones; the Viennese too have a decided tendency to *embonpoint,* but in youth these defects are not accentuated. Amongst the Austrian aristocracy the great beauty of the girls was very noticeable, as was their height, in marked contrast to the short stature of most of the men. I have always heard that one of the first outward signs of the decadence of a race is that the girls grow taller, whilst the men get shorter.

The Vienna theatres are justly celebrated. At the Hof-Burg Theatre may be seen the most finished acting on the German stage. The Burg varied its programme almost nightly, and it was an amusing sight to see the troops of liveried footmen inquiring at the box-office, on behalf of their mistresses, whether the play to be given that night was or was not a *Comtessen-Stück, i.e.,* a play fit for young girls to see. The box-keeper always gave a plain "Yes" or "No" in reply. After Charles Garnier's super-ornate pile in Paris, the Vienna Opera-house is the finest in Europe, and the musical standard reaches the highest possible level, completely eclipsing Paris in that respect. In the "'seventies" Johann Strauss's delightful comic operas still retained their vogue. Bubbling over with merriment, full of delicious ear-tickling melodies, and with a "go" and an irresistible intoxication about them that no French composer has ever succeeded in emulating, these operettas, "Die Fledermaus," "Prinz Methusalem," and "La Reine Indigo," would well stand revival. When the "Fledermaus" was revived in London some ten years ago it ran, if my memory serves me right, for nearly a year. Occasionally Strauss himself conducted one of his own operettas; then the orchestra, responding to his magical baton, played like very demons. Strauss had one peculiarity. Should he be dissatisfied with the vim the orchestra put into one of his favourite numbers, he would snatch the instrument from the first violin and play it himself. Then the orchestra answered like one man, and one left the theatre with the entrancing strains still tingling in one's ears.

The family houses of most of the Austrian nobility were in the Inner Town, the old walled city, where space was very limited. These fine old houses, built for the greater part in the Italian *baroque* style, though splendid for entertaining, were almost pitch dark and very airless in the daytime. Judging, too, from the awful smells in them, they must have been singularly insanitary dwellings. The Lobkowitz Palace, afterwards the French Embassy, was so dark by day that artificial light had always to be used. In the great seventeenth century ball-room of the Lobkowitz Palace there was a railed off oak-panelled alcove containing a bust of Beethoven, an oak table, and three chairs. It was in that alcove, and at that table, that Beethoven, when librarian to Prince Lobkowitz, composed some of his greatest works.

Our own Embassy in the Metternichgasse, built

by the British Government, was rather cramped and could in no way compare with the Berlin house.

I remember well a ball given by Prince S——, head of one of the greatest Austrian families, in his fine but extremely dark house in the Inner Town. It was Prince S——'s custom on these occasions to have three hundred young peasants sent up from his country estates, and to have them all thrust into the family livery. These bucolic youths, looking very sheepish in their unfamiliar plush breeches and stockings, with their unkempt heads powdered, and with swords at their sides, stood motionless on every step of the staircase. I counted one hundred of these rustic retainers on the staircase alone. They would have looked better had their liveries occasionally fitted them. The ball-room at Prince S——'s was hung with splendid Brussels seventeenth century tapestry framed in mahogany panels, heavily carved and gilt. I have never seen this combination of mahogany, gilding, and tapestry anywhere else. It was wonderfully decorative, and with the elaborate painted ceiling made a fine setting for an entertainment. It was a real pleasure to see how wholeheartedly the Austrians threw themselves into the dancing. I think they all managed to retain a child's power of enjoyment, and they never detracted from this by any unnecessary brainwork. Still they were delightfully friendly, easy-going people. A distinctive feature of every Vienna ball was the "Comtessen-Zimmer," or room reserved for girls. At the end of every dance they all trooped in there, giggling and gossiping, and remained there till the music for the next dance struck up. No married woman dared intrude into the "Comtessen-Zimmer," and I shudder to think of what would have befallen the rash male who ventured to cross that jealously-guarded threshold. I imagine that the charming and beautifully-dressed Austrian married women welcomed this custom, for between the dances at all events they could still hold the field, free from the competition of a younger and fresher generation.

At Prince S——'s, at midnight, armies of rustic retainers, in their temporary disguise, brought battalions of supper tables into the ball-room, and all the guests sat down to a hot supper at the same time. As an instance of how Austrians blended simplicity with a great love of externals, I see from my diary that the supper consisted of bouillon, of plain-boiled carp with horse-radish, of thick slices of hot roast beef, and a lemon ice —and nothing else whatever. A sufficiently substantial repast, but hardly in accordance with modern ideas as to what a ball-supper should consist of. The young peasants, considering that it was their first attempt at waiting, did not break an undue number of plates; they tripped at times, though, over their unaccustomed swords, and gaped vacantly, or would get hitched up with each other, when more dishes crashed to their doom.

In Vienna there was a great distinction drawn between a "Court Ball" (Hof-Ball) and a "Ball at the Court" (Ball bei Hof). To the former everyone on the Palace list was invited, to the latter only a few people; and the one was just as crowded and disagreeable as the other was the reverse. The great rambling pile of the Hof-Burg contains some very fine rooms and a marvellous collection of works of art, and the so-called "Ceremonial Apartments" are of quite Imperial magnificence, but the general effect was far less striking than in Berlin.

In spite of the beauty of the women, the *coup d'œil* was spoilt by the ugly Austrian uniforms. After the disastrous campaign of 1866, the traditional white of the Austrian Army was abolished, and the uniforms were shorn of all unnecessary trappings. The military tailors had evolved hideous garments, ugly in colour, unbecoming in cut. One can only trust that they proved very economical, but the contrast with the splendid and admirably made uniforms of the Prussian Army was very marked. The Hungarian magnates in their traditional family costumes (from which all Hussar uniforms are derived) added a note of gorgeous colour, with their gold-laced tunics and their many-hued velvet slung-jackets. I remember, on the occasion of Queen Victoria's Jubilee in 1887, the astonishment caused by a youthful and exceedingly good-looking Hungarian who appeared at Buckingham Palace in skin-tight blue breeches lavishly embroidered with gold over the thighs, entirely gilt Hessian boots to the knee, and a tight-fitting tunic cut out of a real tiger-skin, fastened with some two dozen turquoise buttons the size of five-shilling pieces. When this resplendent youth reappeared in London ten years later at the Diamond Jubilee, it was with a tonsured head, and he was wearing the violet robes of a prelate of the Roman Church.

As an instance of the inflexibility of the cast-iron rules of the Hapsburg Court: I may mention that the beautiful Countess Karolyi, Austrian Ambassadress in Berlin, was never asked to Court in Vienna, as she lacked the necessary "sixteen quarterings." To a non-Austrian mind it seems illogical that the lovely lady representing Austria in Berlin should have been thought unfitted for an invitation from her own Sovereign.

The immense deference paid to the Austrian Archdukes and Archduchesses was very striking after the comparatively unceremonious fashion in which minor German royalties (always excepting the Emperor and the Crown Prince) were treated in Berlin. The Archduchesses especially were very tenacious of their privileges. They never could forget that they were Hapsburgs, and exacted all the traditional signs of respect.

The unfortunate Empress Elisabeth, destined years after to fall under the dagger of an assassin at Geneva, made but seldom a public appearance in her husband's dominions. She had an almost morbid horror of fulfilling any of the duties of her position. During my stay in the Austrian capital I only caught one glimpse of her, driving through the streets. She was astonishingly handsome, with coiled masses of dark hair, and a very youthful and graceful figure, but the face was so impassive that it produced the effect of a beautiful, listless mask. The Empress was a superb horsewoman, and every single time she rode she was literally sewn into her habit by a tailor, in order to ensure a perfect fit.

The innumerable cafés of Vienna were crowded from morning to night. Seeing them crammed with men in the forenoon, one naturally wondered how the business of the city was transacted. Probably, in typical Austrian fashion, these worthy Viennese left their businesses to take care of themselves whilst they enjoyed themselves in the cafés. The super-excellence of the Vienna coffee would afford a more or less legitimate excuse for this. Nowhere in the world is such coffee made, and a "Capuziner," or a "Melange," the latter with thick whipped cream on the top of it, were indeed things of joy.

Few capitals are more fortunate in their environs than Vienna. The beautiful gardens and park of Schönbrunn Palace have a sort of intimate charm which is wholly lacking at Versailles. They are stately, yet do not overwhelm you with a sense of vast spaces. They are crowned by a sort of temple, known as the Gloriette, from which a splendid view is obtained. In less than three hours from the capital, the railway climbs 3,000 feet to the Semmering, where the mountain scenery is really grand. During the summer months the whole of Vienna empties itself on to the Semmering and the innumerable other hill-resorts within easy distance from the city.

When the time came for my departure, I felt genuinely sorry at leaving this merry, careless, music and laughter-loving town, and these genial, friendly, hospitable incompetents. I feel some compunction in using this word, as people had been very good to me. I cannot help feeling, though, that it is amply warranted. A bracing climate is doubtless wholesome; but a relaxing one can be very pleasant for a time. I went back to Berlin feeling like a boy returning to school after his holidays.

The Viennese had but little love for their upstart rival on the Spree. They had invented the name "Parvenupopolis" for Berlin, and a little popular song, which I may be forgiven for quoting in the original German, expressed their sentiments fairly accurately:

Es gibt nur eine Kaiserstadt,
Es gibt nur ein Wien;
Es gibt nur ein Raübernest,
Und das heisst Berlin.

I had a Bavarian friend in Berlin. We talked over the amazing difference in temperament there was between the Austrians and the Prussians, and the curious charm there was about the former, lacking in intellect though they might be, a charm wholly lacking in the pushful, practical Prussians. My friend agreed, but claimed the same attractive qualities for his own beloved Bavarians; "but," he added impressively, "mark my words, in twenty years from now the whole of Germany will be Prussianised!" (*"Ganz Deutschland wird verpreussert werden."*) Events have shown how absolutely correct my Bavarian friend was in his forecast.

In June, 1878, the great Congress for the settlement of the terms of peace between Russia and Turkey assembled in Berlin. It was an extraordinarily interesting occasion, for almost every single European notability was to be seen in the German capital. The Russian plenipotentiaries were the veteran Prince Gortchakoff and Count Peter Schouvaloff, that most genial *faux-bonhomme;* the Turks were championed by Ali Pasha and by Katheodory Pasha. Great Britain was represented by Lords Beaconsfield and Salisbury; Austria by Count Andrassy, the Prime Minister; France by M. Waddington. In spite of the very large staff brought out from London by the British plenipotentiaries, an enormous amount of work fell upon us at the Embassy.

To a youngster there is something very fascinating in being regarded as so worthy of confidence that the most secret details of the great game of diplomacy were all known to him from day to day. A boy of twenty-one feels very proud of the trust reposed in him, and at being the repository of such weighty and important secrets. That is the traditional method of the British Diplomatic Service.

As all the Embassies gave receptions in honour of their own plenipotentiaries, we met almost nightly all the great men of Europe, and had occasional opportunities for a few words with them. Prince Gortchakoff, who fancied himself Bismarck's only rival, was a little, short, tubby man in spectacles; wholly undistinguished in appearance, and looking for all the world like an average French provincial *notaire.* Count Andrassy, the Hungarian, was a tall, strikingly handsome man, with an immense head of hair. To me, he always recalled the leader of a "Tzigane" orchestra. M. Waddington talked English like an Englishman, and was so typically British in appearance that it was almost impossible to realise that he was a Frenchman. Our admiration for him was increased when we learnt that he had rowed in the Cambridge Eight. But without any question whatever, the personality which excited the greatest interest at the Berlin Congress was that of Lord Beaconsfield, the Jew who by sheer force of intellect had raised himself from nothing into his present commanding position. His peculiar, colourless, inscrutable face, with its sphinx-like impassiveness; the air of mystery which somehow clung about him; the romantic story of his career; even the remnants of dandyism which he still retained in his old age—all these seemed to whet the insatiable public curiosity about him. Some enterprising Berlin tradesmen had brought out fans, with leaves composed of plain white vellum, designed expressly for the Congress. Armed with one of these fans, and with pen and ink, indefatigable feminine autograph-hunters moved about at these evening receptions, securing the signatures of the plenipotentiaries on the white vellum leaves. Many of those fans must still be in existence, and should prove very interesting to-day. Bismarck alone invariably refused his autograph.

At all these gatherings, M. de Blowitz, the then Paris correspondent of the *Times*, was much to the fore. In the "'seventies" the prestige of the *Times* on the Continent of Europe was enormous. In reality the influence of the *Times* was very much overrated, since all Continentals persisted in regarding it as the inspired mouthpiece of the British Government. Great was the *Times*, but greater still was de Blowitz, its prophet. This most remarkable man was a veritable prince of newspaper correspondents. There was no move on the European chess-board of which he was not cognisant, and as to which he did not keep his paper well informed, and his information was always accurate. De Blowitz knew no English, and his lengthy daily telegrams to the *Times* were always written in French and were translated in London. He was really a Bohemian Jew of the name of

Oppen, and he had bestowed the higher-sounding name of de Blowitz on himself. He was a very short, fat little man, with immensely long grey side-whiskers, and a most consequential manner. He was a very great personage indeed in official circles. De Blowitz has in his Memoirs given a full account of the trick by which he learnt of the daily proceedings of the Congress and so transmitted them to his paper. I need not, therefore, go into details about this; it is enough to say that a daily exchange of hats, in the lining of the second of which a summary of the day's deliberations was concealed, played a great part in it.

When the Treaty had been drawn up in French, Lord Salisbury rather startled us by saying that he wished it translated into English and cyphered to London that very evening *in extenso.* This was done to obviate the possibility of the newspaper correspondents getting a version of the Treaty through to London before the British Government had received the actual text. As the Treaty was what I, in the light of later experiences, would now describe as of fifteen thousand words length, this was a sufficiently formidable undertaking. Fifteen of us sat down to the task about 6 p. m., and by working at high pressure we got the translation finished and the last cyphered sheet sent off to the telegraph office by 5 a.m. The translation done at such breakneck speed was possibly a little crude in places. One clause in the Treaty provided that ships in ballast were to have free passage through the Dardanelles. Now the French for "ships in ballast," is "*navires en lest.*" The person translating this (who was *not* a member of the British Diplomatic Service) rendered "*navires en lest*" as "ships in the East," and in this form it was cyphered to London. As, owing to the geographical position of the Dardanelles, any ship approaching them would be, in one sense of the term, a "ship in the East," there was considerable perturbation in Downing Street over this clause, until the mistake was discovered.

Berlin has wonderful natural advantages, considering that it is situated in a featureless, sandy plain. In my day it was quite possible to walk from the Embassy into a real, wild pine-forest, the Grünewald. The Grünewald, being a Royal forest, was unbuilt on, and quite unspoilt. It extended for miles, enclosing many pretty little lakelets. Now I understand that it has been invaded by "villa colonies," so its old charm of wildness must have vanished. The Tiergarten, too, the park of Berlin, retains in places the look of a real country wood. It is inadvisable to venture into the Tiergarten after nightfall, should you wish to retain possession of your watch, purse, and other portable property. The sandy nature of the soil makes it excellent for riding. Within quite a short distance of the city you can find tracts of heathery moor, and can get a good gallop almost anywhere.

There is quite fair partridge-shooting, too, within

a few miles of Berlin, in the immense potato fields, though the entire absence of cover in this hedgeless land makes it very difficult at times to approach the birds. It is pre-eminently a country for "driving" partridges, though most Germans prefer the comparatively easy shots afforded by "walking the birds up."

Potsdam has had but scant justice done it by foreigners. The town is almost surrounded by the river Havel, which here broadens out into a series of winding, wooded lakes, surrounded by tree-clad hills. The Potsdam lakes are really charmingly pretty, and afford an admirable place for rowing or sailing. Neither of these pursuits seems to make the least appeal to Germans. The Embassy kept a small yacht at Potsdam, but she was practically the only craft then on the lakes. As on all narrow waters enclosed by wooded hills, the sailing was very tricky, owing to the constant shifting of the wind. Should it be blowing fresh, it was advisable to sail under very light canvas; and it was always dangerous to haul up the centre-board, even when "running," as on rounding some wooded point you would get "taken aback" to a certainty. Once in the fine open stretch of water between Wansee and Spandau, you could hoist every stitch of canvas available, and indulge with impunity in the most complicated nautical manœuvres. Possibly my extreme fondness for the Potsdam lakes may be due to their extraordinary resemblance to the lakes at my own Northern country home.

The Embassy also owned a light Thames-built four-oar. At times a short, thick-set young man of nineteen pulled bow in our four. The short young man had a withered arm, and the doctors hoped that the exercise of rowing might put some strength into it. He seemed quite a commonplace young man, yet this short, thick-set youth was destined less than forty years after to plunge the world into the greatest calamity it has ever known; to sacrifice millions and millions of human lives to his own inordinate ambition; and to descend to posterity as one of the most sinister characters in the pages of history.

Moored in the "Jungfernsee," one of the Potsdam lakes, lay a miniature sailing frigate, a complete model of a larger craft down to the smallest details. This toy frigate had been a present from King William IV of England to the then King of Prussia. The little frigate had been built in London, and though of only 30-tons burden, had been sailed down the Thames, across the North Sea, and up the Elbe and Havel to Potsdam, by a British naval officer. A pretty bit of seamanship! I have always heard that it was the sight of this toy frigate, lying on the placid lake at Potsdam, that first inspired William of Hohenzollern with the idea of building a gigantic navy.

The whole history of the world might have been changed by an incident which occurred on these same Potsdam lakes in 1880. I have already said that William of Hohenzollern, then only Prince

William, pulled at times in our Embassy four, in the hope that it might strengthen his withered arm. He was very anxious to see if he could learn to scull, in spite of his physical defect, and asked the Ambassadress, Lady Ampthill, whether she would herself undertake to coach him. Lady Ampthill consented, and met Prince William next day at the landing-stage with a light Thames-built skiff, belonging to the Embassy. Lady Ampthill, with the caution of one used to light boats, got in carefully, made her way aft, and grasped the yoke-lines. She then explained to Prince William that this was not a heavy boat such as he had been accustomed to, that he must exercise extreme care, and in getting in must tread exactly in the centre of the boat. William of Hohenzollern, who had never taken advice from anyone in his life, and was always convinced that he himself knew best, responded by jumping into the boat from the landing-stage, capsizing it immediately, and throwing himself and Lady Ampthill into the water. Prince William, owing to his malformation, was unable to swim one stroke, but help was at hand. Two of the Secretaries of the British Embassy had witnessed the accident, and rushed up to aid. The so-called "Naval Station" was close by, where the Emperor's Potsdam yacht lay, a most singularly shabby old paddle-boat. Some German sailors from the "Naval Post" heard the shouting and ran up, and a moist, and we will trust a chastened William and a dripping Ambassadress were eventually rescued from the lake. Otherwise William of Hohenzollern might have ended his life in the "Jungfernsee" at Potsdam that day, and millions of other men would have been permitted to live out their allotted span of existence.

Potsdam itself is quite a pleasing town, with a half-Dutch, half-Italian physiognomy. Both were deliberately borrowed; the first by Frederick William I, who constructed the tree-lined canals which give Potsdam its half-Batavian aspect; the second by Frederick the Great, who fronted Teutonic dwellings with façades copied from Italy to add dignity to the town. It must in justice be added that both are quite successful, though Potsdam, like most other things connected with the Hohenzollerns, has only a couple of hundred years' tradition behind it. The square opposite the railway really does recall Italy. The collection of palaces at Potsdam is bewildering. Of these, three are of the first rank: the Town Palace, Sans-souci, and the great pile of the "New Palace." Either Frederick the Great was very fortunate in his architects, or else he chose them with great discrimination. The Town Palace, even in my time but seldom inhabited, is very fine in the finished details of its decoration. Sans-souci is an absolute gem; its rococo style may be a little over-elaborate, but it produces the effect of a finished, complete whole, in the most admirable taste; even though the exuberant imagination of the eighteenth century has been allowed to run riot in it. The gardens of Sans-souci, too, are most attractive. The immense red-brick building of the New Palace was erected by Frederick the Great during the Seven Years' War, out of sheer bravado. He was anxious to impress on his enemies the fact that his financial resources were not yet exhausted. Considering that he already possessed two stately palaces within a mile of it, the New Palace may be looked upon as distinctly a work of supererogation, also as an appalling waste of money. As a piece of architecture, it is distinctly a success. This list does not, however, nearly exhaust the palatial resources of Potsdam. The eighteenth century had contributed its successes; it remained for the nineteenth to add its failures. Babelsberg, the old Emperor William's favourite residence, was an awful example of a ginger-bread pseudo-Gothic castle. The Marble Palace on the so-called "Holy Lake" was a dull, unimaginative building; and the "Red Prince's" house at Glienicke was frankly terrible. The main features of this place was an avenue of huge cast-iron gilded lions. These golden lions were such a blot on an otherwise charming landscape that one felt relieved by recalling that the apparently ineradicable tendency of the children of Israel to erect Golden Calves at various places in olden days had always been severely discountenanced.

In spite of the carpenter-Gothic of Babelsberg, and of the pinchbeck golden lions of Glienicke, Potsdam will remain in my mind, to the end of my life, associated with memories of fresh breezes and bellying sails; of placid lakes and swift-gliding keels responding to the straining muscles of back and legs; a place of verdant hills dipping into clear waters; of limbs joyously cleaving those clear waters with all the exultation of the swimmer; a place of rest and peace, with every fibre in one's being rejoicing in being away, for the time being, from crowded cities and stifling streets, in the free air amidst woods, waters, and gently-swelling, tree-clad heights.

A year later, I was notified that I was transferred to Petrograd, then of course still known as St. Petersburg. This was in accordance with the dearest wish of my heart. Ever since my childhood's days I had been filled with an intense desire to go to Russia. Like most people unacquainted with the country, I had formed the most grotesquely incorrect mental pictures of Russia. I imagined it a vast Empire of undreamed of magnificence, pleasantly tempered with relics of barbarism; and all these glittering splendours were enveloped in the snow and ice of a semi-Arctic climate, which gave additional piquancy to their glories. I pictured huge tractless forests, their dark expanse only broken by the shimmering golden domes of the Russian churches. I fancied this glamour-land peopled by a species of transported French, full of culture, and all of them polyglot, more brilliant and infinitely more intellectual than their West European prototypes. I imagined this hyperborean paradise served by a race of super-astute diplomatists and officials, with whom we poor Westerners could not hope to contend, and by Generals whom no one could withstand. The evident awe with which Germans envisaged their Eastern neighbours strengthened this idea, and both in England and in France I had heard quite responsible persons gloomily predict, after contemplating the map, that the Northern Colossus was fatally destined at some time to absorb the whole of the rest of Europe.

Apart then from its own intrinsic attraction, I used to gaze at the map of Russia with some such feelings as, I imagine, the early Christians experienced when, on their Sunday walks in Rome, they went to look at the lions in their dens in the circus, and speculated as to their own sensations when, as seemed but too probable, they might have to meet these interesting quadrupeds on the floor of the arena, in a brief, exciting, but definitely final encounter.

Everything I had seen or heard about this mysterious land had enhanced its glamour. The hair-raising rumours which reached Berlin as to revolutionary plots and counter-plots; the appalling stories one heard about the terrible secret police; the atmosphere of intrigue which seemed indigenous to the place—all added to its fascinations. Even the externals were attractive. I had attended weddings and funeral services at the chapel of the Russian Embassy. Here every detail was exotic, and utterly dissimilar to anything in one's previous experience. The absence of seats, organ, or pulpit in the chapel itself; the elaborate Byzantine decorations of the building; the exquisitely beautiful but quite unfamiliar singing; the long-bearded priests in their archaic vestments of unaccustomed golden brocades—everything struck a novel note. It all came from a world apart, centuries removed from the prosaic routine of Western Europe.

Even quite minor details, such as the curiously sumptuous Russian national dresses of the ladies of the Embassy at Court functions, the visits to Berlin of the Russian ballets and troupes of Russian singing gipsies, had all the same stamp of strong racial individuality, of something temperamentally different from all we had been accustomed to.

I was overjoyed at the prospect of seeing for myself at last this land of mingled splendour and barbarism, this country which had retained its traditional racial characteristics in spite of the influences of nineteenth century drab uniformity of type.

As the Petrograd Embassy was short-handed at the time, it was settled that I should postpone my leave for some months and proceed to Russia without delay.

The Crown Prince and Crown Princess, who had been exceedingly kind to me during my stay in Berlin, were good enough to ask me to the New Palace at Potsdam for one night, to take leave of them.

I had never before had an opportunity of going all over the New Palace. I thought it wonderfully fine, though quite French in feeling. The rather faded appearance of some of the rooms increased their look of dignity. It was not of yesterday. The great " Shell Hall," or " Muschel-Saal," much admired of Prussians, is frankly horrible; one of the unfortunate aberrations of eighteenth century taste of which several examples occur in English country-houses of the same date.

My own bedroom was charming; of the purest Louis XV, with apple-green polished panelling and heavily silvered mouldings and mirrors.

Nothing could be more delightful than the Crown Prince's manner on occasions such as this. The short-lived Emperor Frederick had the knack of blending absolute simplicity with great dignity, as had the Empress Frederick. For the curious in such matters, and as an instance of the traditional frugality of the Prussian Court, I may add that supper that evening, at which only the Crown Prince and Princess, the equerry and lady-in-waiting, and myself were present, consisted solely of curds and whey, veal cutlets, and a rice pudding. Nothing else whatever. We sat afterwards in a very stately, lofty, thoroughly French room. The Crown Prince, the equerry, and myself drank beer, whilst the Prince smoked his long pipe. It seemed incongruous to drink beer amid such absolutely French surroundings. I noticed that the Crown Princess always laid down her needlework to refill her husband's pipe and to bring him a fresh tankard of beer. The "Kronprinzliches Paar," as a German would have described them, were both perfectly charming in their conversation with a dull, uninteresting youth of twenty-one. They each had marvellous memories, and recalled many trivial half-forgotten details about my own family. That evening in the friendly atmosphere of the great, dimly-lit room in the New Palace at Potsdam will always live in my memory.

Two days afterwards I drove through the trim, prosaic, well-ordered, stuccoed streets of Berlin to the Eastern Station; for me, the gateway to the land of my desires, vast, mysterious Russia.

CHAPTER III

The Russian frontier—Frontier police—Disappointment at aspect of Petrograd—Lord and Lady Dufferin—The British Embassy — St. Isaac's Cathedral — Beauty of Russian Church-music — The Russian language — The delightful "Blue-stockings" of Petrograd—Princesse Châtean—Pleasant Russian Society—The Secret Police—The Countess's hurried journey—The Yacht Club—Russians really Orientals—Their limitations—The "Intelligenzia"—My Nihilist friends—Their lack of constructive power—Easter Mass at St. Isaac's—Two comical incidents—The Easter supper —The red-bearded young priest—An Empire built on shifting sand.

PETROGRAD is 1,050 miles from Berlin, and forty years ago the fastest trains took forty-five hours to cover the distance between the two capitals. In later years the "Nord-Express" accomplished the journey in twenty-nine hours.

Rolling through the flat fertile plains of East Prussia, with their neat, prosperous villages and picturesque black-and-white farms, the surroundings had such a commonplace air that it was difficult to realise that one was approaching the very threshold of the great, mysterious Northern Empire.

Eydkuhnen, the last Prussian station, was as other Prussian stations, built of trim red brick, neat, practical, and very ugly; with crowds of red-faced, amply-paunched officials, buttoned into the tightest of uniforms, perpetually saluting each other.

Wierjbolovo, or Wirballen Station as the Germans call it, a huge white building, was plainly visible only a third of a mile away. At Wirballen the German train would stop, for whereas the German railways are built to the standard European gauge of 4 feet 8½ inches, the Russian lines were laid to a gauge of 5 feet 1 inch.

This gauge had been deliberately chosen to prevent the invasion of Russia by her Western neighbour. This was to prove an absolutely illusory safeguard, for, as events have shown, nothing is easier than to *narrow* a railway track. To *broaden* it is often quite impossible. The cunning little Japs found this out during the Russo-Japanese War. They narrowed the broad Russian lines to their own gauge of 3 feet 6 inches, *and then sawed off the ends of the sleepers* with portable circular saws, thus making it impossible for the Russians to relay the rails on the broad gauge. I believe that the Germans adopted the same device more recently.

I think at only one other spot in the world does a short quarter of a mile result in such amazing differences in externals as does that little piece of line between Eydkuhnen and Wirballen; and that is at Linea, the first Spanish village out of Gibraltar.

Leaving the prim and starched orderliness of Gibraltar, with its thick coating of British veneer, its tidy streets and buildings enlivened with the scarlet tunics of Mr. Thomas Atkins and his brethren, you traverse the "Neutral Ground" to an iron railing, and literally pass into Spain through an iron gate. The contrast is extraordinary. It would be unfair to select Linea as a typical Spanish village; it is ugly, and lacks the picturesque features of the ordinary Andalusian village; it is also unquestionably very dirty, and very tumble-down. Between Eydkuhnen and Wirballen the contrast is just as marked. As the German train stopped, hosts of bearded, shaggy-headed individuals in high boots and long white aprons (surely a curious article of equipment for a railway porter) swooped down upon the hand-baggage; I handed my passport to a gendarme (a term confined in Russia to frontier and railway police) and passed through an iron gate into Russia.

Russia in this case was represented by a gigantic whitewashed hall, ambitious originally in design and decoration, but, like most things in Russia, showing traces of neglect and lack of cleanliness. The first exotic note was struck by a full-length, life-size ikon of the Saviour, in a solid silver frame, at the end of the hall. All my Russian fellow-travellers devoutly crossed themselves before this ikon, purchased candles at an adjoining stall, and fixed them in the silver holders before the ikon.

Behind the line of tables serving for the Customs examinations was a railed-off space, containing many desks under green-shaded lamps. Here some fifteen green-coated men whispered mysteriously to each other, referring continually to huge registers.

I felt a thrill creep down my back; here I found myself at last face to face with the omnipotent Russian police. The bespectacled green-coated men scrutinised passports intently, conferred amongst themselves in whispers under the green-shaded lamps, and hunted ominously through the big registers. For the first time I became unpleasantly conscious of the existence of such places as the Fortress of St. Peter and St. Paul, and of a country called Siberia. I speculated as to whether the drawbacks of the Siberian climate had not been exaggerated, should one be compelled to make a possibly prolonged sojourn in that genial land. Above all, I was immensely impressed with the lynx-eyed vigilance and feverish activity of these green-coated guardians of the Russian frontier. From my subsequent knowledge of the ways of Russian officials, I should gather that all this feverish activity began one minute after the whistle announced the approach of the Berlin train, and ceased precisely one minute after the Petrograd train had pulled out, and that never, by any chance, did the frontier police succeed in stopping the entry of any really dangerous conspirator.

Diplomats with official passports are exempt from Customs formalities, so I passed on to the platform, thick with pungent wood-smoke, where the huge blue-painted Russian carriages smoked like volcanoes from their heating apparatus, and the gigantic wood-burning engine (built in Germany) vomited dense clouds from its funnel, crowned with a spark-arrester shaped like a mammoth tea urn, or a giant's soup tureen. Everything in this country seemed on a large scale.

In the gaunt, bare, whitewashed restaurant (these three epithets are applicable to almost every public room in Russia) with its great porcelain stove, and red lamps burning before gilded ikons, I first made the acquaintance of fresh caviar and raw herrings, of the national cabbage soup, or "shtchee," of roast ryabchiks and salted cucumbers, all destined to become very familiar. Railway restaurants in Russia are almost invariably quite excellent.

And so the train clanked out through the night, into the depths of this mysterious glamour-land.

The railway from the frontier to Petrograd runs for 550 miles through an unbroken stretch of interminable dreary swamp and forest, such as would in Canada be termed "muskag," with here and there a poor attempt at cultivation in some clearing, set about with wretched little wooden huts. After a twenty-four hours' run, without any preliminary warning whatever in the shape of suburbs, the train emerges from the forest into a huge city, with tramcars rolling in all directions, and the great golden dome of St. Isaac's blazing like a sun against the murky sky.

I had pictured Petrograd to myself as a second Paris; a city glittering with light and colour, but conceived on an infinitely more grandiose scale than the French capital.

We emerged from the station into an immensely

broad street bordered by shabbily-pretentious buildings all showing signs of neglect. The atrociously uneven pavements, the general untidiness, the broad thoroughfare empty except for a lumbering cart or two, the absence of foot-passengers, and the low cotton-wool sky, all gave an effect of unutterable dreariness. And this was the golden city of my dreams! this place of leprous-fronted houses, of vast open spaces full of drifting snowflakes, and of an immense emptiness. I never was so disappointed in my life. The gilt and coloured domes of the Orthodox churches, the sheepskin-clad, red-shirted moujiks, the occasional swift-trotting Russian carriages, with their bearded and padded coachmen, were the only local touches that redeemed the streets from the absolute commonplace. The Russian lettering over the shops, which then conveyed nothing whatever to me, suggested that the alphabet, having followed the national custom and got drunk, had hastily re-affixed itself to the houses upside down. Although as the years went on I grew quite attached to Petrograd, I could never rid myself of this impression of its immense dreariness. This was due to several causes. There are hardly any stone buildings in the city, everything is of brick plastered over. Owing to climatic reasons the houses are not painted, but are daubed with colour-wash. The successive coats of colour-wash clog all the architectural features, and give the buildings a shabby look, added to which the wash flakes off under the winter snows. There is a natural craving in human nature for colour, and in a country wrapped in snow for at least four months in the year this craving finds expression in painting the roofs red, and in besmearing the houses with crude shades of red, blue, green, and yellow. The result is not a happy one. Again, owing to the intense cold, the shop-windows are all very small, and there is but little display in them. Streets and shops were alike very dimly lighted in my day, and as there is an entire absence of cafés in Petrograd, there is none of the usual glitter and glare of these places to brighten up the streets. The theatres make no display of lights, so it is not surprising that the general effect of the city is one of intense gloom. The very low, murky winter sky added to this effect of depression. Peter the Great had planned his new capital on such a gigantic scale that there were not enough inhabitants to fill its vast spaces. The conceptions were magnificent; the results disappointing. Nothing grander could be imagined than the design of the immense *place* opposite the Winter Palace, with Alexander I's great granite monolith towering in the midst of it, and the imposing semicircular sweep of Government Offices of uniform design enclosing it, pierced in the centre by a monumental triumphal arch crowned with a bronze quadriga. The whole effect of this was spoilt by the hideous crude shade of red with which the buildings were daubed, by the general untidiness, and by the broken, uneven pavement; added to which this huge area was usually untenanted, except by a lumbering cart or two, by a solitary stray "istvoschik," and an occasional muffled-up pedestrian. The Petrograd of reality was indeed very different from the sumptuous city of my dreams.

For the second time I was extraordinarily lucky in my Chief. Our relations with Russia had, during the "'seventies," been strained almost to the breaking point. War had on several occasions seemed almost inevitable between the two countries.

Russians, naturally enough, had shown their feelings of hostility to their potential enemies by practically boycotting the entire British Embassy. The English Government had then made a very wise choice, and had appointed to the Petrograd Embassy the one man capable of smoothing these troubled relations. The late Lord Dufferin was not then a diplomat by profession. He had just completed his term of office as Governor-General of Canada, where, as in every position he had previously occupied, he had been extraordinarily successful. Lord Dufferin had an inexhaustible fund of patience, blended with the most perfect tact; he had a charm of manner no human being could resist; but under it all lay an inflexible will. No man ever understood better the use of the iron hand under the velvet glove, and in a twelvemonth from the date of his arrival in Petrograd he had succeeded not only in gaining the confidence of official Russia, but also in re-establishing the most cordial relations with Russian society. In this he was very ably seconded by Lady Dufferin, who combined a perfectly natural manner with quiet dignity and a curious individual charm. Both Lord and Lady Dufferin enjoyed dancing, skating, and tobagganing as wholeheartedly as though they were children.

Our Petrograd Embassy was a fine old house, with a pleasant intimate character about it lacking in the more ornate building at Berlin. It contained a really beautiful snow-white ball-room, and all the windows fronted the broad, swift-flowing Neva, with the exquisitely graceful slender gilded spire of the Fortress Church, towering three hundred feet aloft, opposite them. We had a very fine collection of silver plate at the Embassy. This plate, valued at £30,000, was the property of our Government, and had been sent out sixty years previously by George IV, who understood the importance attached by Russians to externals. We had also a small set, just sufficient for two persons, of real gold plates. These solid gold plates were only used by the Emperor and Empress on the very rare occasions when they honoured the Embassy with their presence. I wonder what has happened to that gold service now!

Owing to the constant tension of the relations between Great Britain and Russia, our work at the Petrograd Embassy was very heavy indeed at that time. We were frequently kept up till 2 a.m. in the Chancery, cyphering telegrams. All important written despatches between London and Petrograd either way were sent by Queen's Messenger open to Berlin, "under Flying Seal," as it is termed. The Berlin Embassy was thus kept constantly posted as to Russian affairs. After reading our open despatches, both to and from London, the Berlin Embassy would seal them up in a special way. We also got duplicates, in cypher, of all telegrams received in London the previous day from the Paris, Vienna, Berlin, and Constantinople Embassies which bore in any way on Russia or the Eastern Question. This gave us two or three hours' work decyphering every day. Both cyphering and decyphering require the closest concentration, as one single mistake may make nonsense of the whole thing; it is consequently exhausting work. We were perfectly well aware that the Russian Government had somehow obtained possession of one of our codes. This particular "compromised code" was only used by us for transmitting intelligence which the Russians were *intended* to know. They could hardly blame us should they derive false impressions from a telegram of ours which they had decyphered with a stolen code, nor could they well admit that they had done this.

As winter came on, I understood why Russians are so fond of gilding the domes and spires of their churches. It must be remembered that Petrograd lies on parallel 60° N. In December it only gets four hours of very uncertain daylight, and the sun is so low on the horizon that its rays do not reach the streets of the city. It is then that the gilded domes flash and glitter, as they catch the beams of the unseen sun. When the long golden needle of the Fortress Church blazed like a flaming torch or a gleaming spear of fire against the murky sky, I thought it a splendid sight, as was the great golden dome of St. Isaac's scintillating like a second sun over the snow-clad roofs of the houses.

Soon after my arrival I went to the vast church under the gilded dome to hear the singing of the far-famed choir of St. Isaac's.

Here were none of the accessories to which I had been accustomed; no seats; no organ; no pulpit; no side-chapels. A blue haze of incense drifted through the twilight of the vague spaces of the great building; a haze glowing rosily where the red lamps burning before the jewelled ikons gave a faint-dawn-like effect in the semi-darkness. Before me the great screen of the "ikonostas" towered to the roof, with its eight malachite columns forty feet high, and its two smaller columns of precious lapis lazuli flanking the "Royal doors" into the sanctuary. Surely Montferrand, the Frenchman, had designedly steeped the cathedral he had built in perpetual twilight. In broad daylight the juxtaposition of these costly materials, with their discordant colours, would have been garish, even vulgar. Now, barely visible in the shadows, they, the rich mosaics, the masses of heavily-gilt bronze work in the ikonostas, gave an impression of barbaric magnificence and immense splendour. The jasper and polychrome Siberian marbles with which the cathedral was lined, the gold and silver of the jewelled ikons, gleaming faintly in the candle-light, strengthened this impression of sumptuous opulence. Then the choir, standing before the ikonostas, burst into song. The exquisitely beautiful singing of the Russian Church was a perfect revelation to me. I would not have believed it possible that unaccompanied human voices could have produced so entrancing an effect. As the "Cherubic Hymn" died away in softest *pianissimo,* its echoes floating into the misty vastness of the dome, a deacon thundered out prayers in a ringing bass, four tones deeper than those a Western European could compass. The higher clergy, with their long flowing white beards, jewelled crowns, and stiffly-archaic vestments of cloth of gold and silver, seemed to have stepped bodily out of the frame of an ikon; and the stately ritual of the Eastern Church gave me an impression as of something of immemorial age, something separated by the gap of countless centuries from our own prosaic epoch; and through it all rose again and again the plaintive response of the choir, "Gospodi pomiloi," "Lord have mercy," exquisitely sung with all the tenderness and pathos of muted strings.

This was at last the real Russia of my dreams. It was all as I had vaguely pictured it to myself; the densely-packed congregation, with sheepskin-clad peasant and sable-coated noble standing side by side, all alike joining in the prescribed genuflections and prostrations of the ritual; the singing-boys, with their close-cropped heads and curious long blue dressing-gowns; the rolling consonants of the Old Slavonic chanted by the priests; all this was really Russia, and not a bastard imitation of an exotic

Western civilisation like the pseudo-classic city outside.

Two years later, Arthur Sullivan, the composer, happened to be in Petrograd, and I took him to the practice of the Emperor's private church choir. Sullivan was passionately devoted to unaccompanied part-singing, and those familiar with his delightful light operas will remember how he introduced into almost every one of them an unaccompanied madrigal, or a sextet. Sullivan told me that he would not have believed it possible for human voices to obtain the string-like effect of these Russian choirs. He added that although six English singing-boys would probably evolve a greater body of sound than twelve Russian boys, no English choir-boy could achieve the silvery tone these musical little Muscovites produced.

People ignorant of the country have a foolish idea that all Russians can speak French. That may be true of one person in two thousand of the whole population. The remainder only speak their native Russ. Not one cabman in Petrograd could understand a syllable of any foreign language, and though in shops, very occasionally, someone with a slight knowledge of German might be found, it was rare. All the waiters in Petrograd restaurants were yellow-faced little Mohammedan Tartars, speaking only Russian and their own language. I determined therefore to learn Russian at once, and was fortunate in finding a very clever teacher. All men should learn a foreign language from a lady, for natural courtesy makes one listen to what she is saying; whereas with a male teacher one's attention is apt to wander. The patient elderly lady who taught me knew neither English nor French, so we used German as a means of communication. Thanks to Madame Kumin's intelligence, and a considerable amount of hard work on my own part, I was able to pass an examination in Russian in eleven months, and to qualify as Interpreter to the Embassy. The difficulties of the Russian language are enormously exaggerated. The pronunciation *is* hard, as are the terminations; and the appalling length of Russian words is disconcerting. In Russian, great emphasis is laid on *one* syllable of a word, and the rest is slurred over. It is therefore vitally important (should you wish to be understood) to get the emphasis on the right syllable, and for some mysterious reason no foreigner, even by accident, *ever succeeds in pronouncing a Russian name right.* It is Schouvàl-off, not Schòuvaloff; Brusìl-off, not Brùsiloff; Demìd-off, not Dèmidoff. The charming dancer's name is Pàv-Lova, not Pavlòva; her equally fascinating rival is Karsàv-ina, not Karsavìna. I could continue the list indefinitely. Be sure of one thing; however the name is pronounced by a foreigner, it is absolutely certain to be wrong.

What a wise man he was who first said that for every fresh language you learn you acquire a new pair of eyes and a new pair of ears; I felt immensely elated when I found that I could read the cabalistic signs over the shops as easily as English lettering.

A relation of mine had given me a letter of introduction to Princess B——. Now this old lady, though she but seldom left her own house, was a very great power indeed in Petrograd, and was universally known as the "Princesse Château." For some reason or another, I was lucky enough to find favour in this dignified old lady's eyes. She asked me to call on her again, and at our second meeting invited me to her Sunday evenings. The Princesse Château's Sunday evenings were a thing quite apart. They were a survival in Petrograd of the French eighteenth century literary "salons," but devoid of the faintest flavour of pedantry or priggism. Never in my life, before or since, have I heard such wonderfully brilliant conversation, for, with the one exception of myself, the Princesse Château tolerated no dull people at her Sundays. She belonged to a generation that always spoke French amongst themselves, and imported their entire culture from France. Peter the Great had designed St. Petersburg as a window through which to look on Europe, and the tradition of this amongst the educated classes was long in dying out. The Princess assembled some thirty people every Sunday, all Russians, with the exception of myself. These people discussed any and every subject—literature, art, music, and philosophy—with sparkling wit, keen critical instinct, and extraordinary felicity of phrase, usually in French, sometimes in English, and occasionally in Russian. Their knowledge seemed encyclopædic, and they appeared equally at home in any of the three languages. They greatly appreciated a neatly-turned epigram, or a novel, crisply-coined definition. Any topic, however, touching directly or indirectly on the external or internal policy of Russia was always tacitly avoided. My *rôle* was perforce reduced to that of a listener, but it was a perfectly delightful society. Princesse Château had a very fine suite of rooms on the first floor of her house, decorated "at the period" in Louis XVI style by imported French artists; these rooms still retained their original furniture and fittings, and were a museum of works of art; but her Sunday evenings were always held in the charming but plainly-furnished rooms which she herself inhabited on the ground floor. We had one distinct advantage over the old French *salons,* for Princesse Château entertained her guests every Sunday to suppers which were justly celebrated in the gastronomic world of Petrograd. During supper the conversation proceeded just as brilliantly as before. There were always two or three Grand Duchesses present, for to attend Princesse Château's Sundays was a sort of certificate of culture. The Grand Duchesses were treated quite unceremoniously, beyond receiving a perfunctory "Madame" in each sentence addressed to them. How curious that, both in English and French, the highest title of respect should be plain "Madame"! As the Russian equivalent is "Vashoe Imperatorskoe Vuisochestvo," a considerable expenditure of time and breath was saved by using the terser French term. And through it all moved the mistress of the house, the stately little smiling old lady, in her plain black woollen dress and lace cap, dropping here a quaint criticism, there an apt *bon-mot.* Perfectly charming people!

The relatives and friends of Princesse Château whom I met at her house, when they discovered that I had a genuine liking for their country, and that I did not criticise details of Russian administration, were good enough to open their houses to me in their turn. Though most of these people owned large and very fine houses, they opened them but rarely to foreigners. They gave, very occcasionally, large entertainments to which they invited half Petrograd, including the Diplomatic Body, but there they stopped. They did not care, as a rule, to invite foreigners to share the intimacy of their family life. I was very fortunate therefore in having an opportunity of seeing a phase of Russian life which few foreigners have enjoyed. Russians seldom do things by halves. I do not believe that in any other country in the world could a stranger have been made to feel himself so thoroughly at home amongst people of a different nationality, and with such totally different racial ideals; or have been treated with such constant and uniform kindness. There was no ceremony whatever on either side, and on the Russian side, at times, an outspokenness approaching bluntness. As I got to know these cultivated, delightful people well, I grew very fond of them. They formed a clique, possibly a narrow clique, amongst themselves, and had that complete disregard for outside criticism which is often found associated with persons of established position. They met almost nightly at each others' houses, and I could not but regret that such beautiful and vast houses should be seen by so few people. One house, in particular, contained a staircase in exact replica of a Grecian temple in white statuary Carrara marble, a thing of exquisite beauty. In their perpetual sets of intellectual lawn tennis, if I may coin the term, the superiority of the feminine over the male intellects was very marked. This is, I believe, a characteristic of all Slavonic countries, and I recalled Bismarck's dictum that the Slav peoples were essentially feminine, and I wondered whether there could be any connection between the two points. Living so much with Russians, it was impossible not to fall into the Russian custom of addressing them by their Christian names and patronymics; such as "Maria Vladìmirovna" (Mary daughter of Vladimir) or "Olga Andreèvna" (Olga daughter of Andrew) or "Pavel Alexàndrovitch" (Paul son of Alexander). I myself became Feòdor Yàkovlevitch, (Frederic son of James, those being the nearest Russian equivalents). On arriving at a house, the proper form of inquiry to the hall porter was, "Ask Mary daughter of Vladimir if she will receive Frederic son of James." In due time the answer came, "Mary daughter of Vladimir begs Frederic son of James to go upstairs." My own servants always addressed me punctiliously as Feòdor Yàkovlevitch. On giving them an order they would answer in Moscovite fashion, "I hear you, Frederic son of James," the equivalent to our prosaic, "Very good, sir."

Amongst my new friends, as at the Princesse Château's, no allusions whatever, direct or indirect, were made to internal conditions in Russia. Apart from the fact that one of these new friends was himself Minister of the Interior at the time, it would not have been safe. In those days the Secret Police, or "Third Section," as they were called, were very active, and their ramifications extended everywhere. One night at a supper party a certain Countess B—— criticised in very open and most unflattering terms a lady to whom the Emperor Alexander II was known to be devotedly attached. Next morning at 8 a.m. the Countess was awakened by her terrified maid, who told her that the "Third Section" were there and demanded instant admittance. Two men came into the Countess's bedroom and informed her that their orders were that she was to take the 12.30 train to Europe that morning. They would remain with her till then, and would accompany her to the frontier. As she would not be allowed to return to Russia for twelve months, they begged her to order her maid to pack what was necessary; and no one knew better than Countess B—— how useless any attempted resistance would be.

This episode made a great stir at the time. As the words complained of had been uttered about 3 a.m., the police action had been remarkably prompt. The informant must have driven straight from the supper party to the "Third Section," and everyone in Petrograd had a very distinct idea who the informant was. Is it necessary to add that she was a lady?

Some of my new friends volunteered to propose and second me for the Imperial Yacht Club. This was not the club that the diplomats usually joined; it was a purely Russian club, and, in spite of its name, had no connection with yachting. It had also the reputation of being extremely exclusive, but thanks to my Russian sponsors, I got duly elected to it. This was, I am sure, the most delightful club in Europe. It was limited to 150 members of whom only two, besides myself, were foreigners, and the most perfect *camaraderie* existed between the members. The atmosphere of the place was excessively friendly and intimate, and the building looked more like a private house than a club, as deceased members had bequeathed to it pictures, a fine collection of old engravings, some splendid old Beauvais tapestry, and a great deal of Oriental porcelain. Above all, we commanded the services of the great Armand, prince of French chefs. Associating so much with Russians, it was possible to see things from their point of view. They all had an unshakable belief in the absolute invincibility of Russia, and in her complete invulnerability, for it must not be forgotten that in 1880 Russia had never yet been defeated in any campaign, except partially in the Crimean War of 1854-56. My friends did not hide their convictions that it was Russia's manifest destiny to absorb in time the whole of the Asiatic Continent, including India, China, and Turkey. There were grounds for this article of faith, for in 1880 Russia's bloodless absorption of vast territories in Central Asia had been astounding. It was not until the Russo-Japanese War of 1904-1905 that the friable clay feet of the Northern Colossus were revealed to the outside world, though those with a fairly intimate knowledge of the country quite realised how insecure were the foundations on which the stupendous structure of modern Russia had been erected.

I am deeply thankful that the great majority of my old friends had passed away in the ordinary course of nature before the Great Catastrophe overwhelmed the mighty Empire in which they took such deep pride; and that they were spared the sight and knowledge of the awful orgy of blood, murder, and spoliation which followed the ruin of the land they loved so well. Were they not now at rest, it would be difficult for me to write of those old days.

To grasp the Russian mentality, it must be remembered that they are essentially Orientals. Russia is not the most Eastern outpost of Western civilisation; it is the most Western outpost of the East. Russians have all the qualities of the Oriental, his fatalism, his inertness, and, I fear, his innate pecuniary corruption. Their fatalism makes them accept their destiny blindly. What has been ordained from the beginning of things is useless to fight against; it must be accepted. The same inertness characterises every Eastern nation, and the habit of "baksheesh" is ingrained in the Oriental blood. If the truth were known, we should probably find that the real reason why Cain killed Abel was that the latter had refused him a commission on some transaction or other. The fatalism and lack of initiative are not the only Oriental traits in the Russian character. In a hundred little ways they show their origin: in their love of uncut jewels; in their lack of sense of time (the Russian for "at once" is "si chas," which means "this hour"; an instructive commentary); in the reluctance South Russians show in introducing strangers to the ladies of their household, the Oriental peeps out everywhere. Peter the Great could order his Boyards to abandon their fur-trimmed velvet robes, to shave off their beards, powder their heads, and array themselves in the satins and brocades of Versailles. He could not alter the men and women inside the French imported finery. He could abandon his old capital, matchless, many-pinnacled Moscow, vibrant with every instinct of Russian nationality; he could create a new pseudo-Western, sham-classical city in the frozen marshes of the Neva; but even the Autocrat could not change the souls of his people. Easterns they were, Easterns they remained, and that is the secret of Russia, they are not Europeans. Peter himself was so fully aware of the racial limitations of his countrymen that he imported numbers of foreigners to run the country; Germans as Civil and Military administrators; Dutchmen as builders and town-planners; and Englishmen to foster its budding commerce. To the latter he granted special privileges, and even in my time there was a very large English commercial community in Petrograd; a few of them descendants of Peter the Great's pioneers; the majority of them with hereditary business connections with Russia. Their special privileges had gradually been withdrawn, but the official name of the English Church in Petrograd was still "British Factory in St. Petersburg," surely a curious title for a place of worship. The various German-Russian families from the Baltic Provinces, the Adlerbergs, the Benckendorffs, and the Stackelbergs, had served Russia well. Under their strong guidance she became a mighty Power, but when under Alexander III the reins of government were confided to purely Russian hands, rapid deterioration set in. This dreamy nation lacks driving power. In my time, the very able Minister for Foreign Affairs, M. de Giers, was of German origin, and his real name was Hirsch. His extremely wily and astute second in command, Baron Jomini, was a Swiss. Modern Russia was largely the creation of the foreigner.

I saw a great deal, too, of a totally different stratum of Russian society. Mr. X., the head of a large exporting house, was of British origin, the descendant of one of Peter's commercial pioneers. He himself, like his father and grandfather, had been born in Russia, and though he retained his English speech, he had adopted all the points of view of the country of his birth. Madame X. came of a family of the so-called "Intelligenzia." Most of her relatives seemed to have undertaken compulsory journeys to Siberia, not as prisoners, but for a given term of exile. Madame X.'s brother-in-law owned and edited a paper of advanced views, which was being continually suppressed, and had been the cause of two long trips eastward for its editor and proprietor. Neither Mr. nor Madame X. shared their relatives' extreme views. What struck me was that behind the floods of vehement invective of Madame O—— (the editor's wife) there was never the smallest practical suggestion. "You say, Madame O——," I would hazard, "that the existing state of things is intolerable. What remedy do you suggest?" "I am not the Government," would retort Madame O—— with great heat. "It is for the Government to make suggestions. I only denounce an abominable injustice." "Quite so, Madame O——, but how can these conditions be improved. What is your programme of reform?" "We have nothing to do with reforms. Our mission is to destroy utterly. Out of the ruins a better state of things must necessarily arise; as nothing could possibly be worse than present conditions." And so we travelled round and round in a circle. Mr. O——, when appealed to, would blink through his spectacles with his kindly old eyes, and emit a torrent of admirable moral aphorisms, which might serve as unimpeachable copy-book headings, but had no bearing whatever on the subject we were discussing. Never once amidst these floods of bitter invective and cataracts of fierce denunciation did I hear one single practical suggestion made or any outline traced of a scheme to better existing conditions. "We must destroy," shouted Madame O——, and there her ideas stopped. I think the Slavonic bent of mind, like the Celtic, is purely *de*structive, and has little or no *con*structive power in it. This may be due to the ineradicable element of the child in both races. They are "Peter Pans," and a child loves destruction.

Poor dreamy, emotional, hopelessly unpractical Russia! Madame O——'s theories have been put into effect now, and we all know how appalling the result has been.

These conversations were always carried on in French for greater safety in order that the servants might not overhear, but when Mr. and Madame O—— found difficulties in expressing themselves in that language, they both broke into torrents of rapid Russian, to poor Madame X.'s unconcealed terror. The danger was a real one, for the O——'s were well known in police circles as revolutionists, and it must have gone hard with the X.'s had their servants reported to the police the violent opinions that had been expressed in their house.

Many of the Diplomatic Body were in the habit of attending the midnight Mass at St. Isaac's on Easter Day, on account of the wonderfully impressive character of the service. We were always requested to come in full uniform, with decorations; and we stood inside the rails of the ikonostas, behind the choir. The time to arrive was about 11.30 p.m., when the great church, packed to its doors by a vast throng, was wrapped in almost total darkness. Under the dome stood a catafalque bearing a gilt coffin. This open coffin contained a strip of silk, on which was painted an effigy of the dead Christ, for it will be remembered that no carved or graven image is allowed in a church of the Eastern rite. There was an arrangement by which a species of blind could be drawn over the painted figure, thus concealing it. As the eye grew accustomed to the shadows, tens of thousands of unlighted candles, outlining the arches, cornices, and other architectural features of the cathedral, were just visible. These candles each had their wick touched with kerosine and then surrounded with a thread of gun-cotton, which ran continuously from candle to candle right round the building. When the hanging end of the thread of gun-cotton was lighted, the flame ran swiftly round the church, kindling each candle in turn; a very fascinating sight. At half-past eleven, the only light was from the candles surrounding the bier, where black-robed priests were chanting the mournful Russian Office for the Dead. At about twenty minutes to twelve the blind was drawn over the dead Christ, and the priests, feigning surprise, advanced to the rails of the ikonostas, and announced to an Archimandrite that the coffin was empty. The Archimandrite ordered them to search round the church, and the priests perambulated the church with gilt lanterns, during which time the catafalque, bier, and its accessories were all removed. The priests announced to the Archimandrite that their search had been unsuccessful, whereupon he ordered them to make a further search outside the church. They went out, and so timed their return as to arrive before the ikonostas at three minutes before midnight. They again reported that they had been unsuccessful; when, as the first stroke of midnight pealed from the great clock, the Metropolitan of Petrograd announced in a loud voice, "Christ is risen!" At an electric signal given from the cathedral, the great guns of the fortress boomed out in a salute of one hundred and one guns; the gun-cotton was touched off, and the swift flash kindled the tens of thousands of candles running round the building; the enormous congregation lit the tapers they carried; the "Royal doors" of the ikonostas were thrown open, and the clergy appeared in their festival vestments of cloth of gold, as the choir burst into the beautiful Russian Easter anthem, and so the Easter Mass began. Nothing more poignantly dramatic, more magnificently impressive, could possibly be imagined than this almost instantaneous change from intense gloom to blazing light; from the plaintive dirges of the Funeral Service to the jubilant strains of the Easter Mass. I never tired of witnessing this splendid piece of symbolism.

It sounds almost irreverent to talk of comical

incidents in connection with so solemn an occasion, but there are two little episodes I must mention. About 1880 the first tentative efforts were made by France to establish a Franco-Russian alliance. Ideas on the subject were very nebulous at first, but slowly they began to crystallise into concrete shape. A new French Ambassador was appointed to Petrograd in the hope of fanning the faint spark into further life. He, wishing to show his sympathy for the *nation amie,* attended the Easter Mass at St. Isaac's, but unfortunately he was quite unversed in the ritual of the Orthodox Church. In every ikonostas there are two ikons on either side of the "Royal doors"; the Saviour on one side, the Madonna and Child on the other. The new Ambassador was standing in front of the ikon of the Saviour, and in the course of the Mass the Metropolitan came out, and made the three prescribed low bows before the ikon, previous to censing it. The Ambassador, taking this as a personal compliment to France, as represented in his own person, acknowledged the attention with three equally low bows, laying his hand on his heart and ejaculating with all the innate politeness of his nation, "Monsieur! Monsieur! Monsieur!" This little incident caused much amusement, as did a newly-arrived German diplomat, who when greeted by a Russian friend with the customary Easter salutation of "Christ is risen!" ("Kristos voskress!") wished to respond, but, being ignorant of the traditional answer, "He is verily risen," merely made a low bow and said, "Ich auch," which may be vulgarly Englished into "The same here."

The universal Easter suppers at the conclusion of the Mass play an important part in Russian life, for they mean the breaking of the long and rigorous Lenten fast of the Eastern Church, during which all meat, butter, milk, and eggs are prohibited. The peasants adhere rigidly to these rules, so the Easter supper assumes great importance in their eyes. The ingredients of this supper are invariable for high and low, for rich and poor—cold ham, hard-boiled eggs dyed red, a sort of light cake akin to the French *brioche,* and a sour cream-cheese shaped into a pyramid and decorated with little crosses of dried currants. I think that this cake and cream cheese (known as "Paskva") are prepared only at Easter-time. Even at the Yacht Club during Holy Week, meat, butter, milk, and eggs were prohibited, and still Armand, our incomparable French chef, managed to produce *plats* of the most succulent description. Loud praises were lavished upon his skill in preparing such excellent dishes out of oil, fish, flour, and vegetables, the only materials allowed him. I met Armand in the passage one day and asked him how he managed to do it. Looking round to see that no Russians could overhear, Armand replied with a wink, "Voyez-vous Monsieur, le bon Dieu ne regarde pas d'aussi près." Of course he had gone on using cream, butter, and eggs, just as usual, but as the members of the Club did not know this, and thought that they were strictly obeying the rules of their Church, I imagine that no blame could attach to them.

On Easter Eve the two-mile-long Nevsky Perspective was lined with humble folks standing by white napkins on which the materials for their Easter supper were arranged. On every napkin glimmered a lighted taper, and the long line of these twinkling lights produced a very charming effect, as of myriads of glow-worms. Priests would pass swiftly down the line, each attended by an acolyte carrying a *pail* of holy water. The priest would mutter a rapid blessing, sprinkle the food and its owner with holy water, pocket an infinitesimally small fee, and pass on again.

A friend of mine was once down in the fruit-growing districts of the Crimea. Passing through one of the villages of that pleasing peninsula, he found it decorated in honour of a religious festival. The village priest was going to bless the first-fruits of the orchards. The peasants stood in a row down the village street, each one with the first crop of his orchard arranged on a clean napkin before him. The red-bearded priest, quite a young man, passed down the street, sprinkling fruit and grower alike with holy water, and repeating a blessing to each one. The young priest approached, and my friend could hear quite plainly the words of his blessing. No. —— it was quite impossible! It was incredible! and yet he could not doubt the evidence of his own ears! The young priest was speaking in good Scots, and the words of the blessing he bestowed on each parishioner were, "Here, man! tak' it. If it does ye nae guid, it canna possibly dae ye any hairm." The men addressed, probably taking this for a quotation from Scripture in some unknown tongue, bowed reverently as the words were pronounced over them. That a Russian village priest in a remote district of the Crimea should talk broad Scots was a sufficiently unusual circumstance to cause my friend to make some further inquiries. It then appeared that when the Government dockyard at Sebastopol was reopened, several Scottish foremen from the Clyde shipbuilding yards were imported to supervise the Russian workmen. Amongst others came a Glasgow foreman with his wife and a son who was destined for the ministry of the Free Church of Scotland. Once arrived in Russia, they found that facilities for training a youth for the Presbyterian ministry were somewhat lacking in Sebastopol. Sooner than sacrifice their dearest wish, the parents, with commendable broadmindedness, decided that their offspring should enter the Russian Church. He was accordingly sent to a seminary and in due course was ordained a priest and appointed to a parish, but he apparently still retained his Scottish speech and his characteristically Scottish independence of view.

After a year in Petrograd I used to attempt to analyse to myself the complex Russian character. "We are a 'jelly-folk,'" had said one of my friends to me. The Russian term was "Kiselnui narod," and I think there is truth in that. They *are* an invertebrate folk. I cannot help thinking that Peter the Great was one of the worst enemies of his own country. Instead of allowing Russia to develop naturally on lines suited to the racial instincts of her people, he attempted to run the whole country into a West European mould, and to superimpose upon it a veneer imported from the France of Louis Quatorze. With the very few this could perhaps succeed, with the many it was a foregone failure. He tried in one short lifetime to do what it had taken other countries centuries to accomplish. He built a vast and imposing edifice on shifting sand, without any foundations. It might stand for a time; its ultimate doom was certain.

From the windows of our Embassy we looked upon the broad Neva. When fast bound in the grip of winter, sledge-roads were made across the ice, bordered with lamp-posts and marked out with sawn-off fir trees. Little wooden taverns and tea-houses were built on the river, and as soon as the ice was of sufficient thickness the tramcar lines were laid across it. A colony of Laps came yearly and encamped on the river with their reindeer, for the temperature of Petrograd rarely falling more than ten degrees below zero, it was looked upon as a genial winter climate for invalids from Lapland. A stranger from another planet might have imagined that these buildings were permanent, that the fir trees were really growing, and that all the life on the frozen river would last indefinitely. Everyone knew, though, with absolute certainty that by the middle of April the ice would break up, and that these little houses, if not removed in time, would be carried away and engulfed in the liberated stream. By May the river would be running again as freely as though these temporary edifices had never been built on it.

I think these houses built on the ice were very typical of Russia.

CHAPTER IV

The Winter Palace—Its interior—Alexander II—A Russian Court Ball—The "Bals des Palmiers"—The Empress—The blessing of the Neva—Some curiosities of the Winter Palace—The great Orloff diamond—My friend the Lady-in-Waiting—Sugared Compensations—The attempt on the Emperor's life of 1880—Some unexpected finds in the Palace—A most hilarious funeral—Sporting expeditions—Night drives through the forest in mid-winter—Wolves—A typical Russian village—A peasant's house—"Deaf and dumb people"—The inquisitive peasant youth—Curiosity about strangers—An embarrassing situation—A still more awkward one—Food difficulties—A bear hunt—My first bear—Alcoholic consequences—My liking for the Russian peasant—The beneficent india-rubber Ikon—Two curious sporting incidents—Village habits—The great gulf fixed between Russian nobility and peasants.

THE Winter Palace drags its lengthy, uninteresting façade for some five hundred feet along the quays of the Neva. It presents a mere wearisome iteration of the same architectural features repeated again and again, and any effect it might produce is marred by the hideous shade of that crude red, called by the Russians "raspberry colour," with which it is daubed, and for which they have so misplaced an affection.

The interior of the Winter Palace was burned out in 1837, and only a few of the original State rooms survive. These surviving rooms are the only ones of any artistic interest, as the other innumerable and stupendous halls were all reconstructed during the "period of bad taste," and bear ample witness to that fact in every detail of their ornamentation.

The Ambassadors' staircase, part of the original building, is very dignified and imposing with its groups of statuary, painted ceiling, and lavish decoration, as is Peter the Great's Throne room, with jasper columns, and walls hung with red velvet worked in gold with great Russian two-headed eagles. All the tables, chairs, and chandeliers in this room were of solid silver.

St. George's Hall, another of the old rooms, I thought splendid, with its pure white marble walls and columns and rich adornments of gilt bronze, and there was also an agreeably barbaric hall with entirely gilt columns, many banners, and gigantic effigies of ancient Russian warriors. All these rooms were full of collections of the gold and silver-gilt trays on which the symbolical "bread and salt" had been offered to different Emperors in the various towns of their dominions.

The fifty or so other modern rooms were only remarkable for their immense size, the Nicholas Hall, for instance, being 200 feet long and 65 feet wide, though the so-called "Golden Hall" positively dazzled one with its acre or so of gilding. It would have been a happy idea for the Emperor to assemble all the leading financiers of Europe to dine together in the "Golden Hall." The sight of so much of the metal which they had spent their whole lives in amassing would have gratified the financiers, and would probably have stimulated them to fresh exertions.

The Emperor Alexander II always received the diplomats in Peter the Great's Throne room, seated on Peter's throne. He was a wonderfully handsome man even in his old age, with a most commanding manner, and an air of freezing hauteur. When addressing junior members of the Diplomatic Body there was something in his voice and a look in his eye reminiscent of the Great Mogul addressing an earthworm.

I have only seen three Sovereigns who looked their parts quite unmistakably: Alexander II of Russia, William I of Germany, and Queen Victoria. In Queen Victoria's case it was the more remarkable, as she was very short. Yet this little old lady in her plain dress, had the most inimitable dignity, and no one could have mistaken her for anything but a Queen. I remember Queen Victoria attending a concert at the Albert Hall in 1887, two months before the Jubilee celebrations. The vast building was packed to the roof, and the Queen received a tremendous ovation. No one who saw it can ever forget how the little old lady advanced to the front of her box and made two very low sweeping curtsies to the right and to the left of her with incomparable dignity and grace, as she smiled through her tears on the audience in acknowledgment of the thunders of applause that greeted her. Queen Victoria was always moved to tears when she received an unusually cordial ovation from her people, for they loved her, and she loved them.

The scale of everything in the Winter Palace was so vast that it is difficult to compare the Court entertainments there with those elsewhere.

Certainly the Russian ladies looked well in their uniform costumes. The cut, shape, and style of these dresses never varied, be the fashions what they might. The dress, once made, lasted the owner for her lifetime, though with advancing years it might possibly require to be readjusted to an expanding figure. They were enormously expensive to start with—anything from £300 to £1,200. There was a complete under-dress of white satin, heavily embroidered. Over this was worn a velvet dress lavishly trimmed with dark fur. This velvet dress might be of dull red, dark blue, green, or brown, according to the taste of the wearer. It had to have a long train embroidered with gold or silver flowers, or both mixed, as the owner's fancy dictated. On the head was worn the "Kakoshnik," the traditional Russian head-dress, in the form of a crescent. In the case of married women the "Kakoshnik" might be of diamonds, or any gems they fancied, or could compass; for girls the "Kakoshnik" must be of white silk. Girls, too, had to wear white, without the velvet over-dress. The usual fault of Russian faces is their undue breadth across the cheek-bones, and the white " Kakoshnik " worn by the unmarried girls seemed to me to emphasise this defect, whereas a blazing semicircle of diamonds made a most becoming setting for an older face, although at times, as in other cases, the setting might be more ornamental than the object it enshrined. Though the Russian uniforms were mostly copied from German models, the national lack of attention to detail was probably to blame for the lack of effect they produced when compared with their Prussian originals.

There was always something a little slovenly in the way in which the Russian uniforms were worn, though an exception must be made in the case of the resplendent " Chevaliers Gardes," and of the " Gardes à Cheval." The uniform of these two crack cavalry regiments was closely copied from that of the Prussian " Gardes du Corps " and was akin to that of our own Life Guards and Royal Horse Guards; the same leather breeches and long jack-boots, and the same cuirasses; the tunics, though were white, instead of the scarlet or blue of their Engilsh prototypes. The " Chevaliers Gardes " had silvered cuirasses and helmets surmounted with the Russian eagle, whereas those of the " Gardes à Cheval " were gilt. As we know, " all that glitters is not gold," and in spite of their gilding the " Gardes à Cheval " were considered very inferior socially to their rivals. The Emperor's fiercely-moustached Circassian bodyguard struck an agreeably exotic note with their grass-green trousers and long blue kaftans, covered with rows of Persian cartridge-holders in *niello* of black and silver. Others of the Circassians wore coats of chain mail over their kaftans, and these kaftans were always sleeveless, showing the bright green, red, or blue silk shirt-sleeves of their wearers. Another pleasant barbaric touch.

To my mind, the smartest uniforms were those of the Cossack officers; baggy green knickerbockers thrust into high boots, a hooked-and-eyed green tunic without a single button or a scrap of gold lace on it, and a plain white silk belt. No one could complain of a lack of colour at a Petrograd Palace ball. The Russian civil and Court uniforms were ingeniously hideous with their white trousers and long frock-coats covered with broad transverse bars of gold lace. The wearers of these ugly garments always looked to me like walking embodiments of what are known in commercial circles as "gilt-edged securities." As at Berlin, there were hosts of pages at these entertainments. These lads were all attired like miniature "Chevaliers Gardes," in leather breeches and jack-boots, and wore gold-laced green tunics; a singularly unpractical dress, I should have thought, for a growing boy. All Russians of a certain social position were expected to send their sons to be educated at the "School for Imperial Pages," which was housed in an immense and ornate building and counted four hundred pupils. Wise parents mistrusted the education "aux pages" for their sons, knowing that, however little else they might learn there, they would be certain to acquire habits of gross extravagance; the prominence, too, into which these boys were thrust at Court functions tended to make them unduly precocious.

The smaller Court balls were known as "Les Bals des Palmiers." On these occasions, a hundred large palm trees, specially grown for the purpose at Tsarskoe Selo, were brought by road from there in huge vans. Round the palm in its tub supper tables were built, each one accommodating fifteen people. It was really an extraordinarily pretty sight seeing these rows of broad-fronded palms down the great Nicholas Hall, and the knowledge that a few feet away there was an outside temperature of 5° below zero added piquancy to the sight of these exiles from the tropics waving their green plumes so far away in the frozen North. At the "Bals des Palmiers" it was Alexander II's custom to make the round of the tables as soon as his guests were seated. The Emperor would go up to a table, the occupants of which of course all rose at his approach, say a few words to one or two of them, and then eat either a small piece of bread or a little fruit, and just put his lips to a glass of champagne, in order that his guests might say that he had eaten and drank with them. A delicate and graceful attention!

As electric light had not then been introduced into the palace, the entire building was lighted with wax candles. I cannot remember the number I was told was required on these occasions, but I think it was over one hundred thousand. The candles were all lighted with a thread of gun-cotton, as in St. Isaac's Cathedral.

The Empress appeared but very rarely. It was a matter of common knowledge that she was suffering from an incurable disease. All the rooms in which she lived were artifically impregnated with oxygen, continuously released from cylinders in which the gas had been compressed. This, though it relieved the lungs of the sufferer, proved very trying to the Empress's ladies-in-waiting, as this artifical atmosphere with its excess of oxygen after an hour or so gave them all violent headaches and attacks of giddiness.

In spite of the characteristic Russian carelessness about details, these Petrograd Palace entertainments provided a splendid glittering pageant to the eye, for the stage was so vast and the number of performers so great. There was not the same blaze of diamonds as in London, but I should say that the individual jewels were far finer. A stone must be very perfect to satisfy the critical Russian eye, and, true to their Oriental blood, the ladies preferred unfaceted rubies, sapphires, and emeralds. Occasional Emirs from Central Asia served, as do the Indian princes at Buckingham Palace, as a reminder that Russia's responsibilities, like those of Great Britain, did not cease with her European frontiers.

Once a year the diplomats had much the best of the situation. This was at the blessing of the waters of the Neva—"the Jordan," as Russians called it—on January 6, old style, or January 18, according to our reckoning. We saw the ceremonies through the double windows of the great steam-heated Nicholas

Hall, whereas the Emperor and all the Grand Dukes had to stand bareheaded in the snow outside. A great hole was cut in the ice of the Neva, with a temporary chapel erected over it. At the conclusion of the religious service, the Metropolitan of Petrograd solemnly blessed the waters of the river, and dipped a great golden cross into them.

A cordon of soldiers had to guard the opening in the ice until it froze over again, in order to prevent fanatical peasants from bathing in the newly-consecrated waters. Many had lost their lives in this way.

A friend of mine, the Director of the Hermitage Gallery, offered to take me all over the Winter Palace, and the visit occupied nearly an entire day. The maze of rooms was so endless that the mind got a little bewildered and surfeited with the sight of so many splendours. A detail that amused me was a small library on the second floor, opening on to an avenue of lime trees. One of the Empresses had chosen for her private library this room on the second floor, looking into a courtyard. She had selected it on account of its quiet, but expressed a wish to have an avenue of trees, under which to walk in the intervals of her studies. The room being on the second floor, and looking into a yard, the wish appeared to be difficult to execute, but in those days the word "impossible" did not exist for an Empress of Russia. The entire courtyard was filled in with earth, and full-grown lime trees transplanted there. When I saw this aerial grove eighty years afterwards, there was quite a respectable avenue of limes on the second floor of the building, with a gravel walk bordered by grass-plots beneath them. Another Empress wished to have a place to walk in during the winter months, so a very ingenious hanging winter-garden was contrived for her, following all the exterior angles of the building. It was not in the least like an ordinary conservatory, but really did recall an outdoor garden. There were gravel walks, and lawns of lycopodium simulating grass; there were growing orange trees, and quite large palms. For some reason the creepers on the walls of this pseudo-garden were all artifical, being very cleverly made out of painted sheet-iron.

I had an opportunity later of seeing the entire Winter Palace collection of silver plate, and all the Crown jewels, when they were arranged for the inspection of the late Duke of Edinburgh, who was good enough to invite me to come. There were enormous quantities of plate, of Russian, French, and English make, sufficient to stock every silversmith's shop in London. Some of the English plate was of William and Mary's and Queen Anne's date, and there were some fine early Georgian pieces. They would, I confess, have appeared to greater advantage had they conveyed the idea that they had been occasionally cleaned. As it was, they looked like dull pewter that had been neglected for twenty years. Of the jewels, the only things I remember were a superb "corsage" of diamonds and aquamarines—not the pale green stones we associate with the name, but immense stones of that bright blue tint, so highly prized in Russia—and especially the great Orloff diamond. The "corsage" was big enough to make a very ample cuirass for the most stalwart of lifeguardsmen, and the Orloff diamond formed the head of the Russian Imperial sceptre. The history of the Orloff, or Lazareff, diamond is quite interesting. Though by no means the largest, it is considered the most perfect diamond in the world, albeit it has a slight flaw in it. Originally stolen from India, it came into the hands of an Armenian called Lazareff in some unknown manner about A. D. 1750. Lazareff, so the story goes, devised a novel hiding-place for the great stone. Making a deep incision into the calf of his leg, he placed the diamond in the cavity, and lay in bed for three months till the wound was completely healed over. He then started for Amsterdam, and though stripped and searched several times during his journey, for he was strongly suspected of having the stone concealed about his person, its hiding-place was never discovered. At Amsterdam Lazareff had the wound reopened by a surgeon, and the diamond extracted. He then sold it to Count Orloff for 450,000 roubles, or roughly £45,000, and Orloff in his turn made a present of the great stone to Catherine the Great. The diamond is set under a jewelled Russian eagle at the extremity of the sceptre, where it probably shows to greater advantage than it did when concealed for six months in the calf of an Armenian's leg.

The accommodation provided for the suites of the Imperial family is hardly on a par with the magnificence of the rest of the palace. The Duchess of Edinburgh, daughter of Alexander II, made a yearly visit to Petrograd, as long as her mother the Empress was alive. As the Duchess's lady-in-waiting happened to be one of my oldest friends, during her stay I was at the palace at least three days a week, and I retain vivid recollections of the dreary, bare, whitewashed vault assigned to her as a sitting-room. The only redeeming feature of this room was a five-storied glass tray packed with some fifty varieties of the most delicious *bon-bons* the mind of man could conceive. These were all fresh-baked every day by the palace confectioner, and the tray was renewed every morning. There were some sixty of these trays prepared daily, and their arrangement was always absolutely identical, precisely the same number of caramels and *fondants* being placed on each shelf of the tray. Everyone knew that the palace confectioner owned a fashionable sweet shop on the Nevsky, where he traded under a French name, and I imagine that his shop was entirely stocked from the remains of the palace trays.

In the spring of 1880 an attempt was made on Alexander's II's life by a bomb which completely wrecked the white marble private dining-room. The Emperor's dinner hour was 7, and the bomb was timed to explode at 7.20 p.m. The Emperor happened at the time to be overwhelmed with work, and at the last moment he postponed dinner until 7.30.

The bomb exploded at the minute it had been timed for, killing many of the servants. My poor friend the lady-in-waiting was passing along the corridor as the explosion occurred. She fell unhurt amongst the wreckage, but the shock and the sight of the horribly mangled bodies of the servants were too much for her. She never recovered from their effects, and died in England within a year. After this crime, the Winter Palace was thoroughly searched from cellars to attics, and some curious discoveries were made.

Some of the countless moujiks employed in the palace had vast unauthorized colonies of their relatives living with them on the top floor of the building. In one bedroom a full-grown cow was found, placidly chewing the cud. One of the moujiks had smuggled it in as a new-born calf, had brought it up by hand, and afterwards fed it on hay purloined from the stables. Though it may have kept his family well provided with milk, stabling a cow in a bedroom unprovided with proper drainage, on the top floor of a building, is not a proceeding to be unduly encouraged; nor does it tend to add to the sanitary amenities of a palace.

Russians are fond of calling the Nevsky "the street of toleration," for within a third of a mile of its length a Dutch Calvinist, a German Lutheran, a Roman Catholic, and an Armenian church rise almost side by side. "Nevsky" is, of course, only the adjective of "Neva," and the street is termed "Perspective" in French and "Prospect" in Russian. Close to the Armenian church lived M. Delyanoff, who was the Minister of Education in those days. Both M. and Madame Delyanoff were exceedingly hospitable and kind to the Diplomatic Body, so, when M. Delyanoff died, most of the diplomats attended his funeral, appearing, according to Russian custom, in full uniform. The Delyanoffs being Armenians, the funeral took place in the Armenian church, and none of us had had any previous experience of the extraordinary noises which pass for singing amongst Armenians. When six individuals appeared and began bleating like sheep, and followed this by an excellent imitation of hungry wolves howling, it was too much for us. We hastily composed our features into the decorum the occasion demanded, amid furtive little snorts of semi-suppressed laughter. After three grey-bearded priests had stepped from behind the ikonostas, and, putting their chins up in the air, proceeded to yelp together in unison, exactly like dogs baying the moon, the entire Corps Diplomatique broke down utterly. Never have I seen men laugh so unrestrainedly. As we had each been given a large lighted candle, the movements of our swaying bodies were communicated to the tapers, and showers of melted wax began flying in all directions. With the prudence of the land of my birth, I placed myself against a pillar, so as to have no one behind me, but each time the three grey-beards recommenced their comical howling, I must have scattered perfect Niagaras of wax on to the embroidered coat-tails and extensive back of the Swedish Minister in front of me. I should think that I must have expended the combined labours of several hives of bees on his garments, congratulating myself the while that that genial personage, not being a peacock, did not enjoy the advantage of having eyes in his tail. The Swedish Minister, M. Dué, his massive frame quivering with laughter, was meanwhile engaged in performing a like kindly office on to the back of his Roumanian colleague, Prince Ghika, who in his turn was anointing the uniform of M. van der Hooven, the Netherlands Minister. Providentially, the Delyanoff family were all grouped together before the altar, and the farmyard imitations of the Armenian choir so effectually drowned our unseemly merriment that any faint echoes which reached the family were ascribed by them to our very natural emotions in the circumstances. I heard, indeed, afterwards that the family were much touched by our attendance and by our sympathetic behaviour, but never, before or since, have I attended so hilarious a funeral.

Lord Dufferin, in common with most of the members of the Embassy, was filled with an intense desire to kill a bear. These animals, of course, hibernate, and certain peasants made a regular livelihood by discovering bears' lairs (the Russian term, a corruption from the German, is "bear-loge") and then coming to Petrograd and selling the beast at so much per "pood" of forty Russian pounds. The finder undertook to provide sledges and beaters for the sum agreed upon, but nothing was to be paid unless a shot at the bear was obtained. These expeditions involved a considerable amount of discomfort. There was invariably a long drive of from forty to eighty miles to be made in rough country sledges from the nearest available railway station; the accommodation in a peasant's house would consist of the bare floor with some hay laid on it, and every scrap of food, including bread, butter, tea, and sugar, would have to be carried from Petrograd, as European stomachs could not assimilate the sour, wet heavy black bread the peasants eat, and their brick-tea, which contained bullocks' blood, was undrinkable to those unaccustomed to it. It usually fell to my lot, as I spoke the language, to go on ahead to the particular village to which we were bound, and there to make the best arrangements possible for Lord and Lady Dufferin's comfort. My instructions were always to endeavour to get a room in the latest house built, as this was likely to be less infested with vermin than the others. After a four or five hours' run from Petrograd by train, one would find the vendor of the bear waiting at the station with a country sledge. These sledges were merely a few poles tied together, mounted on iron-shod wooden runners, and filled with hay. The sledges were so long that it was possible to lie at full length in them. The rifles, baggage, and food being packed under the hay, one lay down at full length, clad in long felt boots and heavy furs, an air-cushion under one's head, and a Persian "bashilik," or hood of fine camel's hair, drawn over it to prevent ears or nose from being frostbitten. Tucked into a thick fur rug, one composed oneself for an all-night drive through the endless forests. The two drivers sat on a plank in front, and one or other of them was continually dropping off to sleep, and tumbling backwards on to the occupant of the sledge. It was not a very comfortable experience, and sleep was very fickle to woo. In the first place, the sledge-tracks through the forest were very rough indeed, and the jolting was incessant; in the second place, should the actual driver go to sleep as well as his relieving colleague, the sledge would bump against the tree-trunks and overturn, and baggage, rifles and occupants would find themselves struggling in the deep snow. I always tied my baggage together with strings, so as to avoid losing anything in these upsets, but even then it took a considerable time retrieving the impedimenta from the deep snow-drifts.

It always gave me pleasure watching the black conical points of the fir trees outlined against the pale burnished steel of the sky, and in the intense cold the stars blazed like diamonds out of the clear grey vault above. The biting cold burnt like a hot iron against the cheeks, until prudence, and a regard for the preservation of one's ears, dictated the pulling of the "bashilik" over one's face again. The intense stillness, and the absolute silence, for there are no sleigh-bells in Northern Russia, except in the imagination of novelists, had some subtle attraction for me. The silence was occasionally—

very occasionally only—broken by an ominous, long-drawn howl; then a spectral swift-trotting outline would appear, keeping pace easily with the sledge, but half-hidden amongst the tree-trunks. In that case the smooth-bore gun and the buckshot cartridges were quickly disinterred from the hay, and the driver urged his horses into a furious gallop. There was no need to use the whip; the horses knew. Everyone would give a sigh of relief as the silent grey swift-moving spectral figure, with its fox-like lope, vanished after a shot or two had been fired at it. The drivers would take off their caps and cross themselves, muttering "Thanks be to God! Oh! those cursed wolves!" and the horses slowed down of their own accord into an easy amble. There were compensations for a sleepless night in the beauty of the pictures in strong black and white, or in shadowy half-tones of grey which the endless forest displayed at every turn. When the earth is wrapped in its snow-mantle, it is never dark, and the gleams of light from the white carpet down the long-drawn aisles of the dark firs were like the pillared shadows of a great cathedral when the dusk is filling it with mystery and a vague sense of immense size.

All villages that I have seen in Northern Russia are alike, and when you have seen one peasant's house you have seen all.

The village consists of one long street, and in the winter the kindly snow covers much of its unspeakable untidiness. The "isbas," or wooden houses, are all of the same pattern; they are solidly built of rough logs, the projecting ends firmly morticed into each other. Their gable ends all front the street, each with two windows, and every "isba" has its courtyard, where the door is situated. There are no gardens, or attempts at gardens, and the houses are one and all roofed with grey shingles. Each house is raised some six feet from the ground, and they are all water-tight, and most of them air-tight as well. The houses are never painted, and their weathered logs stand out silver-grey against the white background. A good deal of imagination is shown in the fret-saw carving of the barge-boards, which are either ornamented in conventional patterns, or have roughly outlined grotesque animals clambering up their angles; very often too there are fret-saw ornaments round the window-frames as well. Prominent on the gate of every "isba" is the painting, in black on a white ground, of the particular implement each occupant is bound to supply in case of a fire, that dire and relentless foe to Russian wooden-built villages. On some houses a ladder will be depicted; on others an axe or a pail. The interior arrangement of every "isba" I have ever seen is also identical. They always consist of two fair-sized rooms; the "hot room," which the family inhabit in winter, facing the street; the "cold room," used only in summertime, looking into the courtyard. These houses are not uncomfortable, though, a Russian peasant's wants being but few, they are not overburdened with furniture. The disposition of the "hot room" is unvarying. Supposing it facing due south, the door will be in the north-west corner. The north-east corner is occupied by an immense brick stove, filling up one-eighth of the floor-space. These stoves are about five feet high, and their tops are covered with loose sheepskins. Here the entire family sleep in the stifling heat, their resting-place being shared with thousands of voracious, crawling, uninvited guests. In the south-east corner is the ikon shelf, where the family ikons are ranged in line, with a red lamp burning before them. There will be a table and benches in another corner, and a rough dresser, with a samovar, and a collection of those wooden bowls and receptacles, lacquered in scarlet, black, and gold, which Russian peasants make so beautifully; and that is all. The temperature of the "hot room" is overpowering, and the atmosphere fetid beyond the power of description. Every male, on entering takes off his cap and makes a bow before the ikons. I always conformed to this custom, for there is no use in gratuitously wounding people's religious susceptibilities. I invariably slept in the "cold room," for its temperature being probably five or six degrees below freezing point, it was free from vermin, and the atmosphere was purer. The master of the house laid a few armfuls of hay on the floor, and his wife would produce one of those towels Russian women embroider so skilfully in red and blue, and lay it down for the cheek to rest against. I slept in my clothes, with long felt boots on, and my furs thrown over me, and I could sleep there as well as in any bed.

The Russian peasant's idea as to the relation of Holy Russia to the rest of the world is curious. It is rather the point of view of the Chinaman, who thinks that beyond the confines of the " Middle Kingdom " there is only outer barbarism. Everything to the west of Russia is known as " Germania," an intelligible mistake enough when it is remembered that Germany marks Russia's Western frontier. " Slavs " (akin, I think, to " Slova," " a word ") are the only people who can talk; " Germania " is inhabited by deaf and dumb people (" nyémski ") who can only make inarticulate noises. On one of my shooting expeditions, I stopped for an hour at a tea-house to change horses and to get warmed up. The proprietor told me that his son was very much excited at hearing that there was a " deaf and dumb man " in the house, as he had never seen one. Would I speak to the young man, who was then putting on his Sunday clothes on the chance of the interview being granted?

In due course the son appeared; a handsome youth in glorified peasant's costume. The first outward sign of a Russian peasant's rise in the social scale is that he tucks his shirt *into* his trousers, instead of wearing it outside; the second stage is marked by his wearing his trousers *over* his boots, instead of thrusting the trousers into the boots. This young fellow had not reached this point of evolution, and wore his shirt outside, but it was a dark-blue silk shirt, secured by a girdle of rainbow-coloured Persian silk. He still wore his long boots outside too.

but they had scarlet morocco tops, and the legs of them were elaborately embroidered with gold wire. In modern parlance, this gay young spark was a terrific village "nut." Never have I met a youth of such insatiable curiosity, or one so crassly and densely ignorant. He was one perpetual note of interrogation. "Were there roads and villages in Germania?" To the best of my belief there were. "There were no towns though as large as Petrograd." I rather fancied the contrary, and instanced a flourishing little community of some five million souls, situated on an island, with which I was very well acquainted.

The youth eyed me with deep suspicion. "Were there railways in Germania?" Only about a hundred times the mileage of the Russian railways. "There was no electric light though, because Jablochkoff, a Russian, had invented that." (I found this a fixed idea with all Russian peasants.) I had a vague impression of having seen one or two arc lights feebly glimmering in the streets of the benighted cities of Germania. "Could people read and write there, and could they really talk? It was easy to see that I had learned to talk since I had been in Russia." I showed him a copy of the London *Times*. "These were not real letters. Could anyone read these meaningless signs," and so on *ad infinitum*. I am persuaded that when I left that youth he was convinced that I was the nearest relative to Ananias that he had ever met.

No matter which hour of the twenty-four it might

happen to be, ten minutes after my arrival in any of these remote villages the entire population assembled to gaze at the "nyémetz," the deaf and dumb man from remote "Germania," who had arrived in their midst. They crowded into the "hot room," men, women, and children, and gaped on the mysterious stranger from another world, who sat there drinking tea, as we should gaze on a visitor from Mars. I always carried with me on those occasions a small collapsible india-rubber bath and a rubber folding basin. On my first expedition, after my arrival in the village, I procured a bucket of hot water from the mistress of the house, carried it to the "cold room," and, having removed all my garments, proceeded to take a bath. Like wildfire the news spread through the village that the "deaf and dumb" man was washing himself, and they all flocked in to look. I succeeded in "shooing" away the first arrivals, but they returned with reinforcements, until half the population, men, women, and children, were standing in serried rows in my room, following my every movement with breathless interest. I have never suffered from agoraphobia, so I proceeded cheerfully with my ablutions. "Look at him! He is soaping himself!" would be murmured. "How dirty deaf and dumb people must be to want such a lot of washing!" "Why does he rub his teeth with little brushes?" These and similar observations fell from the eager crowd, only broken occasionally by a piercing yell from a child, as she wailed plaintively the Russian equivalent of "Mummy! Sonia not like ugly man!" It was distinctly an embarrassing situation, and only once in my life have I been placed in a more awkward position.

That was at Bahia, in Brazil, when I was at the Rio de Janeiro Legation. I went to call on the British Consul's wife there, and had to walk half a mile from the tram, through the gorgeous tropical vegetation of the charming suburb of Vittoria, amongst villas faced with cool-looking blue and white tiles; the pretty "azulejos" which the Portuguese adopted from the Moors. Oddly enough, a tram and a tramcar are always called "a Bond" in Brazil. The first tram-lines were built out of bonds guaranteed by the State. The people took this to mean the tram itself; so "Bond" it is, and "Bond" it will remain. Being the height of a sweltering Brazilian summer, I was clad in white from head to foot. Suddenly, as happens in the tropics, without any warning whatever, the heavens opened, and solid sheets of water fell on the earth. I reached the Consul's house with my clean white linen soaked through, and most woefully bedraggled. The West Indian black butler (an old acquaintance) who opened the door informed me that the ladies were out. After a glance at my extraordinarily disreputable garments, he added, "You gib me dem clothes, sar, I hab dem all cleaned and ironed in ten minutes, before de ladies come back." On the assurances of this swarthy servitor that he and I were the only souls in the house, I divested myself of every stitch of clothing, and going into the drawing-room, sat down to read a book in precisely the same attire as Adam adopted in the earlier days of his married life. Time went by, and my clothes did not reappear; I should have known that to a Jamaican coloured man measures of time are very elastic. Suddenly I heard voices, and, to my horror, I saw our Consul's wife approaching through the garden with her two daughters and some other ladies.

There was not a moment to lose! In that tropical drawing-room the only available scrap of drapery was a red plush table-cover. Bundling everything on the table ruthlessly to the ground, I had just time to snatch up the table-cloth and drape myself in it (I trust gracefully) when the ladies entered the room. I explained my predicament and lamented my inability to rise, and so we had tea together. It is the only occasion in the course of a long life in which I ever remember taking tea with six ladies, clad only in a red plush table-cloth with bead fringes.

Returning to Russia, the peasants fingered everything I possessed with the insatiable curiosity of children; socks, ties, and shirts. I am bound to say that I never had the smallest thing stolen. As our shooting expeditions were always during Lent, I felt great compunction at shocking the peasants' religious scruples by eating beef, ham, and butter, all forbidden things at that season. I tried hard to persuade one woman that my cold sirloin of roast beef was part of a rare English fish, specially imported, but she was, I fear, of a naturally sceptical bent of mind.

Lady Dufferin had one curious gift. She could spend the night in a rough country sledge, or sleep in her clothes on a truss of hay, and yet appear in the morning as fresh and neat, and spick and span, as though she had had the most elaborate toilet appliances at her disposal. On these occasions she usually wore a Canadian blanket-suit of dark blue and scarlet, with a scarlet belt and hood, and a jaunty little sealskin cap. She always went out to the forest with us.

The procedure on these occasions was invariably the same. An army of beaters was assembled, about two-thirds of them women. This made me uneasy at first, until I learnt that the beaters run no danger whatever from the bear. The beaters form five-sixths, or perhaps less, of a circle round the bear's sleeping place, and the guns are placed in the intervening open space. I may add that, personally, I always used for bear an ordinary smooth-bore sporting gun, with a leaden bullet. I passed every one of these bullets down the barrels of my gun myself to avoid the risk of the gun bursting, before they were loaded into cartridges, and I had them secured with melted tallow. The advantage of a smooth-bore is that at close quarters, as with bear, where you *must* kill your beast to avoid disagreeable consequences, you lose no time in getting your sights on a rapidly-moving object. You shoot as you would a rabbit; and you can make absolutely sure of your animal, *if you keep your head.* A leaden bullet at close quarters has tremendous stopping power. Of course you want a rifle as well for longer shots. I found this method most successful with tiger, later in India, only you *must* remain quite cool.

At a given signal, the beaters begin yelling, beating iron pans with sticks, blowing horns, shouting, and generally making enough pandemonium to awaken the Seven Sleepers. It effectually awakes the bear, who emerges from his bedroom in an exceedingly evil temper, to see what all this fearful din is about. As he is surrounded with noise on three sides, he naturally makes for the only quiet spot, where the guns are posted. By this time he is in a distinctly unamiable mood.

I always took off my ski, and stood nearly waist-deep in the snow so as to get a firm footing. Then you can make quite certain of your shot. Ski or no ski, if it came to running away, the bear would always have the pull on you. The first time I was very lucky. The bear came straight to me. When he was within fifteen feet, and I felt absolutely certain of getting him, I fired. He reared himself on his hind legs to an unbelievable height, and fell stone dead at Lady Dufferin's very feet. That bear's skin is within three feet of me as I write these lines. We went back to the village in orthodox fashion, all with fir-branches in our hands, as a sign of rejoicing; I seated on the dead bear.

As a small boy of nine I had been tossed in a

blanket at school, up to the ceiling, caught again, then up a second time and third time. It was not, and was not intended to be, a pleasant experience, but in my day all little boys had to submit to it. The unhappy little brats stuck their teeth together, and tried hard to grin as they were being hurled skywards. These curious Russians, though, appeared to consider it a delightful exercise.

Arrived at the village again, I was captured by some thirty buxom, stalwart women, and sent spinning up and up, again and again, till I was absolutely giddy. Not only had one to thank them profusely for this honour, but also to disburse a considerable amount of roubles in acknowledgement of it. Poor Lady Dufferin was then caught, in spite of her protests, and sent hurtling skywards through the air half a dozen times. Needless to say that she alighted with not one hair of her head out of place or one fold of her garments disarranged. Being young and inexperienced then, I was foolish enough to follow the Russian custom, and to present the village with a small cask of vodka. I regretted it bitterly. Two hours later not a male in the place was sober. Old grey-beards and young men lay dead drunk in the snow; and quite little boys reeled about hopelessly intoxicated. I could have kicked myself for being so thoughtless. During all the years I was in Russia, I never saw a peasant woman drink spirits, or under the influence of liquor. In my house at Petrograd I had a young peasant as house-boy. He was quite a nice lad of sixteen; clean, willing, and capable, but, young as he was, he had already fallen a victim to the national failing, in which he indulged regularly once a month, when his wages were paid him, and nothing could break him of this habit. I could always tell when Ephim, the boy, had gone out with the deliberate intention of getting drunk, by glancing into his bedroom. He always took the precaution of turning the ikons over his bed, with their faces to the wall, before leaving, and invariably blew out the little red lamp, in order that ikons might not see him reeling into the room upon his return, or deposited unconscious upon his bed. Being a singularly neat boy in his habits, he always put on his very oldest clothes on these occasions, in order not to damage his better ones, should he fall down in the street after losing control of his limbs. This drunkenness spreads like a cancer from top to bottom of Russian society. A friend of mine, who afterwards occupied one of the highest administrative posts, told me quite casually that, on the occasion of his youngest brother's seventeenth birthday, the boy had been allowed to invite six young friends of his own age to dinner; my friend thought it quite amusing that every one of these lads had been carried to bed dead drunk. I attribute the dry-rot which ate into the whole structure of the mighty Empire, and brought it crashing to the ground, in a very large degree to the intemperate habits prevailing amongst all classes of Russian men, which in justice one must add, may be due to climatic reasons.

In the villages our imported food was a constant source of difficulty. We were all averse to shocking the peasants by eating meat openly during Lent, but what were we to do? Out of deference to their scruples, we refrained from buying eggs and milk, which could have been procured in abundance, and furtively devoured ham, cold beef, and pickles behind cunningly contrived ramparts of newspaper, in the hope that it might pass unnoticed. Remembering how meagre at the best of times the diet of these peasants is, it is impossible to help admiring them for the conscientious manner in which they obey the rules of their Church during Lent. I once gave a pretty peasant child a piece of plum cake. Her mother snatched it from her, and asked me whether the cake contained butter or eggs. On my acknowledgement that it contained both, she threw it into the stove, and asked me indignantly how I dared to imperil her child's immortal soul by giving her forbidden food in Lent. Even my sixteen-year-old house-boy in Petrograd, the bibulous Ephim, although he regularly succumbed to the charms of vodka, lived entirely on porridge and dry bread during Lent, and would not touch meat, butter, or eggs on any consideration whatever. The more I saw of the peasants the more I liked them. The men all drank, and were not particularly truthful, but they were like great simple, bearded, unkempt children, with (drunkenness apart) all a child's faults, and all a nice child's power of attraction. I liked the great, stalwart, big-framed women too. They were seldom good-looking, but their broad faces glowed with health and good nature, and they had as a rule very good skins, nice teeth, and beautiful complexions. I found that I could get on with these villagers like a house on fire. However cold the weather, no village girl or woman wears anything on her head but a gaudy folded cotton handkerchief.

I never shared the resentment of my Russian friends at being addressed with the familiar "thou" by the peasants. They intended no discourtesy; it was their natural form of address, and they could not be expected to know that beyond the narrow confines of their village there was another world where the ceremonious "you" was habitually employed. I rather fancy that anyone bred in the country, and accustomed from his earliest childhood to mix with farmers, cottagers, and farm-labourers, can get on with other country-bred people, whether at home, or in Russia, India, or Canada—a town-bred man would not know what to talk about. In spite of the peasants' reputation for pilfering, not one of us ever had the smallest thing stolen. I did indeed lose a rubber air-cushion in the snow, but that was owing to the overturning of a sledge. A colleague of mine, whom I had hitherto always regarded as a truthful man, assured me a year afterwards that he had seen my air-cushion ranged on the ikon shelf in a peasant's house, with *two* red lamps burning before it. The owner of the house declared, according to my friend, that my air-cushion was an ikon of peculiar sanctity, though the painting had in some mysterious manner become obliterated from it. My colleague further assured me that my air-cushion was building up a very gratifying little local connection as a miracle-working ikon of quite unusual efficiency, and that, under its kindly tutelage, crops prospered and flocks and herds increased; of course within reasonable limits only, for the new ikon held essentially moderate views, and was temperamentally opposed to anything in the way of undue optimism. I wished that I could have credited this, for it would have been satisfactory to imagine oneself, through the agency of the air-cushion, a vicarious yet untiring benefactor of a whole countryside.

On one of our shooting expeditions a curious incident occurred. Lord Dufferin had taken a long shot at a bear, and had wounded without killing him. For some reason, the animal stopped, and climbed to the top of a high fir tree. Lord Dufferin approached, fired again, and the bear dropped dead to the ground. It is but seldom that one sees a dead bear fall from the top of a tree. I witnessed an equally strange sporting incident once in India. It was just over the borders of Assam, and we were returning to camp on elephants, after a day's big game shooting. As we approached a hollow clothed with thick jungle, the elephants all commenced trumpeting. Knowing how wonderfully keen the elephant's sense of smell is, that told us that some beast lay concealed in the hollow. Thinking it would prove to be a bear, I took up my favourite smooth-bore charged with leaden bullets, when with a great crashing and rending of boughs the jungle parted, and a galloping rhinoceros charged out, his head well down, making straight for the elephant that was carrying a nephew of mine. My nephew had just time to snatch up a heavy 4-bore elephant rifle. He fired, and by an extraordinary piece of luck succeeded in hitting the huge beast in his one vulnerable spot, just behind the shoulder. The rhinoceros rolled right over like a shot rabbit and lay stone dead. It was a thousand to one chance, and if I live to a hundred I shall never see anything of the sort again. It was also very fortunate, for had he missed his shot, nothing on earth could have saved my nephew's life.

We found that the most acceptable presents in the villages were packets of sugar and tins of sardines. Sugar is costly and difficult to procure in Russian villages. The usual way of employing it, when friends are gathered round the table of some "isba" with the samovar in the middle and steaming glasses of tea before each guest, is for No. 1 to take a piece of sugar, place it between his teeth, and then suck his tea through it. No. 1 quickly passes the piece of sugar to his neighbor, who uses it in the same way, and transfers it to the next person, and so on, till the sugar is all dissolved. This method of using sugar, though doubtless economical, always struck me as being of dubious cleanliness. A gift of a pound of lump sugar was always welcomed with grateful thanks. Sardines were even more acceptable, as they could be eaten in Lent. The grown-ups devoured the fish, lifting them out of the tin with their fingers; and the children were given the oil to smear on their bread, in place of forbidden butter.

After days in the keen fresh air, and in the limitless expanse of forest and snow, life in Petrograd seemed terribly artificial. I used to marvel that my cultured, omniscient, polygot friends were fellow-countrymen of the bearded, red-shirted, illiterate peasants we had just left. The gulf seemed so unbridgable between them, and apart from a common language and a common religion (both, I acknowledge, very potent bonds of union) there seemed no link between them, or any possible community of ideas. Now in England there *is* that community of ideas. All classes, from the highest to the lowest, share to some extent the same tastes and the same prejudices. There is too that most powerful of connecting links, a common love of sport. The cricket ground and the football field are witnesses to this, and it shows in a hundred little ways beside. The freemasonry of sport is very real.

It was perfectly delightful to live with and to mix so much amongst charming people of such wide culture and education, but they seemed to me to bear the same relation to the world outside their own that a rare orchid in its glass shelter bears to a wild flower growing in the open air. The one is indigenous to the soil; the other was originally imported, and can only thrive in an artificial atmosphere, and under artificial conditions. If the glass gets broken, or the fire goes out, the orchid dies, but the wild flower is not affected. After all, man made the towns, but God made the country.

CHAPTER V

The Russian Gipsies—Midnight drives—Gipsy singing—Its fascination—The consequences of a late night—An unconventional luncheon—Lord Dufferin's methods—Assassination of Alexander II—Stürmer—Pathetic incidents in connection with the murder of the Emperor—The funeral procession and service—Details concerning—The Votive Church—The Order of the Garter—Unusual incidents at the Investiture—Precautions taken for Emperor's safety—The Imperial train—Finland—Exciting salmon-fishing there—Harraka Niska—Koltesha—Excellent shooting there—Ski-running—"Ringing the game in"—A wolf-shooting party—The obese General—Some incidents—A novel form of sport—Black game and capercailzie—At dawn in a Finnish forest—Immense charm of it—Ice-hilling or "Montagnes Russes"—Ice-boating on the Gulf of Finland.

In my day there were two or three restaurants on the islands formed by the delta of the Neva, with troupes of singing gipsies attached to them. These restaurants did a roaring trade in consequence, for the singing of the gipsy choirs seems to produce on Russians the same maddening, almost intoxicating effect that the "skirl o' the pipes" does on those with Scottish blood in their veins.

Personally, I thought that one soon tired of this

gipsy singing; not so my Russian friends—it appeared to have an irresistible attraction for them. I always dreaded the consequences when some foolish person, usually at 1 or even 2 a.m., proposed a visit to the gipsies, for all the ladies present would instantly jump at the suggestion, and I knew full well that it entailed a forcible separation from bed until six or possibly seven next morning.

Troikas would at once be sent for. A troika is a thing quite apart. Its horses are harnessed as are no other horses in the world, since the centre horse trots in shafts, whilst the two outside horses, the "*pristashkui*," loose save for long traces, gallop. Driving a troika is a special art. The driver stands; he has a special badge, peacock's feathers set in a round cap; he has a special name, "*yamshchik*," and he charges quite a special price.

To my mind, the drive out to the islands was the one redeeming feature of these expeditions. Within the confines of the city, the pace of the troikas was moderate enough, but as the last scattered houses of the suburbs merged into the forest, the driver would call to his horses, and the two loose horses broke into a furious gallop, the centre horse in shafts moving as swiftly as any American trotter. Smoothly and silently under the burnished steel of the starlit sky, they tore over the snow, the vague outlines of the fir trees whizzing past. Faster and faster, until the wild excitement of it made one's blood tingle within one, even as the bitter cold made one's cheeks tingle, as we raced through the keen pure air. That wild gallop through the forest was perfectly glorious. I believe that on us sons of the North real cold has the same exhilarating effect that warmth and sunshine have on the Lotos-eating dwellers by the blue Mediterranean.

The troika would draw up at the door of a long, low, wooden building, hidden away amongst the fir trees of the forest. After repeated bangings at the door, a sleepy-eyed Tartar appeared, who ushered one into a great gaunt, bare, whitewashed room, where other little yellow, flat-faced, Tartar waiters were lighting countless wax candles, bringing in many slim-shouldered, gold foil-covered bottles of champagne, and a samovar or two, and arranging seats. Then the gipsy troupe strolled in, some twenty-five strong; the younger members passably good-looking, with fine dark eyes, abundant eyelashes, and extremely indifferent complexions. The older members of the company made no attempt at coquetry. They came muffled in woollen shawls, probably to conceal toilet deficiencies, yawning openly and undisguisedly; not concealing their disgust at being robbed of their sleep in order to sing to a pack of uninteresting strangers, to whom, incidentally, they owed their entire means of livelihood. Some ten swarthy, evil-faced, indeterminate males with guitars filled up the background.

One of the younger members of the troupe would begin a song in waltz time, in a curious metallic voice, with a ring in it of something Eastern, barbaric, and utterly strange to European ears, to the thrum of the guitars of the swarthy males in the background. The elderly females looked inexpressibly bored, and hugged their woollen shawls a little closer over their heads. Then the chorus took up the refrain. A tempest of wild, nasal melody arose, in the most perfect harmony. It was metallic, and the din was incredible, but the effect it produced on the listeners was astounding. The old women, dropping their cherished shawls, awoke to life. Their dull eyes sparkled again, they sang madly, frenetically; like people possessed. The un-European *timbre* of the voices conduced doubtless to the effect, but the fact remains that this clamour of nasal, metallic voices, singing in exquisite harmony, had about it something so novel and fresh—or was it something so immemorially old?—that the listeners felt absolutely intoxicated.

On the Russians it acted like hypnotism. After the first song, they all joined in, and even I, the dour and unemotional son of a Northern land, found myself, as words and music grew familiar, shouting the bass parts of the songs with all the strength of my lungs. The Russian language lends itself admirably to song, and the excess of sibilants in it is not noticeable in singing.

These Russian gipsies, like the Austrian bands, produced their effects by very simple means. They harmonised their songs themselves, and they always introduced a succession of "sixths" or "thirds"; emphasising the "sixth" in the tenor part.

One can, however, have too much of a good thing. I used to think longingly of my far-off couch, but there was no tearing Russians away from the gipsies. The clock ticked on; they refused to move. The absorption of much champagne has never afforded me the smallest amusement. The consumption of tea has also its limits, and my longed-for bed was so far away! The really staggering figure one had to disburse as one's share for these gipsy entertainments seemed to me to be a very long price to pay for a sleepless night.

Once a fortnight the "Queen's Messenger" left Petrograd at noon, on his return journey to London. On "Messenger mornings" we had all to be at the Embassy at 9 a.m. punctually. One morning, after a compulsory vigil with the gipsies, I was awakened by my servant with the news that it was close on nine, and that my sledge was already at the door. It was impossible to dress in the time, so after some rapid ablutions, I drew the long felt boots the Russians call "Valinki" over my pyjamas, put on some heavy furs, and jumped into my sledge. Lord Dufferin found me writing hard in the steam-heated Chancery, clad only in silk pyjamas, and with my bare feet in slippers. He made no remark, but I knew that nothing ever escaped his notice. By noon we had the despatches finished, the bags sealed up, the "waybill" made out, various precautionary measures taken as to which it is unnecessary to enlarge, and the Messenger left for London. I called to the hall porter to bring me my furs, and told him to order my sledge round. "His Excellency has sent your sledge home," said the porter, with a smile lurking round the corners of his mouth. "Then call me a hack sledge." "His Excellency hopes that you will give him the pleasure of your company at luncheon." "But I must go home and dress first." "His Excellency's orders were that you are to go as you are," answered the grinning porter. Then I understood. Nothing is ever gained by being shy or self-conscious, so after a hasty toilet, I sent for my heavy fur "shuba." Furs in Russia are intended for use, not ornament, and this "shuba" was an extremely weighty and voluminous garment, designed to withstand the rigours of the North Pole itself. A glance at the mirror convinced me that I was most indelicately *décolleté* about the neck, so I hooked the big collar of the "shuba" together, and strode upstairs. The heat of this fur garment was unendurable, but there was nothing else for it. Certainly the legs of my pyjamas protruded below it, so I congratulated myself on the fact that they were a brand-new pair of very smart striped mauve silk. My bare feet too were encased in remarkably neat Persian slippers of green morocco. Lady Dufferin received me exactly as though I had been dressed in the most immaculate of frock-coats. Her children though, gazed at my huge fur coat, round-eyed with astonishment, for neither man nor woman ever comes into a Russian house with furs on—an arrangement which would not at all suit some of my London friends, who seem to think that furs are designed for being shown off in hot rooms. The governess, an elderly lady, catching sight of my unfortunate pyjama legs below the fur coat, assumed a highly scandalised attitude, as though she could scarcely credit the evidence of her eyes. (I repeat that they were exceptionally smart pyjamas.)

During luncheon Lord Dufferin made himself perfectly charming, and I did my best to act as though it were quite normal to sit down to one's repasts in an immense fur coat.

The Ambassador was very susceptible to cold, and liked the house heated to a great temperature. That day the furnace-man must have been quite unusually active, for the steam hissed and sizzled in the radiators, until the heat of that dining-room was suffocating. Conscious of my extreme *décolletage,* I did not dare unhook the collar of my "shuba," being naturally of a modest disposition, and never, even in later years at Colombo or Singapore, have I suffered so terribly from heat as in that Petrograd dining-room in the depths of a Russian winter. The only cool thing in the room was the governess, who, when she caught sight of my bare feet, froze into an arctic iceberg of disdain, in spite of my really very ornamental Persian slippers. The poor lady had obviously never even caught a glimpse of pyjamas before. After that episode I always came to the Embassy fully dressed.

Another instance of Lord Dufferin's methods occurs to me. We had a large evening party at the Embassy, and a certain very pushing and pertinacious English newspaper correspondent did everything in his power to get asked to this reception. For very excellent reasons, his request was refused. In spite of this, on the night of the party the journalist appeared. I informed Lord Dufferin, and asked what he wished me to do about it. "Let me deal with him myself," answered the Ambassador, and going up to the unbidden guest, he made him a little bow, and said with a bland smile, "May I inquire, sir, to what I owe this most unexpected honour?" Then as the unhappy newspaper-man stuttered out something, Lord Dufferin continued with an even blander smile, "Do not allow me, my dear sir, I beg of you, to detain you from your other doubtless numerous engagements"; then calling me, he added, "Will you kindly accompany this gentleman to the front door, and see that on a cold night like this he gets all his warm clothing." It was really impossible to turn a man out of your house in a more courteous fashion.

There was another plan Lord Dufferin used at times. All despatches, and most of our private letters, were sent home by hand, in charge of the Queen's Messenger. We knew perfectly well that anything sent from the Embassy through the ordinary mails would be opened at the Censor's office, and copies taken. Ministries of Foreign Affairs give at times "diplomatic" answers, and occasionally it was advisable to let the Russian Government know that the Ambassador was quite aware that the assurances given him did not quite tally with the actual facts. He would then write a despatch to London to that effect, and send it by mail, being well aware that it would be opened and a copy sent to the Russian Ministry of Foreign Affairs. In this indirect fashion, he delicately conveyed to the Russian Government that he had not been hoodwinked by the rather fanciful statements made to him.

I was sitting at luncheon with some friends at a colleague's house on Sunday, the fateful 1st of March, 1881 (March 13, new style). Suddenly our white-headed old Chancery messenger burst unceremoniously into the room, and called out, "The Emperor has been assassinated!" We all jumped up; the old man, a German-speaking Russian from the Baltic Provinces, kept on wringing his hands, and moaning, "Unser arme gute Kaiser! unser arme gute Kaiser!" ("Our poor dear Emperor!") We hurried to the Embassy as fast as we could go, and found the Ambassador just stepping into his carriage to get the latest news from the Winter Palace. Lady Dufferin had not seen the actual crime committed, but she had heard the explosion of the bomb, and had seen the wounded horses led past, and was terribly upset in consequence. She was walking along the Catherine Canal with her youngest daughter when the Emperor's carriage passed and the first bomb was thrown. The carriage was one of Napoleon III's special armoured coaches, bought after the fall of the Second French Empire. The bomb shattered the wheels of the carriage, but the Emperor was untouched. He stepped out into the snow, when the second bomb was thrown, which blew his legs to pieces, and the Emperor was taken in a private sledge, in a dying condition, to the Winter Palace. The bombs had been painted white, to look like snowballs.

Ten minutes later one of the Court Chamberlains arrived. I met him in the hall, and he informed me, with the tears streaming down his face, that all was over.

That Chamberlain was a German-Russian named Stürmer, and he was the very same man who thirty-four years later was destined, by his gross incompetence, or worse, as Prime Minister, to bring the mighty Russian Empire crashing in ruins to the ground, and to drive the well-intentioned, irresolute Nicholas II, the grandson of the Sovereign for whom he professed so great an affection, to his abdication, imprisonment, and ignominious death.

There was a Queen's Messenger due in Petrograd from London that same afternoon, and Lord Dufferin, thinking that the police might give trouble, desired me to meet him at the station.

The Messenger refused to believe my news. He persisted in treating the whole thing as a joke, so I ordered my coachman to drive through the great semi-circular *place* in front of the Winter Palace. That *place* presented a wonderful sight. There were tens of thousands of people, all kneeling bare-headed in the snow, in close-packed ranks. I thought the sight of those serried thousands kneeling bare-headed, praying for the soul of their dead Emperor, a strangely moving and beautiful spectacle. When the Messenger saw this, and noted the black and yellow Imperial flag waving at half-mast over the Palace, he no longer doubted.

The Grand Duke Vladimir had announced the Emperor's death to the vast crowds in the traditional Russian fashion. The words "death" or "die" being considered ill-omened by old-fashioned Russians, the actual sentence used by the Grand Duke was, "The Emperor has bidden you to live long." ("Gosudar Imperator vam prikazal dolga jit!") The words conveyed their message.

The body of the Emperor having been embalmed, the funeral did not take place for a fortnight. As the crow flies, the distance between the Winter Palace and the Fortress Church is only about half a mile; it was, however, still winter-time, the Neva was frozen over, and the floating bridges had been removed. It being contrary to tradition to take the body of a dead Emperor of Russia across ice, the funeral procession had to pass over the permanent bridges to the Fortress, a distance of about six miles.

Lady Dufferin and I saw the procession from the corner windows of a house on the quays. On paper it sounded very grand, but like so many things in Russia, it was spoilt by lack of attention to details. The distances were kept irregularly, and many of the officials wore ordinary civilian great-coats over their uniforms, which did not enhance the effect of the *cortège*. The most striking feature of the procession was the "Black Knight" on foot, followed immediately by the "Golden Knight" on horseback. These were, I believe, meant to typify "The Angel of Death" and "The Angel of the Resurrection." Both Knights were clad in armour from head to foot, with the vizors of their helmets down. The "Black Knight's" armour was dull sooty-black all over; he had a long black plume waving from his helmet. The "Golden Knight," mounted on a white horse, with a white plume in his helmet, wore gilded and burnished armour, which blazed like a torch in the sunlight. The weight of the black armour being very great, there had been considerable difficulty in finding a man sufficiently strong to walk six miles, carrying this tremendous burden. A gigantic young private of the Preobrajensky Guards undertook the task for a fee of one hundred roubles, but though he managed to accomplish the distance, he fainted from exhaustion on reaching the Fortress Church, and was, I heard, two months in hospital from the effects of his effort.

We were able to get Lady Dufferin into her place in the Fortress Church, long before the procession arrived, by driving across the ice of the river. The absence of seats in a Russian church, and the extreme length of the Orthodox liturgy, rendered these services very trying for ladies. The Fortress Church had been built by a Dutch architect, and was the most un-Eastern-looking Orthodox church I ever saw. It actually contained a pulpit! In the north aisle of the church all the Emperors since Peter the Great's time lie in uniform plain white marble tombs, with gilt-bronze Russian eagles at their four corners. The Tsars mostly rest in the Cathedral of the Archangel, in the Moscow Kremlin. I have before explained that Peter was the last of the Tsars and the first of the Emperors. The regulations for Court mourning in Petrograd were most stringent. All ladies had to appear in perfectly plain black, lustreless woollen dresses, made high to the throat. On their heads they wore a sort of Mary Queen of Scots pointed cap of black crape, with a long black crape veil falling to their feet. The only detail of the funeral which struck me was the perfectly splendid pall of cloth of gold. This pall had been specially woven in Moscow, of threads of real gold. When folded back during the ceremony it looked exactly like gleaming waves of liquid gold.

A memorial church in old-Russian style has been erected on the Catherine Canal on the spot where Alexander II was assassinated. The five onion-shaped domes of this church, of copper enamelled in stripes and spirals of crude blue and white, green and yellow, and scarlet and white, may possibly look less garish in two hundred years' time than they do at present. The severely plain Byzantine interior, covered with archaic-looking frescoes on a gold ground, is effective. The ikonostas is entirely of that vivid pink and enormously costly Siberian marble that Russians term "heavy stone." Personally I should consider the huge sum it cost as spent in vain.

Edward VII and Queen Alexandra, in those days, of course, Prince and Princess of Wales, represented Great Britain at Alexander II's funeral, and remained in Petrograd a month after it.

A week after the funeral, the Prince of Wales, by Queen Victoria's command, invested Alexander III with the Order of the Garter. As the Garter is the oldest Order of Chivalry in Europe, the ceremonies at its investiture have 570 years of tradition behind them. The insignia, the star, the ribbon, the collar, the sword, and the actual garter itself, are all carried on separate, long, narrow cushions of red velvet, heavily trimmed with gold bullion. Owing to the deep Court mourning, it was decided that the investiture should be private. No one was to be present except the new Emperor and Empress, Queen Alexandra, the Grand Master and Grand Mistress of the Russian Court, the members of the British Embassy, and the Prince of Wales and his staff. This, as it turned out, was very fortunate. The ceremony was to take place at the Anitchkoff Palace on the Nevsky, which Alexander III inhabited throughout his reign, as he preferred it to the huge rambling Winter Palace. On the appointed day, we all marched into the great Throne room of the Anitchkoff Palace, the Prince of Wales leading the way, with five members of his staff carrying the insignia on the traditional long narrow velvet cushions. I carried nothing, but we made, I thought, a very dignified and effective entrance. As we entered the Throne room, a perfectly audible feminine voice cried out in English, "Oh, my dear! Do look at them. They look exactly like a row of wet-nurses carrying babies!" Nothing will induce me to say from whom the remark proceeded. The two sisters, Empress and Queen, looked at each other for a minute, and then exploded with laughter. The Emperor fought manfully for a while to keep his face, until, catching sight of the member of the Prince of Wales's staff who was carrying his cushion in the peculiarly maternal fashion that had so excited the risibility of the Royal sisters, he too succumbed, and his colossal frame quivered with mirth. Never, I imagine, since its institution in 1349, has the Order of the Garter been conferred amid such general hilarity, but as no spectators were present, this lapse from the ordinary decorum of the ceremonial did not much matter. The general public never heard of it, nor, I trust, did Queen Victoria.

The Emperor Alexander III was a man of great personal courage, but he gave way, under protest, to the wishes of those responsible for his personal safety. They insisted on his always using the armour-plated carriages bought from Napoleon III. These coaches were so immensely heavy that they soon killed the horses dragging them. Again, on railway journeys, the actual time-table and route of the Imperial train between two points was always different from the published time-table and route. Napoleon III's private train had been purchased at the same time as his steel-plated carriages. This train had been greatly enlarged and fitted to the Russian gauge. I do not suppose that any more sumptuous palace on wheels has ever been built than this train of nine vestibuled cars. It was fitted with every imaginable convenience. Alexander III sent it to the frontier to meet his brother-in-law the Prince of Wales, which was the occasion on which I saw it.

During the six months following Alexander II's assassination all social life in Petrograd stopped. We of the Embassy had many other resources, for in those days the British business colony in Petrograd was still large, and flourished exceedingly. They had various sporting clubs, of some of which we were members. There was in particular the Fishing Club at Harraka Niska in Finland, where the river Vuoksi issues from the hundred-mile-long Lake Saima.

It was a curious experience driving to the Finnish railway station in Petrograd. In the city outside, the date would be June 1, Russian style. Inside the station, the date became June 13, European style. In place of the baggy knickerbockers, high boots, and fur caps of the Russian railwaymen, the employees of the Finnish railway wore the ordinary uniforms customary on European railways. The tickets were printed in European, not Russian characters, and the fares were given in marks and pennies, instead of in roubles and kopecks. The notices on the railway were all printed in six languages, Finnish, Swedish, Russian, French, English, and German, and my patriotic feelings were gratified at noting that all the locomotives had been built in Glasgow. I was astonished to find that although Finland formed an integral part of the Russian Empire, there was a Custom House and Customs examination at the Finnish frontier.

Finland is a country of endless little hills, and endless forests, all alike bestrewn with huge granite boulders; it is also a land of endless rivers and lakes. It is pretty in a monotonous fashion, and looks wonderfully tidy after Russia proper. The wooden houses and villages are all neatly painted a chocolate brown, and in spite of its sparse population it seems very prosperous. The Finns are all Protestants; the educated classes are mostly Swedish-speaking, the others talking their own impossible Ural-Altaic language. At the extremely comfortable club-house at Harraka Niska none of the fishermen or boatmen could talk anything but Finnish. We all had little conversation books printed in Russian and Finnish, but we usually found the language of signs more convenient. In later years, in South America, it became my duty to interview daily the Legation cook, an accomplished but extremely adipose female from Old Spain. I had not then learnt Spanish, and she understood no other tongue, so we conversed by signs. It is extremely derogatory to one's personal dignity to be forced to imitate in succession a hen laying an egg, a sheep bleating, or a duck quacking, and yet this was the only way in which I could order dinner. No one who has not tried it can believe how difficult it is to indicate in pantomime certain comestibles, such, for instance, as kidneys, liver and bacon, or a Welsh rarebit.

The fish at Harraka would not look at a fly, and could only be hooked on a phantom-minnow. The fishing there was very exciting. The big fish all lay where Lake Saima debouched into the turbulent Vuoksi river. There was a terrific rapid there, and the boatmen, who knew every inch of the ground, would head the boat straight for that seething white caldron of raging waves, lashing and roaring down the rocky gorge, as they dashed up angry spurts of white spray. Just as it seemed that nothing could save one from being hurled into that mad turmoil of leaping waters, where no human being could hope to live for a minute, a back-current shot the boat swiftly across to the other bank. That was the moment when the fish were hooked. They were splendid fighters, and played magnificently. These Harraka fish were curiously uniform in size, always running from 18 to 22 lb. Though everyone called them salmon, I think myself that they were really bull-trout, or *Salmo ferox.* A salmon would have had to travel at least 400 miles from salt water, and I do not believe that any fish living could have got up the tremendous Imatra waterfall, some six miles lower down the Vuoksi. These fish invariably had lice on them. In Great Britain sea-lice on a salmon are taken as a certain indication that the fish is fresh-run. These fish cannot possibly have been fresh-run, so I think it probable that in these great lakes there may be a fresh-water variety of the parasite. Another peculiarity of the Harraka fish was that, though they were excellent eating, they would not keep above two days. I have myself caught eleven of these big fellows in one day. During June there was capital grayling fishing in the lower Vuoksi, the fish running large, and taking the fly readily, though in that heavy water they were apt to break off. There were plenty of small trout too in the Vuoksi, but the densely-wooded banks made fishing difficult, and the water was always crystal-clear, and needed the finest of tackle.

I spent some most enjoyable days at Koltesha, a small English shooting-club of ten members, about twenty miles out of Petrograd. During September, for one fortnight, the marshes round Koltesha were alive with "double-snipe." This bird migrates in thousands from the Arctic regions to the far South, at the approach of autumn. They alighted in the Koltesha marshes to recruit themselves after their journey from the North Pole, and owing to circumstances beyond their control, few of them continued their journey southward. This confiding fowl has never learnt to zig-zag like the other members of the snipe family, and they paid the penalty for this omission by usually proceeding to the kitchen. A "double-snipe" is most delicious eating. The winter shooting at Koltesha was most delightful. The art of "ski-walking" had first to be learnt, and on commencing this unaccustomed method of locomotion, various muscles, which its use called into play for the first time, showed their resentment by aching furiously. The ground round Koltesha being hilly was admirably adapted for coasting on ski. It was difficult at first to shoot from the insecure footing of ski, and the unusual amount of clothing between one's shoulder and the stock of one's gun did not facilitate matters. Everything, however, can be learnt in time. I can claim to be the pioneer of ski on the American Continent, for in January, 1887, I brought over to Canada the very first pair of ski ever seen in America. I used to coast down the toboggan slides at Ottawa on them, amidst universal derision. I was told that, however useful ski might be in Russia, they were quite unsuited to Canadian conditions, and would never be popular there, as the old-fashioned "raquettes" were infinitely superior. Humph! *Qui vivra verra!*

Koltesha abounded in black game, "ryabchiks," or hazel-grouse, and ptarmigan. Russian hares turn snow-white in winter, and are very difficult to see against a snowy background in consequence. It is almost impossible to convey on paper any idea of the intense delight of those days in the sun and the cold, when the air had that delicious clean smell that always goes with intense frost, the dark fir woods, with their purple shadows, stood out in sharp contrast to the dazzling sheet of white snow, and the sunlight gilded the patches of oak and birch scrub that climbed down the hollows of the low hills. One returned home glowing from head to foot. We got larger game too by "ringing them." The process of "ringing" is as follows. No four-footed creature can travel over the snow without leaving his tracks behind him. Let us suppose a small wood, one mile in circumference. If a man travels round this on ski, and if the track of any animal crosses his trail, going *into* the wood, and this track does not again come *out* of the wood, it is obvious that that particular animal is still taking cover there. Measures to drive him out are taken accordingly. We got in this way at Koltesha quite a number of elks, lynxes, and wolves.

The best wolf-shooting I ever got was at the invitation of the Russian Minister of Finance. Great packs of these ravenous brutes were playing havoc on his estate, two hundred miles from Petrograd, so he invited a large shooting party to his country house. We travelled down in a private sleeping-car, and had over twenty miles to drive in rough country sledges from the station. One of the guests was an enormously fat Russian General, a perfect mammoth of a man. As I was very slim in those days, I was told off as this gigantic warrior's fellow-passenger. Although he took up nine-tenths of the sledge, I just managed to creep in, but every time we jolted—and as the track was very rough, this was pretty frequently—I got 250 lb. of Russian General on the top of me, squeezing the life out of me. He was a good-natured Colossus, and apologised profusely for his own obesity, and for his instability, but I was black and blue all over, and since that day I have felt profound sympathy for the little princes in the Tower, for I know what being smothered with a feather-bed feels like.

The Minister's country house was, as are most other Russian country houses, a modest wooden building with whitewashed rooms very scantily furnished. The Minister had, however, thoughtfully brought down his famous Petrograd chef, and I should judge about three-quarters of the contents of his wine-cellar. We had to proceed to our places in the forest in absolute silence, and the wolf being an exceedingly wary animal with a a very keen sense of smell, all smoking was rigorously prohibited.

It was nice open scrubland, undulating gently. The beaters were skilful and we were very lucky, for after an interminable wait, the entire pack of wolves rushed down on us. A wolf is killed with slugs from a smooth-bore. I personally was fortunate, for I got shots at eight wolves, and six of them felt disinclined for further exertions. I still have a carriage-rug made of the skins of the wolves I killed that day. The banging all round meanwhile was terrific. In two days we accounted for fifty-two of these pests. It gave me the utmost pleasure killing these murderous, bloodthirsty brutes; far more than slaying an inoffensive bear. Should a bear encounter a human being in the course of his daily walks, he is certainly apt to hug him to death, as a precautionary measure. He is also addicted to smashing to a jelly, with one blow of his powerful paws, the head of a chance stranger. These peculiarities apart, the bear may be regarded as practically harmless. It is otherwise with the wolf.

Some of the British Colony were fond of going to Finland for a peculiar form of sport. I use the last word dubiously, for to kill any game birds during the breeding season seems a curiously unsportsmanlike act. Circumstances rather excused this. It is well known that black game do not pair, but that they are polygamous. During the breeding season the male birds meet every morning at dawn on regular fighting grounds, and there battle for the attentions of the fairer sex. These fighting grounds are well known to the keepers, who erect there in early autumn conical shelters of fir branches. The birds become familiar with these shelters (called in Russian "shagashki") and pay no attention to them. The "gun" introduces himself into the shelter not later than midnight, and there waits patiently for the first gleam of dawn. He must on no account smoke. With the first grey streak of dawn in the sky there is a great rushing of wings in the air, and dozens of male birds appear from nowhere; strutting up and down, puffing out their feathers, and hissing furiously at each other in challenge. The grey hens meanwhile sit in the surrounding trees, watching, as did the ladies of old at a tournament, the prowess of their men-folk in the lists. The grey hens never show themselves, and make no sound; two things, one would imagine, contrary to every instinct of their sex. A challenge once accepted, two males begin fighting furiously with wings, claws, and beaks. So absorbed are the birds in their combat, that they neither see nor hear anything, and pay no attention to a gun-shot. Should they be within reach of the "shagashka," that is the time to fire. It sounds horribly unsportsmanlike, but it must be remembered that the birds are only just visible in the uncertain dawn. As dawn matures into daylight, the birds suddenly stop fighting, and all fly away simultaneously, followed by the grey hens. I never would kill more than two as specimens, for this splendid bird is such a thing of joy in his breeding plumage, with his glossy dark blue satin coat, and white velvet waistcoat, that there is some excuse for wanting to examine him closer. Ladies, too, loved a blackcock's tail or wings for their hats. It was also the only way in which this curious and little-known phase of bird life could be witnessed.

The capercailzie is called in Russian "the deaf one." Why this name should be given to a bird of abnormally acute hearing seems at first sight puzzling. The explanation is that the male capercailzie in the breeding season concludes his love-song with a peculiar "tchuck, tchuck," impossible to reproduce on paper, moving his head rapidly to and fro the while. During this "tchuck, tchuck," the bird is deaf and blind to the world. The capercailzie hunter goes out into the forest at about 1 a.m. and listens intently. As soon as he hears a capercailzie's song, he moves towards the sound very, very cautiously. When within half a mile of the bird, he must wait for the "tchuck, tchuck," which lasts about two minutes, before daring to advance. The "tchuck" over, he must remain absolutely motionless until it recommences. The snapping of a twig will be enough to silence the bird and to make it fly away. It will be seen then that to approach a capercailzie is a difficult task, and one requiring infinite patience. Once within shot, there is no particular fun in shooting a sitting bird the size of a turkey, up at the top of a tree, even though it only appears as a dusky mass against the faint beginnings of dawn.

The real charm of this blackcock and capercailzie shooting was that one would not otherwise have been out in the great forest at break of day.

To me there was always an infinite fascination in seeing these great Northern tracts of woodland awakening from their long winter sleep. The sweetness of the dawn, the delicious smell of growing things, the fresh young life springing up under one's feet, all these appealed to every fibre in my being. Nature always restores the balance of things. In Russia, as in Canada, after the rigours of the winter, once the snow has disappeared, flowers carpet the ground with a rapidity of growth unknown in more temperate climates. These Finland woods were covered with a low creeping plant with masses of small, white, waxy flowers. It was, I think, one of the smaller cranberries. There was an orange-flowering nettle, too, the leaves of which changed from green to vivid purple as they climbed the stalk, making gorgeous patches of colour, and great drifts of blue hepaticas on the higher ground. To appreciate Nature properly, she must be seen at unaccustomed times, as she bestirs herself after her night's rest whilst the sky brightens.

In Petrograd itself the British Colony found plenty of amusement. We had an English ice-hill club to which all the Embassy belonged. The elevation of a Russian ice-hill, some forty feet only, may seem tame after the imposing heights of Canadian toboggan slides, but I fancy that the pace travelled is greater in Russia. The ice-hills were always built in pairs, about three hundred yards apart, with two parallel runs. Both hills and runs were built of solid blocks of ice, watered every day, and the pitch of the actual hill was very steep. In the place of a toboggan we used little sleds two feet long, mounted on skate-runners, which were kept constantly sharpened. These travelled over the ice at a tremendous pace, and at the end of the straight run, the corresponding hill had only to be mounted to bring you home again to the starting-point. The art of steering these sleds was soon learnt, once the elementary principle was grasped that after a turn to the left, a corresponding turn to the right must be made to straighten up the machine, exactly as is done instinctively on a bicycle. A wave of the hand or of the foot was enough to change the direction, the ice-hiller going down head foremost, with the sled under his chest.

Longer sleds were used for taking ladies down. The man sat cross-legged in front, whilst the lady knelt behind him with both her arms round his neck. Possibly the enforced familiarity of this attitude was what made the amusement so popular.

We gave at times evening parties at the ice-hills, when the woods were lit up with rows of Chinese lanterns, making a charming effect against the snow, and electric arcs blazed from the summits of the slides. To those curious in such matters, I may say that as secondary batteries had not then been invented, and we had no dynamo, power was furnished direct by powerful Grove two-cell batteries. One night our amateur electrician was nearly killed by the brown fumes of nitrous acid these batteries give off from their negative cells.

We had an ice-boat on the Gulf of Finland as well. It is only in early spring, and very seldom then, that this amusement can be indulged in. The necessary conditions are (1) a heavy thaw to melt all the snow from the surface of the ice, followed by a sharp frost; (2) a strong breeze. Nature is not often obliging enough to arrange matters in this sequence. We had some good sailing, though, and could get forty miles an hour out of our craft with a decent breeze. Our boat was of the Dutch, not the Canadian type. I was astonished to find how close an ice-boat could lay to the wind, for obviously anything in the nature of leeway is impossible with a boat on runners. Ice-sailing was bitterly cold work, and the navigation of the Gulf of Finland required great caution, for in early spring great cracks appeared in the ice. On one occasion, in avoiding a large crack, we ran into the omnibus plying on runners between Kronstadt and the mainland. The driver of the coach was drunk, and lost his head, to the terror of his passengers, but very little damage was done. It may be worth while recording this, as it is but seldom that a boat collides with an omnibus.

It will be seen that in one way and another there was no lack of amusement to be found round Petrograd, even during the entire cessation of Court and social entertainments.

CHAPTER VI

Love of Russians for children's games—Peculiarities of Petrograd balls—Some famous beauties of Petrograd Society—The varying garb of hired waiters—Moscow—Its wonderful beauty—The forest of domes—The Kremlin—The three famous "Cathedrals"—The Imperial Treasury—The Sacristy—The Palace—Its splendour—The Terem—A Gargantuan Russian dinner—An unusual episode at the French Ambassador's ball—Bombs—Tsarskoe Selo—Its interior—Extraordinary collection of curiosities in Tsarskoe Park—Origin of term "Vauxhall" for railway station in Russia—Peterhof—Charm of park there—Two Russian illusions—A young man of 25 delivers an Ultimatum to Russia—How it came about—M. de Giers—Other Foreign Ministers—Paraguay—The polite Japanese dentist—A visit to Gatchina—Description of the Palace—Delights of the children's play-room there.

The lingering traces of the child which are found in most Russian natures account probably for their curious love of indoor games. Lady Dufferin had weekly evening parties during Lent, when dancing was rigidly prohibited. Quite invariably, some lady would go up to her and beg that they might be allowed to play what she would term "English running games." So it came about that bald-headed Generals, covered with Orders, and quite elderly ladies, would with immense glee play "Blind-man's buff," "Musical chairs," "Hunt the slipper," and "General post." I believe that they would have joined cheerfully in "Ring a ring of roses," had we only thought of it.

I think it is this remnant of the child in them which, coupled with their quick-working brains, wonderful receptivity, and absolute naturalness, makes Russians of the upper class so curiously attractive.

At balls in my time, oddly enough, quadrilles were the most popular dances. There was always a "leader" for these quadrilles, whose function it was to invent new and startling figures. The "leader" shouted out his directions from the centre of the room, and however involved the figures he devised, however complicated the manœuvres he evolved, he could rely on being implicitly obeyed by the dancers, who were used to these intricate entanglements, and enjoyed them. Woe betide the "leader" should he lose his head, or give a wrong direction! He would find two hundred people inextricably tangled up. I calculate that many years have been taken off my own life by the responsibilities thrust upon me by being frequently made to officiate in this capacity. Balls in Petrograd in the "'eighties" invariably concluded with the "Danse Anglaise," our own familiar "Sir Roger de Coverley."

I never saw an orchestra at a ball in Petrograd, except at the Winter Palace. All Russians preferred a pianist, but a pianist of a quite special brand. These men, locally known as "tappeurs," cultivated a peculiar style of playing, and could get wonderful effects out of an ordinary grand piano. There was in particular one absolute genius called Altkein. Under his superlatively skilled fingers the piano took on all the resonance and varied colour of a full orchestra. Altkein told me that he always played what he called "four-handed," that is doubling the parts of each hand. By the end of the evening he was absolutely exhausted.

The most beautiful woman in Petrograd Society was unquestionably Countess Zena Beauharnais, afterwards Duchess of Leuchtenberg; a tall, queenly blonde with a superb figure. Nature had been very generous to her, for in addition to her wonderful beauty, she had a glorious soprano voice. I could not but regret that she and her sister, Princess Bieloselskaya, had not been forced by circumstances to earn their living on the operatic stage, for the two sisters, soprano and contralto, would certainly have achieved a European reputation with their magnificent voices. How they would have played Amneris and the title-rôle in "Aïda"! The famous General Skobeleff was their brother.

Two other strikingly beautiful women were Princess Kitty Dolgorouki, a piquant little brunette, and her sister-in-law, winning, golden-haired Princess Mary Dolgorouki. After a lapse of nearly forty years, I may perhaps be permitted to express my gratitude to these two charming ladies for the consistent kindness they showered on a peculiarly uninteresting young man, and I should like to add to their names that of Countess Betsy Schouvaloff. I may remark that the somewhat homely British forms of their baptismal names which these *grandes dames* were fond of adopting always amused me. Our two countries were in theory deadly enemies, yet they borrowed little details from us whenever they could. I think that the racial animosity was only skin-deep. This custom of employing English diminutives for Russian names extended to the men too, for Prince Alexander Dolgorouki, Princess Kitty's husband, was always known as " Sandy," whilst Countess Betsy's husband was invariably spoken of as "Bobby" Schouvaloff. Countess Betsy, mistress of one of the stateliest houses in Petrograd, was acknowledged to be the best-dressed woman in Russia. I never noticed whether she were really good-looking or not, for such was the charm of her animation, and the sparkle of her vivacity and quick wit, that one remarked the outer envelope less than the nimble intellect and extraordinary attractiveness that underlay it. She was a daughter of that "Princesse Château" to whom I referred earlier in these reminiscences.

In the great Russian houses there were far fewer liveried servants than is customary in other European countries. This was due to the difficulty of finding sufficiently trained men. The actual work of the house was done by hordes of bearded, red-shirted shaggy-headed moujiks, who, their household duties over, retired to their underground fastnesses. Consequently when dinners or other entertainments were given recourse was had to hired waiters, mostly elderly Germans. It was the curious custom to dress these waiters up in the liveries of the family giving the entertainment. The liveries seldom fitted, and the features of the old waiters were quite familiar to most of us, yet politeness dictated that we should pretend to consider them as servants of the house. Though perfectly conscious of having seen the same individual who, arrayed in orange and white, was standing behind one's chair, dressed in sky-blue only two evenings before, and equally aware of the probability of meeting him the next evening in a different house, clad in crimson, it was considered polite to compliment the mistress of the house on the admirable manner in which her servants were turned out.

There is in all Russian houses a terrible place known as the "buffetnaya." This is a combination of pantry, larder, and serving-room. People at all particular about the cleanliness of their food, or the nicety with which it is served, should avoid this awful spot as they would the plague. A sensitive nose can easily locate the whereabouts of the "buffetnaya" from a considerable distance.

From Petrograd to Moscow is only a twelve hours' run, but in those twelve hours the traveller is transported into a different world. After the soulless regularity of Peter the Great's sham classical creation on the banks of the Neva, the beauty of the semi-Oriental ancient capital comes as a perfect revelation. Moscow, glowing with colour, is seated like Rome on gentle hills, and numbers over three hundred churches. These churches have each the orthodox five domes, and this forest of domes, many of them gilt, others silvered, some blue and gold, or striped with bands and spirals of vivid colour, when seen amongst the tender greenery of May, forms a wonderful picture, unlike anything else in the world. The winding, irregular streets lined with buildings in every imaginable style of architecture, and of every possible shade of colour; the remains of the ancient city walls with their lofty watch-towers crowned with curious conical roofs of grass-green tiles; the great irregular bulk of the Kremlin, towering over all; make a whole of incomparable beauty. There is in the world but one Moscow, as there is but one Venice, and one Oxford.

The great sea of gilded and silvered domes is best seen from the terrace of the Kremlin overlooking the river, though the wealth of detail nearer at hand is apt to distract the eye. The soaring snow-white shaft of Ivan Veliki's tower with its golden pinnacles dominates everything, though the three "Cathedrals," standing almost side by side, hallowed by centuries of tradition, are very sacred places to a Russian, who would consider them the heart of Moscow, and of the Muscovite world. "Mother Moscow," they call her affectionately, and I understand it.

The Russian word "Sobor" is wrongly translated as "Cathedral." A "sobor" is merely a church of peculiar sanctity or of special dignity. The three gleaming white, gold-domed churches of the Kremlin are of quite modest dimensions, yet their venerable walls are rich with the associations of centuries. In the Church of the Assumption the Tsars, and later the Emperors, were all crowned; in the Church of the Archangel the Tsars were buried, though the Emperors lie in Petrograd. The dim Byzantine interior of the Assumption Church, with its faded frescoes on a gold ground, and its walls shimmering with gold, silver, and jewels, is immensely impressive. Here is the real Russia, not the Petrograd stuccoed veneered Russia of yesterday, but ancient Muscovy, sending its roots deep down into the past.

Surely Peter prepared the way for the destruction of his country by uprooting this tree of ancient growth, and by trying to create in one short lifetime a new pseudo-European Empire, with a new capital.

The city should be seen from the Kremlin terrace as the light is fading from the sky and the thousands of church-bells clash out their melodious evening hymn. The Russians have always been master bell-founders, and their bells have a silvery tone unknown in Western Europe. In the gloaming, the Eastern character of the city is much more apparent. The blaze of colour has vanished, and the dusky silhouettes of the church domes take on the onion-shaped forms of the Orient. Delhi, as seen in later years from the fort at sunset was curiously reminiscent of Moscow. I do not suppose that more precious things have ever been gathered together under one roof than the Imperial Treasury at Moscow contained in those days. The eye got surfeited with the sight of so many splendours, and I can only recall the great collection of crowns and thrones of the various Tsars. One throne of Persian workmanship was studded with two thousand diamonds and rubies; another, also from Persia, contained over two thousand large turquoises. There must have been at least a dozen of these glittering thrones, but the most interesting of all was the original ivory throne of the Emperors of Byzantium, brought to Moscow in 1472 by Sophia Palaeologus, wife of Ivan III. Constantine the Great may have sat on that identical throne. It seems curious that the finest collection in the world of English silver-ware of Elizabeth's, James I's, and Charles I's time should be found in the Kremlin at Moscow, till it is remembered that nearly all the plate of that date in England was melted down during the Civil War of 1642—1646. I wonder what has become of all these precious things now!

The sacristy contains an equally wonderful collection of Church plate. I was taken over this by an Archimandrite, and I had been previously warned that he would expect a substantial tip for his services. The Archimandrite's feelings were, however, to be spared by my representing this tip as my contribution to the poor of his parish. The Archimandrite was so immensely imposing, with his violet robes, diamond cross, and long flowing beard, that I felt quite shy of offering him the modest five roubles which I was told would be sufficient. So I doubled it. The Archimandrite pocketed it joyfully, and so moved was he by my unexpected *largesse,* that the excellent ecclesiastic at once motioned me to my knees, and gave me a most fervent blessing, which I am persuaded was well worth the extra five roubles.

The Great Palace of the Kremlin was rebuilt by Nicholas I about 1840. It consequently belongs to the "period of bad taste"; in spite of that it is extraordinarily sumptuous. The St. George's Hall is 200 feet long and 60 feet high; the other great halls, named after the Russian Orders of Chivalry, are nearly as large. Each of these is hung with silk of the same colour as the ribbon of the Order; St. George's Hall, orange and black; St. Andrew's Hall, sky-blue; St. Alexander Nevsky's, pink; St. Catherine's, red and white. I imagine that every silkworm in the world must have been kept busy for months in order to prepare sufficient material for these acres of silk-hung walls. The Kremlin Palace may not be in the best of taste, but these huge halls, with their jasper and malachite columns and profuse gilding, are wonderfully gorgeous, and exactly correspond with one's preconceived ideas of what an Emperor of Russia's palace ought to be like. There is a chapel in the Kremlin Palace with the quaint title of

"The Church of the Redeemer behind the Golden Railing."

The really interesting portion of the Palace is the sixteenth century part, known as the "Terem." These small, dim, vaulted halls with their half-effaced frescoes on walls and ceilings are most fascinating. It is all mediæval, but not with the mediævalism of Western Europe; neither is it Oriental; it is pure Russian; simple, dignified, and delightfully archaic. One could not imagine the old Tsars in a more appropriate setting. Compared with the strident splendours of the modern palace, the vaulted rooms of the old Terem seem to typify the difference between Petrograd and Moscow.

It so happened that later in life I was destined to become very familiar with the deserted palace at Agra, in India, begun by Akbar, finished by Shah Jehan. How different the Oriental conception of a palace is from the Western! The Agra Palace is a place of shady courts and gardens, dotted with exquisitely graceful pavilions of transparent white marble roofed with gilded copper. No two of these pavilions are similar, and in their varied decorations an inexhaustible invention is shown. The white marble is so placed that it is seen everywhere in strong contrast to Akbar's massive buildings of red sandstone. During the Coronation ceremonies, King-Emperor George V seated himself, of right, on the Emperor Akbar's throne in the great Hall of Audience in Agra Palace.

Though Moscow may appear a dream-city when viewed from the Kremlin, it is an eminently practical city as well. It was, in my time, the chief manufacturing centre of Russia, and Moscow business-men had earned the reputation of being well able to look after themselves.

Another side of the life of the great city could be seen in the immense Ermitage restaurant, where Moscow people assured you with pride that the French cooking was only second to Paris. The little Tartar waiters at the Ermitage were, drolly enough, dressed like hospital orderlies, in white linen from head to foot. There might possibly be money in an antiseptic restaurant, should some enterprising person start one. The idea would be novel, and this is an age when new ideas seem attractive.

A Russian merchant in Moscow, a partner in an English firm, imagined himself to be under a great debt of gratitude to the British Embassy in Petrograd, on account of a heavy fine imposed upon him, which we had succeeded in getting remitted. This gentleman was good enough to invite a colleague and myself to dine at a certain "Traktir," celebrated for its Russian cooking. I was very slim in those days, but had I had any idea of the Gargantuan repast we were supposed to assimilate, I should have borrowed a suit of clothes from the most adipose person of my acquaintance, in order to secure additional cargo-space.

In the quaint little " Traktir " decorated in old-

Russian style, after the usual fresh caviar, raw herrings, pickled mushrooms, and smoked sturgeon of the "zakuska," we commenced with cold sucking-pig eaten with horse-radish. Then followed a plain little soup, composed of herrings and cucumbers stewed in sour beer. Slices of boiled salmon and horse-radish were then added, and the soup was served iced. This soup is distinctly an acquired taste. This was succeeded by a simple dish of sterlets, boiled in wine, with truffles, crayfish, and mushrooms. After that came mutton stuffed with buckwheat porridge, pies of the flesh and isinglass of the sturgeon, and Heaven only knows what else. All this accompanied by red and white Crimean wines, Kvass, and mead. I had always imagined that mead was an obsolete beverage, indulged in principally by ancient Britons, and drunk for choice out of their enemies' skulls, but here it was, foaming in beautiful old silver tankards; and perfectly delicious it was! Oddly enough, the Russian name for it, "meod," is almost identical with ours.

Only once in my life have I suffered so terribly from repletion, and that was in the island of Barbados, at the house of a hospitable planter. We sat down to luncheon at one, and rose at five. The sable serving-maids looked on the refusal of a dish as a terrible slur on the cookery of the house, and would take no denial. "No, you like dis, sar, it real West India dish. I gib you lilly piece." What with turtle, and flying-fish, and calipash and calipee, and pepper-pot, and devilled land-crabs, I felt like the boa-constrictor in the Zoological Gardens after his monthly meal.

I was not fortunate enough to witness the coronation of either Alexander III or that of Nicholas II. In the perfect setting of "the Red Staircase," of the ancient stone-built hall known as the "Granovitaya Palata," and of the "Gold Court," the ceremonial must be deeply impressive. On no stage could more picturesque surroundings possibly be devised. During the coronation festivities, most of the Ambassadors hired large houses in Moscow, and transferred their Embassies to the old capital for three weeks. At the coronation of Nicholas II, of unfortunate memory, the French Ambassador, the Comte de Montebello, took a particularly fine house in Moscow, the Shérémaitieff Palace, and it was arranged that he should give a great ball the night after the coronation, at which the newly-crowned Emperor and Empress would be present. The French Government own a wonderful collection of splendid old French furniture, tapestries, and works of art, known as the "Garde Meubles." Under the Monarchy and Empire, these all adorned the interiors of the various palaces. To do full honour to the occasion, the French Government dispatched vanloads of the choicest treasures of the "Garde Meubles" to Moscow, and the Shérémaitieff Palace became a thing of beauty, with Louis Quatorze Gobelins, and furniture made for Marie-Antoinette. To enhance the effect, the Comte and Comtesse de Montebello arranged the most elaborate floral decorations, and took immense pains over them. On the night of the ball, two hours before their guests were due, the Ambassador was informed that the Chief of Police was outside and begged for permission to enter the temporary Embassy. Embassies enjoying what is known as "exterritoriality," none of the police can enter except on the invitation of the Ambassador; much as vampires, according to the legend, could only secure entrance to a house at the personal invitation of the owner. It will be remembered that these unpleasing creatures displayed great ingenuity in securing this permission; indeed the really expert vampires prided themselves on the dexterity with which they could inveigle their selected victim into welcoming them joyfully into his domicile. The Chief of Police informed the French Ambassador that he had absolutely certain information that a powerful bomb had been introduced into the Embassy, concealed in a flower-pot. M. de Montebello was in a difficult position. On the previous day the Ambassador had discovered that every single electric wire in the house had been deliberately severed by some unknown hand. French electricians had repaired the damage, but it was a disquieting incident in the circumstances. The policeman was positive that his information was correct, and the consequences of a terrific bomb exploding in one's house are eminently disagreeable, so he gave his reluctant permission to have the Embassy searched, though his earlier guests might be expected within an hour. Armies of police myrmidons appeared, and at once proceeded to unpot between two and three thousand growing plants, and to pick all the floral decorations to pieces. Nothing whatever was found, but it would be unreasonable to expect secret police, however zealous, to exhibit much skill as trained florists. They made a frightful hash of things, and not only ruined the elaborate decorations, but so managed to cover the polished floors with earth that the rooms looked like ploughed fields, dancing was rendered impossible, and poor Madame de Montebello was in tears. As the guests arrived, the police had to be smuggled out through back passages. This was one of the little amenities of life in a bomb-ridden land.

During the summer months I was much at Tsarskoe Selo. Tsarskoe is only fourteen miles from Petrograd, and some of my Russian friends had villas there. The gigantic Old Palace of Tsarskoe is merely an enlarged Winter Palace, and though its garden façade is nearly a quarter of a mile long, it is uninteresting and unimpressive, being merely an endless repetition of the same details. I was taken over the interior several times, but such a vast quantity of rooms leaves only a confused impression of magnificence. I only recall the really splendid staircase and the famous lapis-lazuli and amber rooms. The lapis-lazuli room is a blaze of blue and gold, with walls, furniture, and chandeliers encrusted with that precious substance.

The amber room is perfectly beautiful. All the walls, cabinets, and tables are made of amber of every possible shade, from straw-colour to deep orange. There are also great groups of figures carved entirely out of amber. Both the lapis and the amber room have curious floors of black ebony inlaid with mother-of-pearl, forming a very effective colour scheme. I have vague memories of the "gold" and "silver" rooms, but very distinct recollections of the bedroom of one of the Empresses, who a hundred years before the late Lord Lister had discovered the benefits of antiseptic surgery had with some curious prophetic instinct had her sleeping-room constructed on the lines of a glorified modern operating theatre. The walls of this quaint apartment were of translucent opal glass, decorated with columns of bright purple glass, with a floor of inlaid mother-of-pearl. Personally, I should always have fancied a faint smell of chloroform lingering about the room.

Catherine the Great had her monogram placed everywhere at Tsarskoe Selo, on doors, walls, and ceilings. It was difficult to connect her with the interlaced "E's," until one remembered that the Russian form of the name is "Ekaterina." How wise the Russians have been in retaining the so-called Cyrillian alphabet in writing their tongue!

In other Slavonic languages, such as Polish and Czech, where the Roman alphabet has been adopted, unholy combinations of "cz," "zh," and "sz" have to be resorted to to reproduce sounds which the

Cyrillian alphabet could express with a single letter; and the tragic thing is that, be the letters piled together never so thickly, they invariably fail to give the foreigner the faintest idea of how the word should really be pronounced. Take the much-talked-of town of Przemysl, for instance.

The park of Tsarskoe is eighteen miles in circumference, and every portion of it is thrown open freely to the public. In spite of being quite flat, it is very pretty with its lake and woods, and was most beautifully kept. To an English eye its trees seemed stunted, for in these far Northern regions no forest trees attain great size. Limes and oaks flourish moderately well, but the climate is too cold for beeches. At the latitude of Petrograd neither apples, pears, nor any kind of fruit tree can be grown; raspberries and strawberries are the only things that can be produced, and they are both superlatively good. The park at Tsarskoe was full of a jumble of the most extraordinarily incongruous buildings and monuments; it would have taken a fortnight to see them all properly. There was a Chinese village, a Chinese theatre, a Dutch dairy, an English Gothic castle, temples, hanging gardens, ruins, grottoes, fountains, and numbers of columns, triumphal arches, and statues. On the lake there was a collection of boats of all nations, varying from a Chinese sampan to an English light four-oar; from a Venetian gondola to a Brazilian catamaran. There was also a fleet of miniature men-of-war, and three of Catherine's great gilt state-barges on the lake. One arm of the lake was spanned by a bridge of an extremely rare blue Siberian marble. Anyone seeing the effect of this blue marble bridge must have congratulated himself on the fact that it was extremely improbable that any similar bridge would ever be erected elsewhere, so rare was the material of which it was constructed.

I never succeeded in finding the spot in Tsarskoe Park where a sentry stands on guard over a violet which Catherine the Great once found there. Catherine, finding the first violet of spring, ordered a sentry to be placed over it, to protect the flower from being plucked. She forgot to rescind the order, and the sentry continued to be posted there. It developed at last into a regular tradition of Tsarskoe, and so, day and night, winter and summer, a sentry stood in Tsarskoe Park over a spot where, 150 years before, a violet once grew.

The Russian name for a railway station is "Vauxhall," and the origin of this is rather curious. The first railway in Europe opened for passenger traffic was the Liverpool and Manchester, inaugurated in 1830. Five years later, Nicholas I, eager to show that Russia was well abreast of the times, determined to have a railway of his own, and ordered one to be built between Petrograd and Tsarskoe Selo, a distance of fourteen miles. The railway was opened in 1837, without any intermediate stations. Unfortunately, with the exception of a few Court officials, no one ever wanted to go to Tsarskoe, so the line could hardly be called a commercial success. Then someone had a brilliant idea! Vauxhall Gardens in South London were then at the height of their popularity. The Tsarskoe line should be extended two miles to a place called Pavlosk, where the railway company would be given fifty acres of ground on which to construct a "Vauxhall Gardens," outbidding its London prototype in attractions. No sooner said than done! The Pavlosk "Vauxhall" became enormously popular amongst Petrogradians in summer-time; the trains were crowded and the railway became a paying proposition. As the Tsarskoe station was the only one then in existence in Petrograd, the worthy citizens got into the habit of directing their own coachmen or cabdrivers simply to go "to Vauxhall." So the name got gradually applied to the actual station building in Petrograd. When the Nicholas railway to Moscow was completed, the station got to be known as the "Moscow Vauxhall." And so it spread, until it came about that every railway station in the Russian Empire, from the Baltic to the Pacific, derived its name from a long-vanished and half-forgotten pleasure-garden in South London, the memory of which is only commemorated to-day by a bridge and a railway station on its site. The name "Vauxhall" itself is, I believe, a corruption of "Folks-Hall," or of its Dutch variant "Volkshall." Even in my day the Pavlosk Vauxhall was a most attractive spot, with an excellent orchestra, myriads of coloured lamps, and a great semicircle of restaurants and refreshment booths. When I knew it, the Tsarskoe railway still retained its original rolling-stock of 1837; little queer over-upholstered carriages, and quaint archaic-looking engines. It had, I think, been built to a different gauge to the standard Russian one; anyhow it had no physical connection with the other railways. It was subsequently modernised.

Peterhof is far more attractive than Tsarskoe as it stands on the Gulf of Finland, and the coast, rising a hundred feet from the sea, redeems the place from the uniform dead flat of the other environs of Petrograd. As its name implies, Peterhof is the creation of Peter himself, who did his best to eclipse Versailles. His fountains and waterworks certainly run Versailles very close. The Oriental in Peter peeped out when he constructed staircases of gilt copper, and of coloured marbles for the water to flow over, precisely as Shah Jehan did in his palaces at Delhi and Agra. As the temperature both at Delhi and Agra often touches 120° during the summer months, these decorative cascades would appear more appropriate there than at Peterhof, where the summer temperature seldom rises to 70°.

The palace stands on a lofty terrace facing the sea. A broad straight vista has been cut through the fir-woods opposite it, down to the waters of the Gulf. Down the middle of this avenue runs a canal flanked on either side by twelve fountains. When *les grandes eaux* are playing, the effect of this perspective of fountains and of Peter's gilded water-chutes is really very fine indeed. I think that the

Oriental in Peter showed itself again here. There is a long single row of almost precisely similar fountains in front of the Taj at Agra.

As at Tsarskoe, the public have free access to every portion of the park, which stretches for four miles along the sea, with many gardens, countless fountains, temples and statues. There was in particular a beautiful Ionic colonnade of pink marble, from the summit of which cataracts of water spouted when the fountains played. The effect of this pink marble temple seen through the film of falling water was remarkably pretty. What pleased me were the two small Dutch châteaux in the grounds, "Marly" and "Monplaisir," where Peter had lived during the building of his great palace. These two houses had been built by imported Dutch craftsmen, and the sight of a severe seventeenth-century Dutch interior with its tiles and sober oak-panelling was so unexpected in Russia. It was almost as much of a surprise as is Groote Constantia, some sixteen miles south of Cape Town. To drive down a mile-long avenue of the finest oaks in the world, and to find at the end of it, amidst hedges of clipped pink oleander and blue plumbago, a most perfect Dutch château, exactly as Governor Van der Stell left it in 1667, is so utterly unexpected at the southern extremity of the African Continent! Groote Constantia, the property of the Cape Government, still contains all its original furniture and pictures of 1667. It is the typical seventeenth-century Continental château, the main building with its façade elaborately decorated in plaster, flanked by two wings at right angles to it, but the last place in the world where you would look for such a finished whole is South Africa. To add to the unexpectedness, the vines for which Constantia is famous are grown in fields enclosed with hedges, with huge oaks as hedgerow timber. This gives such a thoroughly English look to the landscape that I never could realise that the sea seen through the trees was the Indian Ocean, and that the Cape of Good Hope was only ten miles away. Macao, the ancient Portuguese colony forty-five miles from Hong-Kong, is another "surprise-town." It is as though Aladdin's Slave of the Lamp had dumped a seventeenth-century Southern European town down in the middle of China, with churches, plazas, and fountains complete.

There is really a plethora of palaces round Peterhof. They grow as thick as quills on a porcupine's back. One of them, I cannot recall which, had a really beautiful dining-room, built entirely of pink marble. In niches in the four angles of the room were solid silver fountains six feet high, where Naiads and Tritons spouted water fed by a running stream. I should have thought this room more appropriate to India than to Northern Russia, but one of the fondest illusions Russians cherish is that they dwell in a semi-tropical climate.

In Petrograd, as soon as the temperature reached 60°, old gentlemen would appear on the Nevsky dressed in white linen, with Panama hats, and white umbrellas, but still wearing the thickest of overcoats. Should the sun's rays become just perceptible, iced Kvass and lemonade were at once on sale in all the streets. On these occasions I made myself quite popular at the Yacht Club by observing, as I buttoned up my overcoat tightly before venturing into the open air, that this tropical heat was almost unendurable. This invariably provoked gratified smiles of assent.

Another point as to which Russians were for some reason touchy was the fact that the water of the Gulf of Finland is perfectly fresh. Ships can fill their tanks from the water alongside for ten miles below Kronstadt, and the catches of the fishing-boats that came in to Peterhof consisted entirely of pike, perch, eels, roach, and other freshwater fish. Still Russians disliked intensely hearing their sea alluded to as fresh-water. I tactfully pretended to ignore the fringe of fresh-water reeds lining the shore at Peterhof, and after bathing in the Gulf would enlarge on the bracing effect a swim in real salt-water had on the human organism. This, and a few happy suggestions that after the intense brine of the Gulf the waters of the Dead Sea would appear insipidly brackish, conduced towards making me amazingly popular.

In my younger days I was never really happy without a daily swim during the summer months.

The woods sloping down to the Gulf are delightful in summer-time, and are absolutely carpeted with flowers. The flowers seem to realise how short the span of life allotted to them is, and endeavour to make the most of it. So do the mosquitoes.

I have very vivid recollections of one especial visit to Peterhof. In the summer of 1882, the Ambassador and two other members of the Embassy were away in England on leave. The Chargé d'Affaires, who replaced the Ambassador, was laid up with an epidemic that was working great havoc then in Petrograd, as was the Second Secretary. This epidemic was probably due to the extremely unsatisfactory sanitary condition of the city. Consequently no one was left to carry on the work of the Embassy but myself and the new Attaché, a mere lad.

The relations of Great Britain and France in the "'eighties" were widely different from those cordial ones at present prevailing between the two countries. Far from being trusted friends and allies, the tension between England and France was often strained almost to the breaking-point, especially with regard to Egyptian affairs. This was due in a great measure to Bismarck's traditional foreign policy of attempting to embroil her neighbours, to the greater advantage of Germany. In old-fashioned surgery, doctors frequently introduced a foreign body into an open wound in order to irritate it, and prevent its healing unduly quickly. This was termed a seton. Bismarck's whole policy was founded on the introduction of setons into open wounds, to prevent their healing. His successors in office endeavoured to continue this policy, but did not succeed, for though they might share Bismarck's entire want of scruples, they lacked his commanding genius.

Ismail, Khedive of Egypt since 1863, had brought his country to the verge of bankruptcy by his gross extravagance. Great Britain and France had established in 1877 a Dual Control of Egyptian affairs in the interest of the foreign bondholders, but the two countries did not pull well together. In 1879 the incorrigible Ismail was deposed in favour of Tewfik, and two years later a military revolt was instigated by Arabi Pasha. Very unwisely, attempts were made to propitiate Arabi by making him a member of the Egyptian Cabinet, and matters went from bad to worse. In May, 1882, the French and British fleets appeared before Alexandria and threatened it, and on June 11, 1882, the Arab population massacred large numbers of the foreign residents of Alexandria. Still the French Government refused to take any definite action, and systematically opposed every proposal made by the British Government. We were perfectly well aware that the opposition of the French to the British policy was consistently backed up by Russia, Russia being in its turn prompted from Berlin. All this we knew. After the massacre of June 11, the French fleet, instead of acting, sailed away from Alexandria.

Amongst the usual daily sheaf of telegrams from London which the Attaché and I decyphered on July 12, 1882, was one announcing that the British Mediterranean Squadron had on the previous day bombarded and destroyed the forts of Alexandria, and that in two days' time British marines would be landed and the city of Alexandria occupied. There were also details of further steps that would be taken, should circumstances render them necessary. All these facts were to be communicated to the Russian Government at once. I went off with this weighty telegram to the house of the Chargé d'Affaires, whom I found very weak and feverish, and quite unable to rise from his bed. He directed me to go forthwith to Peterhof, to see M. de Giers, the Russian Minister for Foreign Affairs, who was there in attendance on the Emperor, and to make my statement to him. I placed the Attaché in charge of the Chancery, and had time admitted of it, I should certainly have smeared that youth's cheeks and lips with some burnt cork, to add a few years to his apparent age, and to delude people into the belief that he had already begun to shave. The dignity of the British Embassy had to be considered. I begged of him to refrain from puerile levity in any business interviews he might have, and I implored him to try to conceal the schoolboy under the mask of the zealous official. I then started for Peterhof. It is not often that a young man of twenty-five is called upon to deliver what was virtually an Ultimatum to the mighty Russian Empire, and I had no illusions whatever as to the manner in which my communication would be received.

I saw M. de Giers at Peterhof, and read him my message. I have never in my life seen a man so astonished; he was absolutely flabbergasted. The Gladstone Government of 1880-85 was then in power in England, and it was a fixed axiom with every Continental statesman (and not, I am bound to admit, an altogether unfounded one) that under no circumstances whatever would the Gladstone Cabinet ever take definite action. They would talk eternally; they would never act. M. de Giers at length said to me, "I have heard your communication with great regret. I have noted what you have said with even deeper regret." He paused for a while, and then added very gravely, "The Emperor's regret will be even more profound than my own, and I will not conceal from you that his Majesty will be highly displeased when he learns the news you have brought me." I inquired of M. de Giers whether he wished me to see the Emperor, and to make my communication in person to His Imperial Majesty, and felt relieved when he told me that it was unnecessary, as I was not feeling particularly anxious to face an angry Autocrat alone. I left a transcript I had myself made of the telegram I had decyphered with M. de Giers, and left. A moment's reflection will show that to leave a copy of a decoded telegram with anyone would be to render the code useless. The original cypher telegram would be always accessible, and a decypher of it would be tantamount to giving away the code. It was our practice to make transcripts, giving the sense in totally different language, and with the position of every sentence altered.

After that, as events in Egypt developed, and until the Chargé d' Affaires was about again, I journeyed to Peterhof almost daily to see M. de Giers. We always seemed to get on very well together, in spite of racial animosities.

The clouds in Egypt rolled away, and with them the very serious menace to which I have alluded. Events fortunately shaped themselves propitiously. On September 13, 1882, Sir Garnet Wolseley utterly routed Arabi's forces at Tel-el-Kebir; Arabi was deported to Ceylon, and the revolt came to an end.

A diplomat naturally meets Ministers of Foreign Affairs of many types. There was a strong contrast between the polished and courtly M. de Giers, who in spite of his urbanity could manage to infuse a very strong sub-acid flavour into his suavity when he chose, and some other Ministers with whom I have come in contact. A few years later, when at Buenos Ayres, preliminary steps were taken for drawing up an Extradition Treaty between Great Britain and Paraguay, and as there were details which required adjusting, I was sent 1,100 miles up the river to Asuncion, the unsophisticated capital of the Inland Republic. Dr. ——, at that time Paraguayan Foreign Minister, was a Guarani, of pure Indian blood. He did not receive me at the Ministry for Foreign Affairs, for the excellent reason that there was no such place in that primitive republic, but in his own extremely modest residence. When his Excellency welcomed me in the whitewashed *sala* of that house, sumptuously furnished with four wooden chairs, and nothing else whatever, he had on neither shoes, stockings, nor shirt, and wore merely a pair of canvas trousers, and an unbuttoned coat of the same material, affording ample glimpses of his somewhat dusky skin. In the suffocating heat of Asuncion such a costume has its obvious advantages; still I cannot imagine, let us say, the French Minister for Foreign Affairs receiving the humblest member of a Foreign Legation at the Quai d'Orsay with bare feet, shirtless, and clad only in two garments.

Dr. ——, in spite of being Indian by blood, spoke most correct and finished Spanish, and had all the courtesy which those who use that beautiful language seem somehow to acquire instinctively. It is to be regretted that the same cannot be said of all those using the English language. Not to be outdone by this polite Paraguayan, I responded in the same vein, and we mutually smothered each other with the choicest flowers of Castilian courtesy. These little amenities, though doubtless tending to smooth down the asperities of life, are apt to consume a good deal of time.

Once at Kyoto in Japan, I had occasion for the services of a dentist. As the dentist only spoke Japanese, I took my interpreter with me. After removing my shoes at the door—an unusual preliminary to a visit to a dentist—we went upstairs, where we found a dapper little individual in kimono and white socks, surrounded by the most modern and up-to-date dental paraphernalia, sucking his breath, and rubbing his knees with true Japanese politeness. Eager to show that a foreigner could also have delightful manners, I sucked my breath, if anything, rather louder, and rubbed my knees a trifle harder. "Dentist says," came from the interpreter, "will you honourably deign to explain where trouble lies in honourable tooth?"

"If the dentist will honourably deign to examine my left-hand lower molar," I responded with charming courtesy, "he will find it requires stopping, but for Heaven's sake, Mr. Nakimura, ask him to be careful how he uses his honourable drill, for I am terrified to death at that invention of the Evil One." Soon the Satanic drill got well into its stride, and began boring into every nerve of my head. I jumped out of the chair. "Tell the dentist, Mr. Nakimura, that he is honourably deigning to hurt me like the very devil with his honourable but wholly damnable drill." "Dentist says if you honourably deign to reseat yourself in chair, he soon conquer difficulties in your honourable tooth." "Certainly. But dentist must not give me honourable hell any more," and so on, and so on. I am bound to admit that the little Jap's workmanship was so good that it has remained intact up to the present day. I wonder if Japs, when annoyed, can ever relieve themselves by the use of really strong language, or whether the crust of conventional politeness is too thick to admit of it. In that case they must feel like a lobster afflicted with acute eczema, unable to obtain relief by scratching himself, owing to the impervious shell in which Nature has encased him.

I dined with the British Consul at Asuncion, after my interview with Dr. ——. The Consul lived three miles out of town, and the coffee we drank after dinner, the sugar we put into the coffee, and the cigars we smoked with it, had all been grown in his garden, within sight of the windows. I had ridden out to the Quinta in company with a young Australian, who will reappear later on in these pages in his proper place; one Dick Howard. It was the first but by no means the last time in my life that I ever got on a horse in evening clothes. Dick Howard, having no evening clothes with him, had arrayed himself in one of his favourite cricket blazers, a pleasantly vivid garment. On our way out, my horse shied violently at a snake in the road. The girths slipped on the grass-fed animal, and my saddle rolled gently round and deposited me, tail-coat, white tie and all, in some four feet of dust. The snake, however, probably panic-stricken at the sight of Howard's blazer, had tactfully withdrawn; otherwise, as it happened to be a deadly Jararaca, it is highly unlikely that I should have been writing these lines at the present moment. The ineradicable love of Dick Howard, the cheery, laughing young Antipodean, for brilliant-hued blazers of various athletic clubs will be enlarged on later. In Indian hill stations all men habitually ride out to dinner-parties.

whilst ladies are carried in litters. During the rains, men put a suit of pyjamas over their evening clothes to protect them, before drawing on rubber boots and rubber coats and venturing into the pelting downpour. The Syce trots behind, carrying his master's pumps in a rubber sponge-bag.

All this, however, is far afield from Russia. Alexander III preferred Gatchina to any of his other palaces as a residence, as it was so much smaller, Gatchina being a cosy little house of 600 rooms only. I never saw it except once in mid-winter, when the Emperor summoned the Ambassador there, and I was also invited. As the far-famed beauties of Gatchina Park were covered with four feet of snow, it would be difficult to pronounce an opinion upon them. The rivers and lakes, the haunts of the celebrated Gatchina trout, were, of course, also deep-buried.

Alexander III was a man of very simple tastes, and nothing could be plainer than the large study in which he received us. Alexander III, a Colossus of a man, had great dignity, combined with a geniality of manner very different from the glacial hauteur of his father, Alexander II. The Emperor was in fact rather partial to a humorous anecdote, and some I recalled seemed to divert his Majesty. Outside his study-door stood two gigantic negroes on guard, in Eastern dresses of green and scarlet. The Empress Marie, though she did not share her sister Queen Alexandra's wonderful beauty, had all of her subtle and indescribable charm of manner, and she was very gracious to a stupid young Secretary-of-Embassy.

The bedroom given to me at Gatchina could hardly be described by the standardised epithets for Russian interiors "bare, gaunt, and whitewashed," as it had light blue silk walls embroidered with large silver wreaths. The mirrors were silvered, and the bed stood in a species of chancel, up four steps, and surrounded by a balustrade of silvered carved wood. Both the Ambassador and I agreed that the Imperial cellar fully maintained its high reputation. We were given in particular some very wonderful old Tokay, a present from the Emperor of Austria, a wine that was not on the market.

We were taken all over the palace, which contained, amongst other things, a large riding-school and a full-sized theatre. The really enchanting room was a large hall on the ground floor where many generations of little Grand-Dukes and Grand-Duchesses had played. As, owing to the severe winter climate, it is difficult for Russian children to amuse themselves much out-of-doors, these large play-rooms are almost a necessity in that frozen land. The Gatchina play-room was a vast low hall, a place of many whitewashed arches. In this delightful room was every possible thing that could attract a child. At one end were two wooden *Montagnes Russes,* the descent of which could be negotiated in little wheeled trollies. In another corner was a fully-equipped gymnasium. There were "giants' strides," swings, swing-boats and a merry-go-round. There was a toy railway with switches and signal-posts complete, the locomotives of which were worked by treadles, like a tricycle. There were dolls' houses galore, and larger houses into which the children could get, with real cooking-stoves in the little kitchens, and little parlours in which to eat the results of their primitive culinary experiments. There were mechanical orchestras, self-playing pianos and barrel-organs, and masses and masses of toys. On seeing this delectable spot, I regretted for the first time that I had not been born a Russian Grand-Duke, between the ages though of five and twelve only.

I believe that there is a similar room at Tsarskoe, although I never saw it.

CHAPTER VII

Lisbon—The two Kings of Portugal, and of Barataria—King Fernando and the Countess—A Lisbon bull-fight—The "hat-trick"—Courtship window-parade—The spurred youth of Lisbon—Portuguese politeness—The De Reszke family—The Opera—Terrible personal experiences in a circus—The bounding Bishop—Ecclesiastical possibilities—Portuguese coinage—Beauty of Lisbon—Visits of the British Fleet—Misguided midshipmen—The Legation Whale-boat—"Good wine needs no bush"—A delightful orange-farm—Cintra—Contrast between the Past and Present of Portugal.

A PROFFESIONAL diplomat becomes used to rapid changes in his environment. He has also to learn to readjust his monetary standards, for after calculating everything in roubles for, let us say, four years, he may find himself in a country where the peseta or the dollar are the units. At every fresh post he has to start again from the beginning, as he endeavours to learn the customs and above all the mentality of the new country. He has to form a brand-new acquaintance, to get to know the points of view of those amongst whom he is living, and in general to shape himself to totally new surroundings. A diplomat in this way insensibly acquires adaptability.

It would be difficult to imagine a greater contrast to Petrograd than Lisbon, which was my next post.

After the rather hectic gaiety of Petrograd, with its persistent flavour of an exotic and artificial civilisation, the placid, uneventful flow of life at Lisbon was restful, possibly even dull.

Curiously enough, in those days there were two Kings of Portugal at the same time. This state of things (which always reminded me irresistibly of the two Kings of Barataria in Gilbert and Sullivan's "Gondoliers") had come about quite naturally. Queen Maria II (Maria da Gloria) had married in 1836 Prince Ferdinand of Saxe-Coburg, who was raised next year to the title of King Consort. Maria II died in 1853 and was succeeded by Pedro V. During his son's minority King Ferdinand acted as Regent, and Pedro, dying unmarried eight years after, was succeeded in turn by his brother Luiz, also a son of King Ferdinand.

When the Corps Diplomatique were received at the Ajuda Palace on New Year's Day, the scene always struck me as being intensely comical. The two Kings (universally known as Dom Fernando and Dom Luiz) entered simultaneously by different doors. When they met Dom Luiz made a low bow to Dom Fernando, and then kissed his father's hand. Dom Fernando responded with an equally low bow, and kissed his son's hand. The two Kings then ascended the throne together. Had "The Gondoliers" been already composed then, I should have expected the two Monarchs to break into the duet from the second act, "Rising early in the Morning," in which the two Kings of Barataria explain their multitudinous duties. As King Luiz had a fine tenor voice, His Majesty could also in that case have brightened up the proceedings by singing us "Take a pair of sparkling eyes."

Dom Fernando was a perfectly delightful old gentleman, very highly cultured, full of humour, and with a charming natural courtesy of manner. The drolly-named Necessidades Palace which he inhabited was an unpretentious house full of beautiful old Portuguese furniture. Most of the rooms were wainscoted with the finest "azulejos" I ever saw; blue and white tiles which the Portuguese adopted originally from the Moors, but learnt later to make for themselves under the tuition of Dutch craftsmen from Delft. These "azulejos" form the most decorative background to a room that can be imagined. A bold pictorial design, a complete and elaborate picture in blue on white, runs along their whole length. It is thus very difficult to remove and re-erect "azulejos," for one broken tile will spoil the whole design. The Portuguese use these everywhere, both for the exteriors and interiors of their houses, and also as garden ornaments, and they are wonderfully effective.

Dom Fernando had married morganatically, as his second wife, a dancer of American origin. This lady had a remarkably strident voice, and was much to the fore on the fortnightly afternoons when Dom Fernando received the men of the Corps Diplomatique. For some reason or other, the ladies of the Diplomatic Body always found themselves unable to attend these gatherings. The courteous, genial old King would move about, smilingly dispensing his truly admirable cigars, and brimful of anecdotes and jokelets. The nasal raucous tones of the ex-dancer, always known as "the Countess," would summon him in English. "Say, King! you just hurry up with those cigars. They are badly wanted here."

I imagine that in the days of her successes on the stage the lady's outline must have been less voluminous than it was when I made her acquaintance. The only other occasion when I heard a monarch addressed as "King" *tout court* was when a small relation of my own, aged five, at a children's garden-party at Buckingham Palace insisted on answering King Edward VII's questions with a "Yes, O King," or "No, O King"; a form of address which had a pleasant Biblical flavour about it.

The Portuguese are a very humane race, and are extraordinarily kind to animals. They are also devoted to bull-fights. These two tendencies seem irreconcilable, till the fact is grasped that a Portuguese bull-fight is absolutely bloodless. Neither bulls nor horses are killed; the whole spectacle resolves itself into an exhibition of horsemanship and skill.

The bulls' horns are padded and covered with leather thongs. The *picador* rides a really good and highly-trained horse. Should he allow the bull even to touch his horse with his padded horns, the unfortunate *picador* will get mercilessly hissed.

These *picadores* do not wear the showy Spanish dresses, but Louis Quinze costumes of purple velvet with large white wigs. The *espada* is armed with a wooden sword only, which he plants innocuously on the neck of the bull, and woe betide him should those tens of thousands of eager eyes watching him detect a deviation of even one inch from the death-dealing spot. He will be hissed out of the ring. On the other hand, should he succeed in touching the fatal place with his harmless weapon, his skill would be rewarded with thunders of applause, and all the occupants of the upper galleries would shower small change and cigarettes into the ring, and would also hurl their hats into the arena, which always struck me as a peculiarly comical way of expressing their appreciation.

The *espada* would gaze at the hundreds of shabby battered bowler hats reposing on the sand of the arena with the same expression of simulated rapture that a *prima donna* assumes as floral tributes are handed to her across the footlights. The *espada,* his hand on his heart, would bow again and again, as though saying, "Are these lovely hats really for me?" But after a second glance at the dilapidated head-gear, covering the entire floor-space of the arena with little sub-fuse hummocks, he would apparently change his mind. "It is really amazingly good of you, and I do appreciate it, but I think on the whole that I will not deprive you of them," and then an exhibition of real skill occurred. The *espada,* taking up a hat, would glance at the galleries. Up went a hand, and the hat hurtled aloft to its owner with unfailing accuracy; and this performance was repeated perhaps a hundred times. I always considered the *espada's* hat-returning act far more extraordinary than his futile manipulation of the inoffensive wooden sword. During the aerial flights of the hats, two small acolytes of the *espada,* his miniature facsimiles in dress, picked up the small change and cigarettes, and, I trust, duly handed them over intact to their master. The bull meanwhile, after his imaginary slaughter, had trotted home contentedly to his underground quarters, surrounded by some twenty gaily-caparisoned tame bullocks. To my mind Spanish bull-fighting is revolting and horrible to the last degree. I have seen it once, and nothing will induce me to assist a second time at so disgusting a spectacle; but the most squeamish person can view a Portuguese bull-fight with impunity. Even though the bull has his horns bandaged, considerable skill and great acrobatic agility come into play. Few of us would care to stand in the path of a charging polled Angus bull, hornless though he be. The *bandarilheros* who plant paper-decorated darts in the neck of the charging bull are as nimble as trained acrobats, and vault lightly out of the ring when hard pressed. Conspicuous at a Lisbon bull-fight are a number of sturdy peasants, tricked out in showy clothes of scarlet and orange. These are "the men of strength." Should a bull prove cowardly in the ring, and decline to fight, the public clamour for him to be caught and expelled ignominiously from the ring by "the men of strength." Eight of the stalwart peasants will then hurl themselves on to the bull and literally hustle him out of the arena; no mean feat. Take it all round, a Portuguese bull-fight was picturesque and full of life and colour, though the neighbouring Spaniards affected an immense contempt for them on account of their bloodlessness and make-belief.

A curious Portuguese custom is one which ordains that a youth before proposing formally for a maiden's hand must do "window parade" for two months (in Portuguese "fazer a janella"). Nature has not allotted good looks to the majority of the Portuguese race, and she has been especially niggardly in this respect to the feminine element of the population. The taste for olives and for caviar is usually supposed to be an acquired one, and so may be the taste for Lusitanian loveliness. Somewhat to the surprise of the foreigner, Portuguese maidens seemed to inspire the same sentiments in the breasts of the youthful male as do their more-favoured sisters in other lands, but in *bourgeois* circles the "window-parade" was an indispensable preliminary to courtship. The youth had to pass backwards and forwards along the street where the dwelling of his *innamorata* was situated, casting up glances of passionate appeal to a window, where, as he knew, the form of his enchantress would presently appear. The maiden, when she judged that she might at length reveal herself without unduly encouraging her suitor, moved to the open window and stood fanning herself, laboriously unconscious of her ardent swain in the street below. The youth would then express his consuming passion in pantomime, making frantic gestures in testimony of his mad adoration. The senhorita in return might favour him with a coy glance, and in token of dismissal would perhaps drop him a rose, which the young man would press to his lips and then place over his heart, and so the performance came to an end, to be renewed again the next evening. The lovesick swain would almost certainly be wearing spurs. At first I could not make out why the young men of Lisbon, who had probably never been on a horse in their whole lives, should habitually walk about the town with spurs on their heels. It was, I think, a survival of the old Peninsular tradition, and was intended to prove to the world that they were "cavalleiros." In Spain an immense distinction was formerly made between the "caballero" and the "peon"; the mounted man, or gentleman, and the man on foot, or day-labourer. The little box-spurs were the only means these Lisbon youths had of proving their quality to the world. They had no horses, but they *had* spurs, which was obviously the next best thing.

Fortunes in Portugal being small, and strict economy having to be observed amongst all classes, I have heard that these damsels of the window-sill only dressed down to the waist. They would assume a *corsage* of scarlet or crimson plush, and, their nether garments being invisible from below, would study both economy and comfort by wearing a flannel petticoat below it. It is unnecessary for me to add that I never verified this detail from personal observation.

Some of the old Portuguese families occupied very fine, if sparsely furnished, houses, with *enfilades* of great, lofty bare rooms. After calling at one of these houses, the master of it would in Continental fashion " reconduct " his vistor towards the front door. At every single doorway the Portuguese code of politeness dictated that the visitor should protest energetically against his host accompanying him one step further. With equal insistence the host expressed his resolve to escort his visitor a little longer. The master of the house had previously settled in his own mind exactly how far he was going towards the entrance, the distance depending on the rank of the visitor, but the accepted code of manners insisted upon these protests and counter-protests at every single doorway.

In Germany " door-politeness " plays a great part. In one of Kotzebue's comedies two provincial notabilities of equal rank are engaged in a duel of " door-politeness." " But I must really insist on your Excellency passing first." " I could not dream of it, your Excellency. I will follow you." " Your Excellency knows that I could never allow that," and so on. The curtain falls on these two ladies each declining to precede the other, and when it rises on the second act the doorway is still there, and the two ladies are still disputing. Quite an effective stage-situation, and one which a modern dramatist might utilise.

In paying visits in Lisbon one was often pressed to remain to dinner, but the invitation was a mere form of politeness, and was not intended to be accepted. You invariably replied that you deeply regretted that you were already engaged. The more you were urged to throw over your engagement, the deeper became your regret that this particular engagement must be fulfilled. The engagament probably consisted in dining alone at the club, but under no circumstances must the invitation be accepted. In view of the straitened circumstances of most Portuguese families, the evening meal would probably consist of one single dish of *bacalhao* or salt cod, and you would have put your hosts to the greatest inconvenience.

With the exception of the Opera, the Lisbon theatres were most indifferent. When I first arrived there the Lisbon Opera had been fortunate enough to secure the services of a very gifted Polish family, a sister and two brothers, the latter of whom were destined later to become the idols of the London public. They were Mlle. de Reszke and Jean and Edouard de Reszke, all three of them then comparatively unknown. Mlle. de Reszke had the most glorious voice. To hear her singing with her brother Jean in "Faust" was a perfect revelation. Mlle. de Reszke appeared to the best advantage when the stalwart Jean sang with her, for she was immensely tall, and towered over the average portly, stumpy, little operatic tenor. The French say, cruelly enough, "bête comme un ténor." This may or may not be true, but the fact remains that the usual stage tenor is short, bull-necked, and conspicuously inclined to adipose tissue. When her brother Jean was out of the cast, it required an immense effort of the imagination to picture this splendid creature as being really desperately enamoured of the little paunchy, swarthy individual who, reaching to her shoulder only, was hurling his high notes at the public over the footlights.

At afternoon parties these three consummate artists occasionally sang unaccompanied trios. I have never heard anything so perfectly done. I am convinced that had Mlle. de Reszke lived, she would have established as great a European reputation as did her two brothers. The Lisbon musical public were terribly critical. They had one most disconcerting habit. Instead of hissing, should an artist have been unfortunate enough to incur their displeasure, the audience stood up and began banging the movable wooden seats of the stalls and dress circle up and down. This produced a deafening din, effectually drowning the orchestra and singers. The effect on the unhappy artist against whom all this pandemonium was directed may be imagined. On gala nights the Lisbon Opera was decorated in a very simple but effective manner. Most Portuguese families own a number of "colchas," or embroidered bed-quilts. These are of satin, silk, or linen, beautifully worked in colours. On a gala night, hundreds of these "colchas" were hung over the fronts of the boxes and galleries, with a wonderfully decorative effect. In the same way, on Church festivals, when religious processions made their way through the streets, many-hued "colchas" were thrown over the balconies of the houses, giving an extraordinarily festive appearance to the town.

As at Berlin and Petrograd, there was a really good circus at Lisbon. I, for one, am sorry that this particular form of entertainment is now obsolete in England, for it has always appealed to me, in spite of some painful memories connected with a circus which, if I may be permitted a long digression, I will relate.

Nearly thirty years ago I left London on a visit to one of the historic châteaux of France, in company with a friend who is now a well-known member of Parliament, and also churchwarden of a famous West-end church. We travelled over by night, and reached our destination about eleven next morning. We noticed a huge circular tent in the park of the château, but paid no particular attention to it. The first words with which our hostess, the bearer of a great French name, greeted us were, "I feel sure that I can rely upon you, *mes amis*. You have to help us out of a difficulty. My son and his friends have been practising for four months for their amateur circus. Our first performance is to-day at two o'clock. We have sold eight hundred tickets for the benefit of the French Red Cross, and yesterday, only yesterday, our two clowns were telegraphed for. They have both been ordered to the autumn manœuvres, and you two must take their places, or our performance is ruined. *Je sais que vous n'allez pas me manquer."* In vain we both protested that we had had no experience whatever as clowns, that branch of our education having been culpably neglected. Our hostess insisted, and would take no denial. "Go and wash; go and eat; and then put on the dresses you will find in your rooms." I never felt so miserable in my life as I did whilst making up my face the orthodox dead white, with scarlet triangles on the cheeks, big mouth, and blackened nose. The clown's kit was complete in every detail, with wig, conical hat, patterned stockings and queer white felt shoes. As far as externals went, I was orthodoxy itself, but the "business," and the "wheezes"! The future churchwarden had been taken in hand by some young Frenchmen. As he was to play "Chocolat," the black clown, they commenced by stripping him and blacking him from head to foot with boot-blacking. They then polished him.

I entered the ring with a sinking heart. I was to remain there two hours, and endeavour to amuse a French audience for that period without any preparation whatever. "Business," "gag," and "patter" had all to be improvised, and the "patter," of course, had to be in French. Luckily, I could then throw "cart-wheels" and turn somersaults to an indefinite extent. So I made my entrance in that fashion. Fortunately I got on good terms with my audience almost at once, and with confidence came inspiration; and with inspiration additional confidence, and a judicious recollection of the stock-tricks of clowns in various Continental capitals. Far greater liberties can be taken with a French audience than would be possible in England, but if anyone thinks it an easy task to go into a circus ring and to clown for two hours on end in a foreign language, without one minute's preparation, let him try it. The ring-master always pretends to flick the clown; it is part of the traditional "business"; but this amateur ring-master (most beautifully got up) handled his long whip so unskilfully that he not only really flicked my legs, but cut pieces out of them. When I jumped and yelled with genuine pain, the audience roared with laughter, so of course the ring-master plied his whip again. At the end of the performance my legs were absolutely raw. The clown came off badly too in some of the "roughs-and-tumbles," for the clown is always fair game. The French amateurs gave a really astonishingly good performance. They had borrowed trained horses from a real circus, and the same young Hungarian to whom I have alluded at the beginning of these reminiscences as having created a mild sensation by appearing at Buckingham Palace in a tiger-skin tunic trimmed with large turquoises, rode round the ring on a pad in sky-blue tights, bounding through paper hoops and over garlands of artificial flowers as easily and gracefully as though he had done nothing else all his life. Later on in the afternoon this versatile Hungarian reappeared in flowing Oriental robes and a false beard as "Ali Ben Hassan, the Bedouin Chief." Riding round the ring at full gallop, and firing from the saddle with a shot-gun, he broke glass balls with all the dexterity of a trained professional. That young Hungarian is now a bishop of the Roman Catholic Church. Before 1914 I had occasion to meet him frequently. Whenever I thought that on the strength of his purple robes he was assuming undue airs of ecclesiastical superiority (to use the word "swanking" would be an unpardonable vulgarism, especially in the case of a bishop), I invariably reminded his lordship of the afternoon, many years ago, when, arrayed in sky-blue silk tights, he had dashed through paper hoops in a French amateur circus. My remarks were usually met with the deprecatory smile and little gesture of protest of the hand so charactertistic of the Roman ecclesiastic, as the bishop murmured, "*Cher ami, tout cela est oublié depuis longtemps.*" I assured the prelate that for my own part I should never forget it, if only for the unexpected skill he had displayed; though I recognise that bishops may dislike being reminded of their past, especially when they have performed in circuses in their youth.

In addition to the Hungarian's "act," there was another beautiful exhibition of horsemanship. A boy of sixteen, a member of an historic French family, by dint of long, patient, and painful practice, was able to give an admirable performance of the familiar circus " turn " known as " The Courier of St. Petersburg," in which the rider, standing a-straddle on two barebacked ponies, drives four other ponies in front of him; an extraordinary feat for an amateur to have mastered. My friend the agile ecclesiastic is portrayed, perhaps a little maliciously, in Abel Hermant's most amusing book " Trains de Luxe," under the name of " Monseigneur Granita de Caffe Nero." It may interest ladies to learn that this fastidious prelate always had his purple robes made by Doucet, the famous Paris dressmaking firm, to ensure that they should " sit " properly. On the whole, our circus was really a very creditable effort for amateurs.

The entertainment was, I believe, pronounced a tremendous success, and at its conclusion the only person who was the worse for it was the poor clown. He had not only lost his voice entirely, from shouting for two hours on end, but he was black and blue from head to foot. Added to which, his legs were raw and bleeding from the ring-master's pitiless whip. I am thankful to say that in the course of a long life that was my one and only appearance in the ring of a circus. My fellow-clown, " Chocolat," the future member of Parliament and churchwarden, had been so liberally coated with boot-blacking by his French friends that it refused to come off, and for days afterwards his face was artistically decorated with swarthy patches.

Before 1914, I had frequently pointed out to my

friend the bishop that should he wish to raise any funds in his Hungarian diocese he could not do better than repeat his performance in the French circus. As a concession to his exalted rank, he might wear tights of episcopal purple. Should he have retained any of the nimbleness of his youth, his flock could not fail to be enormously gratified at witnessing their chief pastor bounding through paper hoops and leaping over obstacles with incredible agility for his age. The knowledge that they had so gifted and supple a prelate would probably greatly increase his moral influence over them and could scarcely fail to render him amazingly popular. Could his lordship have convinced his flock that he could demolish the arguments of any religious opponent with the same ease that he displayed in penetrating the paper obstacles to his equestrian progress, he would certainly be acclaimed as a theological controversialist of the first rank. In the same way, I have endeavoured to persuade my friend the member of Parliament that he might brighten up the proceedings in the House of Commons were he to appear there occasionally in the clown's dress he wore thirty years ago in France. Failing that, his attendance at the Easter Vestry Meeting of his West-end church with a blackened face might introduce that note of hilarity which is often so markedly lacking at these gatherings.

All this has led me far away from Lisbon in the "'eighties." Mark Twain has described, in "A Tramp Abroad," the terror with which a foreigner is overwhelmed on being presented with his first hotel bill on Portuguese territory. The total will certainly run into thousands of reis, and the unhappy stranger sees bankruptcy staring him in the face.

As a matter of fact, one thousand reis equal at par exactly four and twopence. It follows that a hundred reis are the equivalent of fivepence, and that one rei is the twentieth of a penny.

A French colleague of mine insisted that the Portuguese were actuated by national pride in selecting so small a monetary unit. An elementary calculation will show that the proud possessor of £222 10*s*. can claim to be a millionaire in Portugal. According to my French friend, Portugal was anxious to show the world that though a small country, a larger proportion of her subjects were millionaires than any other European country could boast of. In the same way the Frenchman explained the curious Lisbon habit of writing a number over every opening on the ground floor of a house, whether door or window. As a result the numbers of the houses crept up rapidly to the most imposing figures. It was not uncommon to find a house inscribed No. 2000 in a comparatively short street. Accordingly, Lisbon, though a small capital, was able to gain a spurious reputation for immense size.

A peculiarity of Lisbon was the double set of names of the principal streets and squares: the official name, and the popular one. I have never known this custom prevail anywhere else. Thus the principal street was officially known as Rua Garrett, and that name was duly written up. Everyone, though, spoke of it as the "Chiada." In the same way the splendid square facing the Tagus which English people call "Black Horse Square" had its official designation written up as "Praça do Comercio." It was, however, invariably called "Terreiro do Paço." The list could be extended indefinitely. Street names in Lisbon did not err in the matter of shortness. "Rua do Sacramento a Lapa de Baixio" strikes me as quite a sufficiently lengthy name for a street of six houses.

Lisbon is certainly a handsome town. It has been so frequently wrecked by earthquakes that there is very little mediæval architecture remaining, in spite of its great age. Two notable exceptions are the Tower of Belem and the exquisitely beautiful cloisters of the Hieronymite Convent, also at Belem. The tower stands on a promontory jutting into the Tagus, and the convent was built in the late fifteen-hundreds to commemorate the discovery of the sea route to India by Vasco da Gama. These two buildings are both in the "Manoeline" style, a variety of highly ornate late Gothic peculiar to Portugal. It is the fashion to sneer at Manoeline architecture, with its profuse decoration, as being a decadent style. To my mind the cloisters of Belem (the Portuguese variant of Bethlehem) rank as one of the architectural masterpieces of Europe. Its arches are draped, as it were, with a lace-work of intricate and minute stone carving, as delicate almost as jewellers' work. The warm brown colour of the stone adds to the effect, and anyone but an architectural pedant must admit the amazing beauty of the place. The finest example of Manoeline in Portugal is the great Abbey of Batalha, in my day far away from any railway, and very difficult of access.

At the time of the great earthquake of 1755 which laid Lisbon in ruins, Portugal was fortunate enough to have a man of real genius at the head of affairs, the Marquis de Pombal. Pombal not only re-established the national finances on a sound basis, but rebuilt the capital from his own designs. The stately "Black Horse Square" fronting the Tagus and the streets surrounding it were all designed by Pombal. I suppose that there is no hillier capital in the world than Lisbon. Many of the streets are too steep for the tramcars to climb. The Portuguese fashion of coating the exteriors of the houses with bright-coloured tiles of blue and white, or orange and white, gives a cheerful air to the town, —the French word "riant" would be more appropriate—and the numerous public gardens, where the palm-trees apparently grow as contentedly as in their native tropics, add to this effect of sunlit brightness. As in Brazil and other Portuguese-speaking countries, the houses are all very tall, and sash-windows are universal, as in England, contrary to the custom of other Continental countries.

House rent could not be called excessive in Portugal. In my day quite a large house, totally lacking in every description of modern convenience, but with a fine staircase and plenty of lofty rooms, could be hired for £80 a year, a price which may make the Londoner think seriously of transferring himself to the banks of the Tagus.

In the " 'eighties " Lisbon was the winter head-quarters of our Channel Squadron. I once saw the late Admiral Dowdeswell bring his entire fleet up the Tagus under sail; a most wonderful sight! The two five-masted flagships, the *Minotaur* and the *Agincourt,* had very graceful lines, and with every stitch of their canvas set, they were things of exquisite beauty. The *Northumberland* had also been designed as a sister ship, but for some reason had had two of her masts removed. The old *Minotaur,* now alas! a shapeless hulk known as *Ganges II,* is still, I believe, doing useful work at Harwich.

As may be imagined, the arrival of the British Fleet infused a certain element of liveliness into the sleepy city. Gambling-rooms were opened all over Lisbon, and as the bluejackets had a habit of wrecking any place where they suspected the proprietor of cheating them, the Legation had its work cut out for it in endeavouring to placate the local authorities and smooth down their wounded susceptibilities. One gambling-house, known as "Portuguese Joe's," was frequented mainly by midshipmen. They were strictly forbidden to go there, but the place was crammed every night with them, in spite of official prohibition. The British midshipman being a creature of impulse, the moment these youths (every one of whom thought it incumbent on his dignity to have a huge cigar in his mouth, even though he might still be of very tender years) suspected any foul play, they would proceed very systematically and methodically to smash the whole place up to matchwood. There was consequently a good deal of trouble, and the Legation quietly put strong pressure on the Portuguese Government to close these gambling-houses down permanently. This was accordingly done, much to the wrath of the midshipmen, who were, I believe, supplied with free drinks and cigars by the proprietors of these places. It is just possible that the Admiral's wishes may have been consulted before this drastic action was taken. Midshipmen in those days went to sea at fourteen and fifteen years of age, and consequently needed some shepherding.

As our Minister had constantly to pay official visits to the Fleet, the British Government kept a whale-boat at Lisbon for the use of the Legation. The coxswain, an ex-naval petty officer who spoke Portuguese, acted as Chancery servant when not afloat. When the boat was wanted, the coxswain went down to the quay with two bagfuls of blue-jackets' uniforms, and engaged a dozen chance Tagus boatmen. The Lisbon boatman, though skilful, is extraordinarily unclean in his person and his attire. I wish the people who lavished praises on the smart appearance of the Legation whale-boat and of its scratch crew could have seen, as I often did, the revoltingly filthy garments of these longshoremen before they drew the snowy naval white duck trousers and jumpers over them. Their persons were even dirtier, and—for reasons into which I need not enter—it was advisable to smoke a strong cigar whilst they were pulling. The tides in the Tagus run very strong; at spring-tides they will run seven or eight knots, so considerable skill is required in handling a boat. To do our odoriferous whited sepulchres of boatmen justice, they *could* pull, and the real workmanlike man-of-war fashion in which our coxswain always brought the boat alongside a ship, in spite of wind and tremendous tide, did credit to himself, and shed a mild reflected glory on the Legation.

The country round Lisbon is very arid. It produces, however, most excellent wines, both red and white, and in my time really good wine could be bought for fourpence a bottle. At the time of the vintage, all the country taverns and wine shops displayed a bush tied to a pole at their doors, as a sign that they had new wine, "green wine," as the Portuguese call it, for sale. Let the stranger beware of that new wine! Though pleasant to the palate and apparently innocuous, it is in reality hideously intoxicating, as a reference to the 13th verse of the second chapter of the Acts will show. I think that the custom of tying a bush to the door of a tavern where new wine is on sale must be the origin of the expression "good wine needs no bush."

The capabilities of this apparently intractable and arid soil when scientifically irrigated were convincingly shown on a farm some sixteen miles from Lisbon, belonging to a Colonel Campbell, an Englishman. Colonel Campbell, who had permanently settled in Portugal, had bought from the Government a derelict monastery and the lands attached to it at Torres Vedras, where Wellington entrenched himself in his famous lines in 1809-10. A good stream of water ran through the property, and Colonel Campbell diverted it, and literally caused the desert to blossom like the rose. Here were acres and acres of orange groves, and it was one of the few places in Europe where bananas would ripen. Colonel Campbell supplied the whole of Lisbon with butter, and the only mutton worth eating came also from his farm. It was a place flowing, if not with milk and honey, at all events with oil and wine. Here were huge tanks brimful of amber-coloured olive oil; whilst in vast dim cellars hundreds of barrels of red and white wine were slowly maturing in the mysterious shadows. Outside the sunlight fell on crates of ripe oranges and bananas, ready packed for the Lisbon market, and in the gardens tropical and sub-tropical flowering trees had not only thoroughly acclimatised themselves, but had expanded to prima-donna-like dimensions. The great rambling tiled monastery made a delightful dwelling-house, and to me it will be always a place of pleasant memories—a place of sunshine and golden orange groves; of rustling palms and cool blue and white tiles; of splashing fountains and old stonework smothered in a tangle of wine-coloured Bougainvillea.

The environs of all Portuguese towns are made dreary by the miles and miles of high walls which line the roads. These people must surely have some dark secrets in their lives to require these huge barriers between themselves and the rest of the world. Behind the wall were pleasant old *quintas*, or villas, faced with my favourite "azulejos" of blue and white, and surrounded with attractive, ill-kept gardens, where roses and oleanders ran riot amidst groves of orange and lemon trees.

Cintra would be a beautiful spot anywhere, but in this sun-scorched land it comes as a surprising revelation; a green oasis in a desolate expanse of aridity.

Here are great shady oak woods and tinkling fern-fringed brooks, pleasant leafy valleys, and a grateful sense of moist coolness. On the very summit of the rocky hill of Pena, King Fernando had built a fantastic dream-castle, all domes and pinnacles. It was exactly like the "enchanted castle" of one of Gustave Doré's illustrations, and had, I believe, been partly designed by Doré himself. Some of the details may have been a little too flamboyant for sober British tastes, but, perched on its lofty rock, this castle was surprisingly effective from below with its gilded turrets and Moorish tiles. As the castle occupied every inch of the summit of the Pena hill, the only approach to it was by a broad winding roadway tunnelled through the solid rock. Openings had been cut in the sides of the tunnel giving wonderful views over the valleys far down below. This approach was for all the world like the rocky ways up which Parsifal is led to the temple of the Grail in the first act of Wagner's great mystery drama. The finest feature about Pena, to my mind, was the wood of camellias on its southern face. These camellias had grown to a great size, and when in flower in March they were a most beautiful sight.

There was a great deal of work at the Lisbon Legation, principally of a commercial character. There were never-ending disputes between British shippers and the Custom House authorities, and the extremely dilatory methods of the Portuguese Government were most trying to the temper at times.

I shall always cherish mildly agreeable recollections of Lisbon. It was a placid, sunlit, soporific existence, very different from the turmoil of Petrograd life. The people were friendly, and as hospitable as their very limited financial resources enabled them to be. They could mostly speak French in a fashion, still their limited vocabulary was quite sufficient for expressing their more limited ideas.

I never could help contrasting the splendid past of this little nation with its somewhat inadequate present, for it must be remembered that Portugal in the fifteenth and sixteenth centuries was the leading maritime Power of Europe. Portugal had planted her colonies and her language (surely the most hideous of all spoken idioms!) in Asia, Africa, and South America long before Great Britain or France had even dreamed of a Colonial Empire.

They were a race of hardy and fearless seamen. Prince Henry the Navigator, the son of John of Portugal and of John of Gaunt's daughter, discovered Madeira, the Azores, and the Cape Verde islands in the early fourteen-hundreds.

In the same century Diaz doubled the Cape of Good Hope, and Vasco da Gama succeeded in reaching India by sea, whilst Albuquerque founded Portuguese colonies in Brazil and at Goa in India. This race of intrepid navigators and explorers held the command of the sea long before the Dutch or British, and by the middle of the sixteenth century little Portugal ranked as one of the most powerful monarchies in Europe.

Portugal, too, is England's oldest ally, for the Treaty of Windsor establishing an alliance between the two countries was signed as far back as 1386.

This is not the place in which to enter into the causes which led to the gradual decadence of this wonderful little nation, sapped her energies and atrophied her enterprise. To the historian those causes are sufficiently familiar.

Let us only trust that Lusitania's star may some day rise again.

CHAPTER VIII

Brazil—Contrast between Portuguese and Spanish South America—Moorish traditions—Amazing beauty of Rio de Janeiro—Yellow fever—The Commercial Court Chamberlain—The Emperor Pedro—The Botanic Gardens of Rio—The quaint diversions of Petropolis—The liveried young entomologist—Buenos Ayres—The charm of the "Camp"—Water-throwing—A British Minister in Carnival time—Some Buenos Ayres peculiarities—Masked balls—Climatic conditions—Theatres — Restaurants — Wonderful bird-life of the "Camp" — Estancia Negrete — Duck-shooting — My one flamingo—An exploring expedition in the Gran Chaco—Hardships—Alligators and fish—Currency difficulties.

My first impression of Brazil was that it was a mere transplanted Portugal, but a Portugal set amidst the most glorious vegetation and some of the finest scenery on the face of the globe. It is also unquestionably suffocatingly hot.

There is a great outward difference in the appearances of the towns of Portuguese and Spanish South America. In Brazil the Portuguese built their houses and towns precisely as they had done at home. There are the same winding irregular streets; the same tall houses faced with the decorative "azulejos"; the same shutterless sash-windows. A type of house less suited to the burning climate of Brazil can hardly be imagined. There being no outside shutters, it is impossible to keep the heat out, and the small rooms become so many ovens. The sinuosities of the irregular streets give a curiously old-world look to a Brazilian town, so much so that it is difficult for a European to realise that he is on the American Continent, associated as the latter is in our minds with unending straight lines.

In all Spanish-American countries the towns are laid out on the chess-board principle, with long dreary perspectives stretching themselves endlessly. The Spanish-American type of house too is mostly one-storied and flat-roofed, with two iron-barred windows only looking on to the street. The Moorish conquerors left their impress on Spain, and the Spanish pioneers carried across the Atlantic with them the Moorish conception of a house. The "patio" or enclosed court in the centre of the house is a heritage from the Moors, as is the flat roof or "azotea," and the decorated rainwater cistern in the centre of the "patio."

The very name of this tank in Spanish, "aljibe," is of Arabic origin, and it becomes obvious that this type of house was evolved by Mohammedans who kept their womenkind in jealous and strict seclusion. No indiscreet eyes from outside can penetrate into the "patio," and after nightfall the women could be allowed on to the flat roof to take the air. Those familiar with the East know the great part the roof of a house plays in the life of an Oriental. It is their parlour, particularly after dark. As the inhabitants of South America are not Mohammedans, I cannot conceive why they obstinately adhere to this inconvenient type of dwelling. The "patio" renders the house very dark and airless, becomes a well of damp in winter, and an oven in summer. To my mind unquestionably the best form of house for a hot climate is the Anglo-Indian bungalow, with its broad verandahs, thatched roof, and lofty rooms. In a bungalow some of the heat can be shut out.

On my first arrival in Brazil, the tropics and tropical vegetation were an unopened book to me, and I was fairly intoxicated with their beauty.

There is a short English-owned railway running from Pernambuco to some unknown spot in the interior. The manager of this railway came out on the steamer with us, and he was good enough to take me for a run on an engine into the heart of the virgin forest. I shall never forget the impression this made on me. It was like a peep into a wholly unimagined fairyland.

Had the calls of the mail steamer been deliberately designed to give the stranger a cumulative impression of the beauties of Brazil, they could not have been more happily arranged. First of Pernambuco in flat country, redeemed by its splendid vegetation; then Bahia with its fine bay and gentle hills, and lastly Rio the incomparable.

I have seen most of the surface of this globe, and I say deliberately, without any fear of contradiction, that nowhere is there anything approaching Rio in beauty. The glorious bay, two hundred miles in circumference, dotted with islands, and surrounded by mountains of almost grotesquely fantastic outlines, the whole clothed with exuberantly luxurious tropical vegetation, makes the most lovely picture that can be conceived.

The straggling town in my day had not yet blossomed into those vagaries of ultra-ornate architecture which at present characterise it. It was quaint and picturesque, and fitted its surroundings admirably, the narrow crowded Ruado Ouvidor being the centre of the fashionable life of the place.

It will be remembered that when Gonçalves discovered the great bay on January 1st, 1502, he imagined that it must be the estuary of some mighty river, and christened it accordingly "the River of January," "Rio de Janeiro." Oddly enough, only a few insignificant streams empty themselves into this vast landlocked harbour.

During my first fortnight in Rio, I thought the view over the bay more beautiful with every fresh standpoint I saw it from; whether from Botofogo, or from Nichteroy on the further shore, the view seemed more entrancingly lovely every time; and yet over this, the fairest spot on earth, the Angel of Death was perpetually hovering with outstretched wings; for yellow fever was endemic at Rio then, and yellow fever slays swiftly and surely.

One must have lived in countries where the disease is prevalent to realise the insane terror those two words "yellow fever" strike into most people. On my third visit to Rio, I was destined to contract the disease myself, but it dealt mercifully with me, so henceforth I am immune to yellow fever for the remainder of my life. The ravages this fell disease wrought in the West Indies a hundred years ago cannot be exaggerated. Those familiar with Michael Scott's delightful "Tom Cringle's Log" will remember the gruesome details he gives of a severe outbreak of the epidemic in Jamaica. In those days "Yellow Jack" took toll of nearly fifty per cent. of the white civil and military inhabitants of the British West Indies, as the countless memorial tablets in the older West Indian churches silently testify. Before my arrival in Rio, a new German Minister had, in spite of serious warnings, insisted on taking a beautiful little villa on a rocky promontory jutting into the bay. The house with its white marble colonnades, its lovely gardens, and the wonderful view over the mountains, was a thing of exquisite beauty, but it bore a very evil reputation. Within eight months the German Minister, his secretary, and his two white German servants were all dead of yellow fever. The Brazilians declare that the fever is never contracted during the daytime, but that sunset is the dangerous hour. They also warn the foreigner to avoid fruit and acid drinks.

Conditions have changed since then. The cause of the unhealthiness of Rio was a very simple one. All the sewage of the city was discharged into the landlocked, tideless bay, where it lay festering under the scorching sun. An English company tunnelled a way through the mountains direct to the Atlantic, and all the sewage is now discharged there, with the result that Rio is practically free from the dreaded disease.

The customs of a monarchical country are like a deep-rooted oak, they do not stand transplanting. Where they are the result of the slow growth of many centuries, they have adapted themselves, so to speak, to the soil of the country of their origin, have evolved national characteristics, and have fitted themselves into the national life. When transplanted into a new country, they cannot fail to appear anachronisms, and have always a certain element of the grotesque about them. In my time Dom Pedro, the Emperor of Brazil, had surrounded himself with a modified edition of the externals of a European Court. A colleague of mine had recently been presented to the Emperor at the Palace of São Christovão. As is customary on such occasions, my colleague called on the two Court Chamberlains who were on duty at São Christovão, and they duly returned the visit. One of these Chamberlains, whom we will call Baron de Feijão e Farinha, seemed reluctant to take his departure. He finally produced a bundle of price lists from his pocket, and assured my colleague that he would get far better value for his money at his (the Baron's) ready-made clothing store than at any other similar establishment in South America. From another pocket he then extracted a tape measure, and in spite of my colleague's protest passed the tape over his unwilling body to note the stock size, in the event of an order. The Baron de Feijão especially recommended one of his models, "the Pall Mall," a complete suit of which could be obtained for the nominal sum of 80,000 reis. This appalling sum looks less alarming when reduced to British currency, 80,000 Brazilian reis being equal to about £7 7*s.* I am not sure that he did not promise my colleague a commission on any orders he could extract from other members of the Legation. My colleague, a remarkably well-dressed man, did not recover his equanimity for some days, after picturing his neatly-garbed form arrayed in the appallingly flashy, ill-cut, ready-made garments in which the youth of Rio de Janeiro were wont to disport themselves. To European ideas, it was a little unusual to find a Court Chamberlain engaged in the ready-made clothing line.

On State occasions Dom Pedro assumed the most splendid Imperial mantle any sovereign has ever possessed. It was composed entirely of feathers, being made of the breasts of toucans, shaded from pale pink to deep rose-colour, and was the most gorgeous bit of colour imaginable. In the sweltering climate of Brazil, the heat of this mantle must have been unendurable, and I always wondered how Dom Pedro managed to bear it with a smiling face, but it certainly looked magnificent.

One of the industries of Rio was the manufacture of artificial flowers from the feathers of humming-birds. These feather flowers were wonderfully faithful reproductions of Nature, and were practically indestructible, besides being most artistically made. They were very expensive.

The famous avenue of royal palms in the Botanic Gardens would almost repay anyone for the voyage from Europe. These are, I believe, the tallest palms known, and the long avenue is strikingly impressive. The *Oreodoxa regia,* one of the cabbage-palms, has a huge trunk, perfectly symmetrical, and growing absolutely straight. This perspective of giant boles recalls the columns of an immense Gothic cathedral, whilst the fronds uniting in a green arch two hundred feet overhead complete the illusion. The Botanic Gardens have some most attractive ponds of pink and sky-blue water lilies, and the view of the bay from the gardens is usually considered the finest in Rio.

Owing to the unhealthiness of Rio, most of the Foreign Legations had established themselves permanently at Petropolis, in the Organ Mountains, Petropolis being well above the yellow fever zone. On my third visit to Rio, such a terrible epidemic of yellow fever was raging in the capital that the British Minister very kindly invited me to go up straight to the Legation at Petropolis. The latter is three hours' distance from Rio by mountain railway. People with business in the city leave for Rio by the 7 a.m. train, and reach Petropolis again at 7 p.m. The old Emperor, Dom Pedro, made a point of attending the departure and arrival of the train every single day, and a military band played regularly in the station, morning and evening. This struck me as a very unusual form of amusement. The Emperor (who ten months later was quietly deposed) was a tall, handsome old gentleman, of very distinguished appearance, and with charming manners. He had also encyclopædic knowledge on most points. That a sovereign should take pleasure in seeing the daily train depart and arrive seemed to point to a certain lack of resources in Petropolis, and to hint at moments of deadly dulness in the Imperial villa there. Dom Pedro never appeared in public except in evening dress, and it was a novelty to see the head of a State in full evening dress and high hat at half-past six in the morning, listening to an extremely indifferent brass band braying in the waiting-room of a shabby railway station.

Nature seems to have lavished all the most brilliant hues of her palette on Brazil; the plumage of the birds, the flowers, and foliage all glow with vivid colour. Even a Brazilian toad has bright emerald-green spots all over him. The gorgeous butterflies of this highly-coloured land are well known in Europe, especially those lovely creatures of shimmering, iridescent blue.

These butterflies were the cause of a considerable variation in the hours of meals at the British Legation.

The Minister had recently brought out to Brazil an English boy to act as young footman. Henry was a most willing, obliging lad, but these great Brazilian butterflies exercised a quite irresistible fascination over him, and small blame to him. He kept a butterfly-net in the pantry, and the instant one of the brilliant, glittering creatures appeared in the garden, Henry forgot everything. Clang the front-door bell never so loudly, he paid no heed to it; the cook might be yelling for him to carry the luncheon into the dining-room, Henry turned a deaf ear to her entreaties. Snatching up his butterfly-net, he would dart through the window in hot pursuit. As these great butterflies fly like Handley Pages, he had his work cut out for him, and running is exhausting in a temperature of 90 degrees. The usual hour for luncheon would be long past, and the table would still exhibit a virgin expanse of white cloth. Somewhere in the dim distance we could descry a slim young figure bounding along hot-foot, with butterfly-net poised aloft, so we possessed our souls in patience. Eventually Henry would reappear, moist but triumphant, or dripping and despondent, according to his success or failure with his shimmering quarry. After such violent exercise, Henry had to have a plunge in the swimming-bath and a complete change of clothing before he could resume his duties, all of which occasioned some little further delay. And this would happen every day, so our repasts may be legitimately described as "movable feasts." It was no use speaking to Henry. He would promise to be less forgetful, but the next butterfly that came flitting along drove all good resolves out of this ardent young entomologist's head, and off he would go on flying feet in eager pursuit. I recommended Henry when he returned to England to take up cross-country running seriously. He seemed to have unmistakable aptitudes for it.

The streets of Petropolis were planted with avenues of a flowering tree imported from the Southern Pacific. When in bloom, this tree was so covered with vivid pink blossoms that all its leaves were hidden. These rows of bright pink trees gave the dull little town a curious resemblance to a Japanese fan.

There are some lovely little nooks and corners in the Organ Mountains. One ravine in particular was most beautiful, with a cascade dashing down the cliff, and the clear brook below it fringed with eucharis lilies, and the tropical begonias which we laboriously cultivate in stove-houses. Unfortunately, these beauty spots seemed as attractive to snakes as they were to human beings. This entailed keeping a watchful eye on the ground, for Brazilian snakes are very venomous.

No greater contrast can be imagined than that between the forests and mountains of steamy Brazil and the endless, treeless, dead-flat levels of the Argentine Republic, twelve hundred miles south of them.

When I first knew Buenos Ayres in the early "'eighties," it still retained an old-world air of distinction. The narrow streets were lined with sombre, dignified old buildings of a markedly Spanish type, and the modern riot of over-ornate ginger-bread architecture had not yet transformed the city into a glittering, garish trans-Atlantic pseudo-Paris. In the same way newly-acquired wealth had not begun to assert itself as blatantly as it has since done.

I confess that I was astonished to find two daily English newspapers in Buenos Ayres, for I had not realised the size and importance of the British commercial colony there.

The "Camp" (from the Spanish *campo,* country) outside the city is undeniably ugly and featureless, as it stretches its unending khaki-coloured, treeless flatness to the horizon, but the sense of immense space has something exhilarating about it, and the air is perfectly glorious. In time these vast dun-coloured levels exercise a sort of a fascination over one; to me the "Camp" will always be associated with the raucous cries of the thousands of spurred Argentine plovers, as they wheel over the horsemen with their never-ending scream of "téro, téro."

As in most countries of Spanish origin, the Carnival was kept at Buenos Ayres in the old-fashioned style. In my time, on the last day of the Carnival, Shrove Tuesday, the traditional water-throwing was still allowed in the streets. Everyone going into the streets must be prepared for being drenched with water from head to foot. My new Chief, whom I will call Sir Edward (though he happened to have a totally different name), had just arrived in Buenos Ayres. He was quite unused to South American ways. On Shrove Tuesday I came down to breakfast in an old suit of flannels and a soft shirt and collar, for from my experiences of the previous year I knew what was to be expected in the streets. Sir Edward, a remarkably neat dresser, appeared beautifully arrayed in a new suit, the smartest of bow-ties, and a yellow jean waistcoat. I pointed out to my Chief that it was water-throwing day, and suggested the advisability of his wearing his oldest clothes. Sir Edward gave me to understand that he imagined that few people would venture to throw water over her Britannic Majesty's representative. Off we started on foot for the Chancery of the Legation, which was situated a good mile from our house. I knew what was coming. In the first five minutes we got a bucket of water from the top of a house, plumb all over us, soaking us both to the skin. Sir Edward was speechless with rage for a minute or so, after which I will not attempt to reproduce his language. Men were selling everywhere in the streets the large squirts ("*pomitos*" in Spanish) which are used on these occasions. I equipped myself with a perfect Woolwich Arsenal of *pomitos*, but Sir Edward waved them all disdainfully away. Soon two girls darted out of an open doorway, armed with *pomitos,* and caught us each fairly in the face, after which they giggled and ran into their house, leaving the front door open. Sir Edward fairly danced with rage on the pavement, shouting out the most uncomplimentary opinions as to the

Argentine Republic and its inhabitants. The front door having been left open, I was entitled by all the laws of Carnival time to pursue our two fair assailants into their house, and I did so, in spite of Sir Edward's remonstrances. I chased the two girls into the drawing-room, where we experienced some little difficulty in clambering over sofas and tables, and I finally caught them in the dining-room, where a venerable lady, probably their grandmother, was reposing in an armchair. I gave the two girls a thorough good soaking from my *pomitos,* and bestowed the mildest sprinkling on their aged relative, who was immensely gratified by the attention. "Oh! my dears," she cried in Spanish to the girls, "you both consider me so old. You can see that I am not too old for this young man to enjoy paying me a little compliment."

Autres pays, autres mœurs! Just conceive the feelings of an ordinary British middle-class householder, residing, let us say, at Balham or Wandsworth, at learning that the sanctity of "The Laurels" or "Ferndale" had been invaded by a total stranger; that his daughters had been pursued round the house, and then soaked with water in his own dining-room, and that even his aged mother's revered white hairs had not preserved her from a like indignity. I cannot imagine him accepting it as a humorous everyday incident. Our progress to the Chancery was punctuated by several more interludes of a similar character, and I was really pained on reaching the shelter of our official sanctuary to note how Sir Edward's spotless garments had suffered. Personally, on a broiling February day (corresponding with August in the northern hemisphere) I thought the cool water most refreshing. Our Chancery looked on to the fashionable Calle Florida, and a highly respectable German widow who had lived for thirty years in South America acted as our housekeeper. Sir Edward, considerably ruffled in his temper, sat down to continue a very elaborate memorandum he was drawing up on the new Argentine Customs tariff. The subject was a complicated one, there were masses of figures to deal with, and the work required the closest concentration. Presently our housekeeper, Frau Bauer, entered the room demurely, and made her way to Sir Edward's table,

"Wenn Excellenz so gut sein werden um zu entschuldigen," began Frau Bauer with downcast eyes, and then suddenly with a discreet titter she produced a large *pomito* from under her apron and, secure in the license of Carnival time, she thrust it into Sir Edward's collar, and proceeded to squirt half a pint of cold water down his back, retiring swiftly with elderly coyness amid an explosion of giggles. I think that I have seldom seen a man in such a furious rage. I will not attempt to reproduce Sir Edward's language, for the printer would have exhausted his entire stock of "blanks" before I had got halfway through. The Minister, when he had eased his mind sufficiently, snapped out, "It is obvious that with all this condemned (that was not quite the word he used) foolery going on, it is impossible to do any serious work to-day. Where . . . where . . . can one buy the infernal squirts these condemned idiots use?" "Anywhere in the streets. Shall I buy you some, Sir Edward?" "Yes, get me a lot of them, and the biggest you can find." So we parted.

Returning home after a moist but enjoyable afternoon, I saw a great crowd gathered at the junction of two streets, engaged in a furious water-fight. The central figure was a most disreputable-looking individual with a sodden wisp of linen where his collar should have been; remnants of a tie trailed dankly down, his soaked garments were shapeless, and his head was crowned with a sort of dripping poultice. He was spouting water in all directions like the Crystal Palace fountains in their heyday, with shouts of "Take that, you foolish female; and that, you fat feminine Argentine!" With grief I recognised in this damp reveller her Britannic Majesty's Minister Plenipotentiary.

Upon returning home, we found that our two English servants had been having the time of their lives. They had stood all day on the roof of the house, dashing pails of water over passers-by until they had completely emptied the cistern. There was not one drop of water in the house, and we had to borrow three pailfuls from a complaisant neighbour.

A few years later the police prohibited water-throwing altogether, so this feature of a Buenos

Ayres Carnival is now a thing of the past.

As time went on I grew very fond of Sir Edward. His temper may have flared up quickly, but it died down just as rapidly. He was a man with an extraordinarily varied fund of information, and possessed a very original and subtle sense of humour. He was also a great stylist in writing English, and the drafts I wrote for despatches were but seldom fortunate enough to meet with his approval. A split infinitive brought him to the verge of tears. The Argentine authorities were by no means easy to deal with, and Sir Edward handled them in a masterly fashion. His quiet persistence usually achieved its object. It was a real joy to see him dealing with anyone rash enough to attempt to bully or browbeat him. His tongue could sting like a lash on occasions, whilst he preserved an outward air of imperturbable calm. Sir Edward both spoke and wrote the most beautifully finished Spanish.

A ball in a private house at Buenos Ayres had its peculiar features in the "'eighties." In the first place, none of the furniture was removed from the rooms, and so far from taking up carpets, carpets were actually laid down, should the rooms be unprovided with them. This rendered dancing somewhat difficult; in fact a ball resolved itself into a leisurely arm-in-arm promenade to music through the rooms, steering an erratic course between the articles of furniture, "drawing the port," as a Scottish curler would put it. Occasionally a space behind a sofa could be found sufficiently large to attempt a few mild gyrations, but that was all. The golden youth of Buenos Ayres, in the place of the conventional white evening tie, all affected the most deplorable bows of pale pink or pale green satin. A wedding, too, differed from the European routine. The parents of the bride gave a ball. At twelve o'clock dancing, or promenading amidst the furniture, ceased. A portable altar was brought into the room; a priest made his unexpected entry, and the young couple were married at breakneck speed. At the conclusion of the ceremony, all the young men darted at the bride and tore her marriage-veil to shreds. Priest, altar, and the newly-married couple then disappeared; the band struck up again, and dancing, or rather a leisurely progress round the sofas and ottomans, recommenced.

A form of entertainment that appeals immensely to people of Spanish blood is a masked ball. In Buenos Ayres the ladies only were masked, which gave them a distinct advantage over the men. To enjoy a masquerade a good knowledge of Spanish is necessary. All masked women are addressed indiscriminately as "mascarita" and can be "tutoyée'd." Convention permits, too, anything within reasonable limits to be said by a man to "mascaritas," who one and all assume a little high-pitched head-voice to conceal their identities. I fancy that the real attractions masquerades had for most women lay in the opportunity they afforded every "mascarita" of saying with impunity abominably rude things to some other woman whom she detested. I remember one "mascarita," an acquaintance of mine, whose identity I pierced at once, giving another veiled form accurate details not only as to the date when the pearly range of teeth she was exhibiting to the world had come into her possession, but also the exact price she had paid for them.

It takes a stranger from the North some little time to accustom himself to the inversion of seasons and of the points of the compass in the southern hemisphere. For instance, "a lovely spring day in *October*," or "a chilly autumn evening in *May*," rings curiously to our ears; as it does to hear of a room with a cool *southern* aspect, or to hear complaints about the hot *north* wind. Personally I did not dislike the north wind; it was certainly moist and warm, but it smelt deliciously fragrant with a faint spicy odour after its journey over the great Brazilian forests on its way from the Equator. All Argentines seemed to feel the north wind terribly; it gave them headaches, and appeared to dislocate their entire nervous system. In the Law Courts it was held to be a mitigating circumstance should it be proved that a murder, or other crime of violence, had been committed after a long spell of north wind. Many women went about during a north wind with split beans on their temples to soothe their headaches, a comical sight till one grew accustomed to it. The old German housekeeper of the Chancery, Frau Bauer, invariably had split beans adhering to her temples when the north wind blew.

The icy *pampero,* the south wind direct from the Pole, was the great doctor of Buenos Ayres. Darwin used to consider the River Plate the electrical centre of the world. Nowhere have I experienced such terrific thunderstorms as in the Argentine. Sometimes on a stifling summer night, with the thermometer standing at nearly a hundred degrees, one of these stupendous storms would break over the city with floods of rain. Following on the storm would come the *pampero,* gently at first, but increasing in violence until a blustering, ice-cold gale went roaring through the sweltering city, bringing the temperature down in four hours with a run from 100 degrees to 60 degrees. Extremely pleasant for those like myself with sound lungs; very dangerous to those with delicate chests.

The old-fashioned Argentine house had no protection over the *patio.* In bad weather the occupants had to make their way through the rain from one room to another. Some of the newer houses were built in a style which I have seen nowhere else except on the stage. Everyone is familiar with those airy dwellings composed principally of open colonnades one sees on stage back-cloths. These houses were very similar in design, with open halls of columns and arches, and open-air staircases. On the stage it rains but seldom, and the style may be suited to the climatic conditions prevailing there.

In real life it must be horribly inconvenient. The Italian Minister at Buenos Ayres lived in a house of this description. In fine weather it looked extremely picturesque, but I imagine that his Excellency's progress to bed must have been attended with some difficulties when, during a thunderstorm, the rain poured in cataracts down his open-air staircase, and the *pampero* howled through his open arcades and galleries.

The theatres at Buenos Ayres were quite excellent. At the Opera all the celebrated singers of Europe could be heard, although one could almost have purchased a nice little freehold property near London for the price asked for a seat. There were two French theatres, one devoted to light opera, the other to Palais Royal farces, both admirably given; and, astonishingly enough, during part of my stay, there was actually an English theatre with an English stock company. A peculiarly Spanish form of entertainment is the "Zarzuela," a sort of musical farce. It requires a fairly intimate knowledge of the language to follow these pieces with their many topical allusions.

The Spanish-American temperament seems to dislike instinctively any gloomy or morbid dramas, differing widely from the Russians in this respect. At Petrograd, on the Russian stage, the plays, in addition to the usual marital difficulties, were brightened up by allusions to such cheerful topics as inherited tendencies to kleptomania or suicide, or an intense desire for self-mutilation. What appeals to the morbid frost-bound North apparently fails to attract the light-hearted sons of the southern hemisphere.

Buenos Ayres was also a city of admirable restaurants. In the fashionable places, resplendent with mirrors, coloured marbles and gilding, the cooking rivals Paris, and the bill, when tendered, makes one inclined to rush to the telegraph office to cable for further and largely increased remittances from Europe. There were a number, however, of unpretending French restaurants of the most meritorious description. Never shall I forget Sir Edward's face when, in answer to his questions as to a light supper, the waiter suggested a cold armadillo; a most excellent dish, by the way, though after seeing the creature in the Zoological Gardens one would hardly credit it with gastronomic possibilities. The soil of the Argentine is marvellously fertile, and some day it will become a great wine-growing country. In the meantime vast quantities of inferior wine are imported from Europe. After sampling a thin Spanish red wine, and a heavy sweet black wine known as Priorato, and having tested their effects on his digestion, Sir Edward christened them "The red wine of Our Lady of Pain" and "The black wine of Death."

When the President of the Republic appeared in public on great occasions, he was always preceded by a man carrying a large blue velvet bolster embroidered with the Argentine arms. This was clearly an emblem of national sovereignty, but what this blue bolster was intended to typify I never could find out. Did it indicate that it was the duty of the President to bolster up the Republic, or did it signify that the Republic was always ready to bolster up its President? None of my Argentine friends could throw any light upon the subject further than by saying that this bolster was always carried in front of the President; a sufficiently self-evident fact. It will always remain an enigma to me. A bolster seems a curiously soporific emblem for a young, enterprising, and progressive Republic to select as its symbol.

It would be ungallant to pass over without remark the wonderful beauty of the Argentine girls. This beauty is very shortlived indeed, and owing to their obstinate refusal to take any exercise whatever, feminine outlines increase in bulk at an absurdly early age, but between seventeen and twenty-one many of them are really lovely. Lolling in hammocks and perpetual chocolate-eating bring about their own penalties, and sad to say, bring them about very quickly. I must add that the attractiveness of these girls is rather physical than intellectual.

The house Sir Edward and I rented had been originally built for a stage favourite by one of her many warm-hearted admirers. It had been furnished according to the lady's own markedly florid tastes. I reposed nightly in a room entirely draped in sky-blue satin. The house had a charming garden, and Sir Edward and I expended a great deal of trouble and a considerable amount of money on it. That garden was the pride of our hearts, but we had reckoned without the leaf-cutting ant, the great foe of the horticulturist in South America. At Rio, and in other places in Brazil, they had a special apparatus for pumping the fumes of burning sulphur into the ant-holes, and so were enabled to keep these pests in check. In private gardens in Brazil every single specially cherished plant had to have its stem surrounded with unsightly circular troughs of paraffin and water. In front of our windows we had a large bed of gardenias backed by a splendid border of many-hued cannas which were the apple of Sir Edward's eye. He gazed daily on them with an air not only of pride, but of quasi-paternity. The leaf-cutting ants found their way into our garden, and in four days nothing remained of our beautiful gardenias and cannas but some black, leafless stalks. These abominable insects swept our garden as bare of every green thing as a flight of locusts would have done; they even killed the grass where their serried processions had passed.

For me, the great charm of the Argentine lay in the endless expanses of the "Camp," far away from the noisy city. The show *estancia* of the Argentine was in those days "Negrete," the property of Mr. David Shennan, kindest and most hospitable of Scotsmen. Most English residents and visitors out in the Plate cherish grateful recollections of that pleasant spot, encircled by peach orchards, where the genial proprietor, like a patriarch of old, welcomed his guests, surrounded by his vast herds and flocks. I happen to know the exact number of head of cattle Mr. Shennan had on his *estancia* on January 1, 1884, for I was one of the counters at the stocktaking on the last day of the year. The number was 18,731 head.

Counting cattle is rather laborious work, and needs close concentration. Six of us were in the saddle from daybreak to dusk, with short intervals for meals, and December 31 is at the height of the summer in the southern hemisphere, so the heat was considerable.

This is the method employed in a "count." The cattle are driven into "mobs" of some eight hundred ("Rodeo" is the Spanish term for mob) by the "peons." Some twenty tame bullocks are driven a quarter of a mile from the "mob," and the counters line up on their horses between the two, with their pockets full of beans. The "peons" use their whips, and one or two of the cattle break away from the herd to the tame bullocks. They are followed by more and more at an ever-increasing pace. Each one is counted, and when one hundred is reached, a bean is silently transferred from the left pocket to the right. So the process is continued until the entire herd has passed by. Should the numbers given by the six counters tally within reason, the count is accepted. Should it differ materially, there is a recount; then the counters pass on to another "mob" some two miles away. Under a very hot sun, the strain of continual attention is exhausting, and those six counters found their beds unusually welcome that night.

The dwelling-house of Negrete, which was to become very familiar to me, was over a hundred years old, and stretched itself one-storied round a large *patio,* blue and white tiled, with an elaborate well-head in the centre decorated with good iron-work. The *patio* was fragrant with orange and lemon trees, and great bushes of the lovely sky-blue Paraguayan jasmine. I can never understand why this shrub, the "Jasmin del Paraguay," with its deliciously sweet perfume and showy blue flowers, has never been introduced into England. It would have to be grown under glass, but only requires sufficient heat to keep the frost out.

I had never felt the *joie de vivre*—the sheer joy at being alive—thrill through one's veins so exultantly as when riding over the "Camp" in early morning. I have had the same feeling on the High Veldt in South Africa, where there is the same marvellous air, and, in spite of the undulations of the ground, the same sense of vast space. The glorious air, the sunlight, the limitless, treeless expanse of neutral-tinted grass stretching endlessly to the horizon, and the vast hemisphere of blue sky above had something absolutely intoxicating in them. It may have been the delight of forgetting that there were such things as towns, and streets, and tramways. And then the teeming bird-life of the camp! Ibis and egrets flashed bronze-green or snowy-white through the sunlight; the beautiful pink spoon-bills flapped noisily overhead in single file, a lengthy rosy trail of long legs and necks and brilliant colour; the quaint little ground owls blinked from the entrances of their burrows, and dozens of spurred plovers wheeled in incessant gyrations, keeping up their endless, wearying scream of "téro-téro." I always wanted to shout and sing from sheer delight at being part of it all.

The tinamou, the South American partridge, surprisingly stupid birds, rose almost under the horses' feet, and dozens of cheery little sandpipers darted about in all directions. Birds, birds everywhere! Should one pass near one of the great shallow lagoons, which are such a feature of the country, its surface would be black with ducks, with perhaps a regiment of flamingoes in the centre of it, a dazzling patch of sunlit scarlet, against the turquoise blue the water reflected from the sky.

In springtime the "Camp" is covered with the trailing verbena which in my young days was such a favourite bedding-out plant in England, its flowers making a brilliant league-long carpet of scarlet or purple.

There are endless opportunities for shooting on the "Camp" in the Province of Buenos Ayres, only limited by the difficulties in obtaining cartridges, and the fact that in places where it is impossible to dispose of the game the amount shot must depend on what can be eaten locally. Otherwise it is not sport, but becomes wanton slaughter.

The foolish tinamou are easily shot, but are exceedingly difficult to retrieve out of the knee-high grass, and if only winged, they can run like hares. There is also a large black and white migratory bird of the snipe family, the "batitou," which appears from the frozen regions of the Far South, as winter comes on, and is immensely prized for the table. He is unquestionably a delicious bird to eat, but is very hard to approach owing to his wariness. The duck-shooting was absolutely unequalled. I had never before known that there were so many ducks in the world, nor were there the same complicated preliminaries, as with us; no keepers, no beaters, no dogs were required. One simply put twenty cartridges in a bandolier, took one's gun, jumped on a horse, and rode six miles or so to a selected lagoon. Here the horse was tied up to the nearest fence, and one just walked into the lagoon. So warm was the water in these lagoons that I have stood waist-high in it for hours without feeling the least chilly, or suffering from any ill effects whatever. With the first step came a mighty and stupendous roar of wings, and a prodigious quacking, then the air became black with countless thousands of ducks. Mallards, shovellers, and speckled ducks; black ducks with crimson feet and bills; the great black and white birds Argentines call "Royal" ducks, and we "Muscovy" ducks, though with us they are uninteresting inhabitants of a farmyard. Ducks, ducks everywhere! As these confiding fowl never thought of flying away, but kept circling over the lagoon again and again, I am sure that anyone, given sufficient cartridges, and the inclination to do so, could easily have killed five hundred of them to his own gun in one day. We limited ourselves to ten apiece. Splashing about in the lagoon, it was easy to pick up the dead birds without a dog, but no one who has not carried them can have any idea of the weight of eight ducks in a gamebag pressing on one's back, or can conceive how difficult it is to get into the saddle on a half-broken horse with this weight dragging you backwards. In any other country but the Argentine, to canter home six miles dripping wet would have resulted in a severe chill. No one ever seemed the worse for it out there.

At times I went into the lagoons without a gun, just to observe at close quarters the teeming water-life there. The raucous screams of the vigilant "téro-téros" warned the water-birds of a hostile approach, but it was easy to sit down in the shallow warm water amongst the reeds until the alarm had died down, and one was amply repaid for it, though the enforced lengthy abstention from tobacco was trying.

The "Camp" is a great educator. One learnt there to recap empty cartridge-cases with a machine, and to reload them. One learnt too to clean guns and saddlery. When a thing remains undone, unless you take it in hand yourself, you begin wondering why you should ever have left these things to be done for you by others. The novice finds out that a bridle and bit are surprisingly difficult objects to clean, even given unlimited oil and sand-paper. The " Camp " certainly educates, and teaches the neophyte independence.

I shot several pink spoonbills, one of which in a glass case is not far from me as I write, but I simply longed to get a scarlet flamingo. Owing to the spoonbills' habit of flitting from lagoon to lagoon, they are not difficult to shoot, but a flamingo is a very wary bird. Perched on one leg, they stand in the very middle of a lagoon, and allow no one within gunshot. The officious " téro-téros " effectually notify them of the approach of man, and possibly the flamingoes have learnt from " Alice in Wonderland " that the Queen of Hearts is in the habit of utilising them as croquet-mallets. The natural anxiety to escape so ignominious a fate would tend to make them additionally cautious. Anyhow, I found it impossible to approach them. The idea occurred to me of trying to shoot one with a rifle. So I crawled prostrate on my anatomy up to the lagoon. I failed at least six times, but finally succeeded in killing a flamingo. Wading into the lagoon, I triumphantly retrieved my scarlet victim, and took him by train to Buenos Ayres, intending to hand him over to a taxidermist next day. When I awoke next morning, the blue satin bower in which I slept (originally fitted up, as I have explained, as the bedroom of a minor light of the operatic stage) was filled with a pestilential smell of decayed fish. I inquired the reason of my English servant, who informed me that the cook was afraid that there was something wrong about "the queer duck" I had brought home last night, as its odour was not agreeable. (The real expression he used was "smelling something cruel.") Full of horrible forebodings, I jumped out of bed and ran down to the kitchen, to find a little heap of brilliant scarlet feathers reposing on the table, and Paquita, our fat Andalusian cook, regarding with doubtful eyes a carcase slowly roasting before the fire, and filling the place with unbelievably poisonous effluvia. And that was the end of the only flamingo I ever succeeded in shooting.

A London financial house had, by foreclosing a mortgage, come into possession of a great tract of land in the unsurveyed and uncharted Indian Reserve, the Gran Chaco. Anxious to ascertain whether their newly-acquired property was suited for white settlers, the financial house sent out two representatives to Buenos Ayres with orders to fit out a little expedition to survey and explore it. I was invited to join this expedition, and as work was slack at the time, Sir Edward did not require my services and gave me leave to go. I had been warned that conditions would be very rough indeed, but the opportunity seemed one of those that only occur once in a lifetime, and too good to be lost. I do not think the invitation was quite a disinterested one. The leaders of the expedition probably thought that the presence of a member of the British Legation might be useful in case of difficulties with the Argentine authorities. I travelled by steamer six hundred miles up the mighty Paraná, and joined the other members of the expedition at the Alexandra Colony, a little English settlement belonging to the London firm hundreds of miles from anywhere, and surrounded by vast swamps. The Alexandra Colony was a most prosperous little community, but was unfortunately infested with snakes and every imaginable noxious stinging insect. As we should have to cross deep swamps perpetually, we took no wagons with us, but our baggage was loaded on pack-horses. For provisions we took jerked sun-dried beef (very similar to the South African "biltong"), hard biscuit, flour, coffee, sugar, and salt, as well as several bottles of rum, guns, rifles, plenty of ammunition, and two blankets apiece. We had some thirty horses in all; the loose horses trotting obediently behind a bell-mare, according to their convenient Argentine custom. In Argentina mares are never ridden, and a bell-mare serves the same purpose in keeping the "tropilla" of horses together as does a bell-wether in keeping sheep together with us. At night only the bell-mare need be securely picketed; the horses will not stray far from the sound of her tinkling bell. Should the bell-mare break loose, there is the very devil to pay; all the others will follow her. It will thus be seen that the bell-mare plays a very important part. In French families the *belle-mère* fills an equally important position. We were four Englishmen in all; the two leaders, the doctor, and myself. The doctor was quite a youngster, taking a final outing before settling down to serious practice in Bristol. A nice, cheery youth! The first night I discovered how very hard the ground is to sleep upon, but our troubles did not begin till the second day. We were close up to the tropics, and got into great swamps where millions and millions of mosquitoes attacked us day and night, giving us no rest. Our hands got so swollen with bites that we could hardly hold our reins, and sleep outside our blankets was impossible with these humming, buzzing tormentors devouring us. If one attempted to baffle them by putting one's head under the blanket, the stifling heat made sleep equally difficult. In four days we reached a waterless land; that is to say, there were clear streams in abundance, but they were all of salt, bitter, alkaline water, undrinkable by man or beast. Oddly enough, all the clear streams were of bitter water, whereas the few muddy ones were of excellent drinking water. I think these alkaline streams are peculiar to the interior of South America. Our horses suffered terribly; so did we. We had three Argentine gauchos with us, to look after the horses and baggage, besides two pure Indians. One of these Indians, known by the pretty name of Chinche, or "The Bug," could usually find water-holes by watching the flight of the birds. The water in these holes was often black and fetid, yet we drank it greedily. Chinche could also get a little water out of some kinds of aloes by cutting the heart out of the plant. In the resulting cavity about half a glassful of water, very bitter to the taste, but acceptable all the same, collected in time. Prolonged thirst under a hot sun is very difficult to bear. We nearly murdered the doctor, for he insisted on recalling the memories of great cool tankards of shandy-gaff in Thames-side hostelries, and at our worst times of drought had a maddening trick of imitating (exceedingly well too) the tinkling of ice against the sides of a long tumbler.

In spite of thirst and the accursed mosquitoes it was an interesting trip. We were where few, if any, white men had been before us; the scenery was pretty; and game was very plentiful. The open rolling, down-like country, with its little copses and single trees, was like a gigantic edition of some English park in the southern counties. In the early morning certain trees, belonging to the cactus family, I imagine, were covered with brilliant clusters of flowers, crimson, pink, and white. As the sun increased in heat all these flowers closed up like sea anemones, to reopen again after sunset. The place crawled with deer, and so tame and unsophisticated were they that it seemed cruel to take advantage of them and to shoot them. We had to do so for food, for we lived almost entirely on venison, and venison is a meat I absolutely detest. When food is unpalatable, one is surprised to find how very little is necessary to sustain life; an experience most of us have repeated during these last two years, not entirely voluntarily. Chinche, the Indian, could see the tracks of any beasts in the dew at dawn, where my eyes could detect nothing whatever. In this way I was enabled to shoot a fine jaguar, whose skin has reposed for thirty years in my dining-room. One night, too, an ant-eater blundered into our camp, and by some extraordinary fluke I shot him in the dark. His skin now keeps his compatriot company. An ant-eating bear is a very shy and wary animal, and as he is nocturnal in his habits, he is but rarely met with, so this was a wonderful bit of luck. We encountered large herds of peccaries, the South American wild boar. These little beasts are very fierce and extremely pugnacious, and the horses seemed frightened of them. The flesh of the peccary is excellent and formed a most welcome variation to the eternal venison. I never could learn to shoot from the saddle as Argentines do, but had to slip off my horse to fire. I was told afterwards that it was very dangerous to do this with these savage little peccaries.

There are always compensations to be found everywhere. Had not the abominable mosquitoes prevented sleep, one would not have gazed up for hours at the glorious constellations of the Southern sky, including that arch-impostor the Southern Cross, glittering in the dark-blue bowl of the clear tropical night sky. Had we not suffered so from thirst, we should have appreciated less the unlimited foaming beer we found awaiting us on our return to the Alexandra Colony. By the way, all South Americans believe firmly in moon-strokes, and will never let the moon's rays fall on their faces whilst sleeping.

I judged the country we traversed quite unfitted for white settlers, owing to the lack of good water, and the evil-smelling swamps that cut the land up so. That exploring trip was doubtless pleasanter in retrospect than in actual experience. I would not have missed it, though, for anything, for it gave one an idea of stern realities.

On returning to the Alexandra Colony, both I and the doctor, a remarkably fair-skinned young man, found, after copious ablutions, that our faces and hands had been burnt so black by the sun that we could easily have taken our places with the now defunct Moore and Burgess minstrels in the vanished St. James's Hall in Piccadilly without having to use any burnt-cork whatever.

On the evening of our arrival at Alexandra, I was reading in the sitting-room in an armchair against the wall. The doctor called out to me to keep perfectly still, and not to move on any account until he returned. He came back with a pickle-jar and a bottle. I smelt the unmistakable odour of chloroform, and next minute the doctor triumphantly exhibited an immense tarantula spider in the pickle-jar. He had cleverly chloroformed the venomous insect within half an inch of my head, otherwise I should certainly have been bitten. The bite of these great spiders, though not necessarily fatal, is intensely painful.

The doctor had brought out with him a complete anti-snake-bite equipment, and was always longing for an occasion to use it. He was constantly imploring us to go and get bitten by some highly venomous snake, in order to give him an opportunity of testing the efficacy of his drugs, hypodermic syringes, and lancets. At Alexandra a dog did get bitten by a dangerous snake, and was at once brought to the doctor, who injected his snake-bite antidote, with the result that the dog died on the spot.

A river ran through Alexandra which was simply alive with fish, also with alligators. In the upper reaches of the Paraná and its tributaries, bathing is dangerous not only because of the alligators, but on account of an abominable little biting-fish. These biting-fish, which go about in shoals, are not unlike a flounder in appearance and size. They have very sharp teeth and attack voraciously everything that ventures into the water. In that climate their bites are very liable to bring on lockjaw. The doctor and I spent most of our time along this river with fishing lines and rifles, for alligators had still the charm of novelty to us both, and we both delighted in shooting these revolting saurians. I advise no one to try to skin a dead alligator. There are thousands of sinews to be cut through, and the pestilential smell of the brute would sicken a Chinaman. We caught some extraordinary-looking fish on hand lines, including a great golden carp of over 50 lb. ("dorado" in Spanish). It took us nearly an hour to land this big fellow, who proved truly excellent when cooked.

When I first reached the Argentine, travel was complicated by the fact that each province issued its own notes, which were only current within the province itself except at a heavy discount. The value of the dollar fluctuated enormously in the different provinces. In Buenos Ayres the dollar was depreciated to four cents, or twopence, and was treated as such, the ordinary tram fare being one depreciated dollar. In other provinces the dollar stood as high as three shillings. In passing from one province to another all paper money had to be changed, and this entailed the most intricate calculations. It is unnecessary to add that the stranger was fleeced quite mercilessly. The currency has since been placed on a more rational basis. National notes, issued against a gold reserve, have superseded the provincial currency, and pass from one end of the Republic to the other.

Upon returning to Buenos Ayres, my blue-satin bedroom looked strangely artificial and effeminate, after sleeping on the ground under the stars for so long.

CHAPTER IX

Paraguay—Journey up the river—A primitive Capital—Dick the Australian—His polychrome garb—A Paraguayan Race Meeting—Beautiful figures of native women—The "Falcon" adventurers—A quaint railway—Patiño Cué—An extraordinary household—The capable Australian boy—Wild life in the swamps—"Bushed"—A literary evening—A railway record—The Tigre midnight swims—Canada—Maddening flies—A grand salmon-river—The Canadian backwoods—Skunks and bears—Different views as to industrial progress.

As negotiations had commenced in the "'eighties" for a new Treaty, including an Extradition clause, between the British and Paraguayan Governments, several minor points connected with it required clearing up.

I accordingly went up the river to Asuncion, the Paraguayan capital, five days distant from Buenos Ayres by steamer. A short account of that primitive little inland Republic in the days before it was linked up with Argentina by railway may prove of interest, for it was unlike anything else, with its stately two hundred-year-old relics of the old Spanish civilisation mixed up with the roughest of modern makeshifts. The vast majority of the people were Guaranis, of pure Indian blood and speech. The little State was so isolated from the rest of the world that the nineteenth century had touched it very lightly. Since its independence Paraguay had suffered under the rule of a succession of Dictator Presidents, the worst of whom was Francisco Lopez, usually known as Tyrant Lopez. This ignorant savage aspired to be the Napoleon of South America, and in 1864 declared war simultaneously on Brazil, Uruguay, and the Argentine Republic. The war continued till 1870, when, fortunately, Lopez was killed, but the population of Paraguay had diminshed from one and a quarter million to four hundred thousand people, nearly all the males being killed. In my time there were seven women to every male of the population.

The journey up the mighty Paraná is very uninteresting, for these huge rivers are too broad for the details on either shore to be seen clearly. After the steamer had turned up the Paraguay river on the verge of the tropics, it became less monotonous. The last Argentine town is Formosa, a little place of thatched shanties clustered under groves of palms. We arrived there at night, and remained three hours. I shall never forget the eerie, uncanny effect of seeing for the first time Paraguayan women, with a white petticoat, and a white sheet over their heads as their sole garments, flitting noiselessly along on bare feet under the palms in the brilliant moonlight. They looked like hooded silent ghosts, and reminded me irresistibly of the fourth act of "Robert le Diable," when the ghosts of the nuns arise out of their cloister graves at Bertram's command. They did not though, as in the opera, break into a glittering ballet.

On board the steamer there was a young globe-trotting Australian. He was a nice, cheery lad, and, like most Australians, absolutely natural and unaffected. As he spoke no Spanish, he was rather at a loose end, and we agreed to foregather.

Asuncion was really a curiosity in the way of capitals. Lopez the Tyrant suffered from megalomania, as others rulers have done since his day. He began to construct many imposing buildings, but finished none of them. He had built a huge palace on the model of the Tuileries on a bluff over the river. It looked very imposing, but had no roof and no inside. He had also begun a great mausoleum for members of the Lopez family, but that again had only a façade, and was already crumbling to ruin. The rest of the town consisted principally of mud and bamboo shanties, thatched with palm. The streets were unpaved, and in the main street a strong spring gushed up. Everyone rode; there was but one wheeled vehicle in Asuncion, and that was only used for weddings and funerals. The inhabitants spoke of their one carriage as we should speak of something absolutely unique of its kind, say the statue of the Venus de Milo, or of some rare curiosity, such as a great auk's egg, or a twopenny blue Mauritius postage stamp, or a real live specimen of the dodo.

Nothing could be rougher than the accommodation Howard, the young Australian, and I found at the hotel. We were shown into a very dirty brick-paved room containing eight beds. We washed unabashed at the fountain in the *patio,* as there were no other facilities for ablutions at all, and the barefooted, shirtless waiter addressed us each by our Christian names *tout court,* at once, omitting the customary "Don." The Spanish forms of Christian names are more melodious than ours, and Howard failed to recognize his homely name of "Dick" in "Ricardo."

As South American men become moustached and bearded very early in life, I think that our clean-shaved faces, to which they were not accustomed, led the people to imagine us both much younger than we really were, for I was then twenty-seven, and the long-legged Dick was twenty-one. Never have I known anyone laugh so much as that light-hearted Australian boy. He was such a happy, merry, careless creature, brimful of sheer joy at being alive, and if he had never cultivated his brains much, he atoned for it by being able to do anything he liked with his hands and feet. He could mend and repair anything, from a gun to a fence; he could cook, and use a needle and thread as skilfully as he could a stock-whip. I took a great liking to this lean, sun-browned, pleasant-faced lad with the merry laugh and the perfectly natural manner; we got on together as though we had known each other all our lives, in fact we were addressing one another by our Christian names on the third day of our acquaintance.

Dick was a most ardent cricketer, and his baggage seemed to consist principally of a large and varied assortment of blazers of various Australian athletic clubs. He insisted on wearing one of these, a quiet little affair of mauve, blue, and pink stripes, and our first stroll through Asuncion became a sort of triumphal progress. The inhabitants flocked out of their houses, loud in their admiration of the "Gringo's" (all foreigners are "Gringos" in South America) tasteful raiment. So much so that I began to grow jealous, and returning to the hotel, I borrowed another of Howard's blazers (if my memory serves me right, that of the "Wonga-Wonga Wallabies"), an artistic little garment of magenta, orange, and green stripes. We then sauntered about Asuncion, arm-in-arm, to the delirious joy of the populace. We soon had half the town at our heels, enthusiastic over these walking rainbows from the mysterious lands outside Paraguay. These people were as inquisitive as children, and plied us with perpetual questions. Since Howard could not speak Spanish, all the burden of conversation fell on me. As I occupied an official position, albeit a modest one, I thought it best to sink my identity, and became temporarily a citizen of the United States, Mr. Dwight P. Curtis, of Hicksville, Pa., and I gave my hearers the most glowing and rose-coloured accounts of the enterprise and nascent industries of this progressive but, I fear, wholly imaginary spot. I can only trust that no Paraguayan left his native land to seek his fortune in Hicksville, Pa., for he might have had to search the State of Pennsylvania for some time before finding it.

I have already recounted, earlier in these reminiscences, how the Paraguayan Minister for Foreign Affairs received me, and that his Excellency on that occasion dispensed not only with shoes and stockings, but with a shirt as well. He was, however, like most people in Spanish-speaking lands, courtesy itself.

Dick Howard having heard that there were some races in a country town six miles away, was, like a true Australian, wild to go to them. Encouraged by our phenomenal success of the previous day, we arrayed ourselves in two new Australian blazers, and rode out to the races, Howard imploring me all the way to use my influence to let him have a mount there.

The races were very peculiar. The course was short, only about three furlongs, and perfectly straight. Only two horses ran at once, so the races were virtually a succession of "heats," but the excitement and betting were tremendous. The jockeys were little Indian boys, and their "colours" consisted of red, blue, or green bathing drawers. Otherwise they were stark naked, and, of course, bare-legged. The jockeys' principal preoccupation seemed to be either to kick the opposing jockey in the face, or to crack him over the head with the heavy butts of their raw-hide whips. Howard still wanted to ride. I pointed out to him the impossibility of exhibiting to the public his six feet of lean young Australian in nothing but a pair of green bathing drawers. He answered that if he could only get a mount he would be quite willing to dispense with the drawers even. Howard also had a few remarks to offer about the Melbourne Cup, and Flemington Racecourse, and was not wholly complimentary to this Paraguayan country meeting. The ladies present were nearly all bare-foot, and clad in the invariable white petticoat and sheet. It was not in the least like the Royal enclosure at Ascot, yet they had far more on, and appeared more becomingly dressed than many of the ladies parading in that sacrosanct spot in this year of grace 1919. Every single woman, and every child, even infants of the tenderest age, had a green Paraguayan cigar in their mouths.

These Paraguayan women were as beautifully built as classical statues; with exquisitely moulded little hands and feet. Their "attaches," as the French term the wrist and ankles, were equally delicately formed. They were "tea with plenty of milk in it" colour, and though their faces were not pretty, they moved with such graceful dignity that the general impression they left was a very pleasing one.

Our blazers aroused rapturous enthusiasm. I am sure that the members of the "St. Kilda Wanderers" would have forgiven me for masquerading in their colours, could they have witnessed the terrific success I achieved in my tasteful, if brilliant, borrowed plumage.

Asuncion pleased me. This quaint little capital, stranded in its backwater in the very heart of the South American Continent, was so remote from all the interests and movements of the modern world. The big three-hundred-year cathedral bore the unmistakable dignified stamp of the old Spanish "Conquistadores." It contained an altar-piece of solid silver reaching from floor to roof. How Lopez must have longed to melt that altar-piece down for his own use! Round the cathedral were some old houses with verandahs supported on palm trunks, beautifully carved in native patterns by Indians under the direction of the Jesuits. The Jesuits had also originally introduced the orange tree into Paraguay, where it had run wild all over the country, producing delicious fruit, which for some reason was often green, instead of being of the familiar golden colour.

Everyone envies what they do not possess. On the Continent cafés are sometimes decorated with pictures of palms and luxuriant tropical vegetation, in order to give people of the frozen North an illusion of warmth.

In steaming Asuncion, on the other hand, the fashionable café was named, "The North Pole." Here an imaginative Italian artist with a deficient sense of perspective and curious ideas of colour had decorated the walls with pictures of icebergs, snow, and Polar bears, thus affording the inhabitants of this stew-pan of a town a delicious sense of arctic coolness. The "North Pole" was the only place in Paraguay where ice and iced drinks were to be procured.

Being the height of the summer, the heat was almost unbearable, and bathing in the river was risky on account of those hateful biting-fish. There was a spot two miles away, however, where a stream had been brought to the edge of the cliff overhanging the river, down which it dropped in a feathery cascade, forming a large pool below it. Howard and I rode out every morning there to bathe and luxuriate in the cool water. The river made a great bend here, forming a bay half a mile wide. This bay was literally choked with *Victoria regia,* the giant water-lily, with leaves as big as tea-trays, and great pink flowers the size of cabbages. The lilies were in full bloom then, quite half a mile of them, and they were really a splendid sight. I seem somehow in this description of the *Victoria regia* to have been plagiarising the immortal Mrs. O'Dowd, of "Vanity Fair," in her account of the glories of the hot-houses at her "fawther's" seat of Glenmalony.

Few people now remember a fascinating book of the "'eighties," "The Cruise of the Falcon," recounting how six amateurs sailed a twenty-ton yacht from Southampton to Asuncion in Paraguay. Three of her crew got so bitten with Paraguay that they determined to remain there. We met one of these adventurers by chance in Asuncion, Captain Jardine, late of the P. and O. service, an elderly man. He invited us to visit them at

Patiño Cué, the place where they had settled down, some twenty-five miles from the capital, though he warned us that we should find things extremely rough there, and that there was not one single stick of furniture in the house. He asked us to bring out our own hammocks and blankets, as well as our guns and saddles, the saddle being in my time an invariable item of a traveller's baggage.

Dick and I accordingly bought grass-plaited hammocks and blankets, and started two days later, "humping our swags," as the Australian picturesquely expressed the act of carrying our own possessions. That colour-loving youth had donned a different blazer, probably that of the "Coolgardie Cockatoos." It would have put Joseph's coat of many colours completely in the shade any day of the week, and attracted a great deal of flattering attention.

The ambitious Lopez had insisted on having a railway in his State, to show how progressive he was, so a railway was built. It ran sixty miles from Asuncion to nowhere in particular, and no one ever wanted to travel by it; still it was unquestionably a railway. To give a finishing touch to this, Lopez had constructed a railway station big enough to accommodate the traffic of Paddington. It was, of course, not finished, but was quite large enough for its one train a day. The completed portion was imposing with columns and statues, the rest tailed off to nothing. Here, to our amazement, we found a train composed of

English rolling-stock, with an ancient engine built in Manchester, and, more wonderful to say, with an Englishman as engine-driver. The engine not having been designed for burning wood, the fire-box was too small, and the driver found it difficult to keep up steam with wood, as we found out during our journey. We travelled in a real English first-class carriage of immense antiquity, blue cloth and all. So decrepit was it that when the speed of the train exceeded five miles an hour (which was but seldom) the roof and sides parted company, and gaped inches apart. We seldom got up the gradients at the first or second try, but of course allowances must be made for a Paraguayan railway. Lopez had built Patiño Cué, for which we were bound, as a country-house for himself. He had not, of course, finished it, but had insisted on his new railway running within a quarter of a mile of his house, which we found very convenient.

I could never have imagined such a curious establishment as the one at Patiño Cué. The large stone house, for which Jardine paid the huge rent of £5 per annum, was tumbling to ruin. Three rooms only were fairly water-tight, but these had gaping holes in their roofs and sides, and the window frames had long since been removed. The fittings consisted of a few enamelled iron plates and mugs, and of one tin basin. Packing cases served as seats and tables, and hammocks were slung on hooks. Captain Jardine did all the cooking and ran the establishment; his two companions (Howard and I, for convenience's sake, simply termed them "the wasters") lay smoking in their hammocks all day, and did nothing whatever. I may add that "the wasters" supplied the whole financial backing. Jardine wore native dress, with bare legs and sandals, a poncho round his waist, and another over his shoulders. A poncho is merely a fringed brown blanket with hole cut in it for the head to pass through. With his long grey beard streaming over his flowing garments, Jardine looked like a neutral-tinted saint in a stained-glass window. It must be a matter for congratulation that, owing to the very circumstances of the case, saints in stained-glass windows are seldom called on to take violent exercise, otherwise their voluminous draperies would infallibly all fall off at the second step. Jardine was a highly educated and an interesting man, with a love for books on metaphysics and other abstruse subjects. He carried a large library about with him, all of which lay in untidy heaps on the floor. He was unquestionably more than a little eccentric. The "wasters" did not count in any way, unless cheques had to be written. The other members of the establishment were an old Indian woman who smoked perpetual cigars, and her grandson, a boy known as Lazarus, from a physical defect which he shared with a Biblical personage, on the testimony of the latter's sisters—you could have run a drag with that boy.

The settlers had started as ranchers; but the

"wasters" had allowed the cattle to break loose and scatter all over the country. They had been too lazy to collect them, or to repair the broken fences, so just lay in their hammocks and smoked. There were some fifty acres of orange groves behind the house. The energetic Jardine had fenced these in, and, having bought a number of pigs, turned pork butcher. There was an abundance of fallen fruit for these pigs to fatten on, and Jardine had built a smoke-house, where he cured his orange-fed pork, and smoked it with lemon wood. His bacon and hams were super-excellent, and fetched good prices in Asuncion, where they were establishing quite a reputation.

Meanwhile, the "wasters" lay in their hammocks in the verandah and smoked. Jardine told me that one of them had not undressed or changed his clothes for six weeks, as it was far too much trouble. Judging from his appearance, he had not made use of soap and water either during that period.

Dick Howard proved a real "handy man." In two days this lengthy, lean, sunburnt youth had rounded up and driven home the scattered cattle, and then set to work to mend and repair all the broken fences. He caught the horses daily, and milked the cows, an art I was never able myself to acquire, and made tea for himself in a "billy."

Patiño Cué was a wonderful site for a house. It stood high up on rolling open ground, surrounded by intensely green wooded knolls. The virgin tropical forest extended almost up to the dilapidated building on one side, whilst in front of it the ground fell away to a great lake, three miles away. A long range of green hills rose the other side of the water, and everywhere clear little brooks gurgled down to the lake.

I liked the place, in spite of its intense heat, and stayed there over a fortnight, helping with the cattle, and making myself as useful as I could in repairing what the "wasters" had allowed to go to ruin. They reposed meanwhile in their hammocks.

It was very pretty country, and had the immense advantage of being free from mosquitoes. As there are disadvantages everywhere, to make up for this it crawled with snakes.

Jardine's culinary operations were simplicity itself. He had some immense earthen jars four feet high, own brothers to those seen on the stage in "Ali Baba and the Forty Thieves" at pantomime time. These must have been the identical jars in which the Forty Thieves concealed themselves, to be smothered with boiling oil by the crafty Morgiana. By the way, I never could understand until I had seen fields of growing sesame in India why Ali Baba's brother should have mistaken the talisman words "Open Sesame" for "Open Barley." The two grains are very similar in appearance whilst growing, which explains it.

Jardine placed a layer of beef at the bottom of his jar. On that he put a layer of mandioca (the root from which tapioca is prepared), another layer of his own bacon, and a stratum of green vegetables. Then more beef, and so on till the jar was half full. In went a handful of salt, two handfuls of red peppers, and two gallons of water, and then a wood fire was built round the pot, which simmered away day and night till all its contents were eaten. The old Indian woman baked delicious bread from the root of the mandioca mixed with milk and cheese, and that constituted our entire dietary. There were no fixed meals. Should you require food, you took a hunch of mandioca bread and a tin dipper, and went to the big earthen jar simmering amongst its embers in the yard. Should you wish for soup, you put the dipper in at the top; if you preferred stew, you pushed it to the bottom. Nothing could be simpler. As a rough and ready way of feeding a household it had its advantages, though there was unquestionably a certain element of monotony about it.

As a variation from the eternal beef and mandioca, Jardine begged Dick and myself to shoot him as many snipe as possible, in the swamps near the big lake. Those swamps were most attractive, and were simply alive with snipe and every sort of living creature. Dick was an excellent shot, and we got from five to fifteen couple of snipe daily. The tree-crowned hillocks in the swamp were the haunts of macaws, great gaudy, screaming, winged rainbows of green and scarlet, and orange and blue, like some of Dick's blazers endowed with feathers and motion. We had neither of us ever seen wild macaws before, and I am afraid that we shot a good many for the sheer pleasure of examining these garish parrots at close quarters, though they are quite uneatable. I shall carry all my life marks on my left hand where a macaw bit me to the bone. There were great brilliant-plumaged toucans too, droll freaks of nature, with huge horny bills nearly as large as their bodies, given them to crack the nuts on which they feed. They flashed swiftly pink through the air, but we never succeeded in getting one. Then there were coypus, the great web-footed South American water-rat, called "nutria" in Spanish, and much prized for his fur. That marsh was one of the most interesting places I have ever been in. The old Indian woman warned us that we should both infallibly die of fever were we to go into the swamps at nightfall, but though Dick and I were there every evening for a fortnight, up to our middles in water, we neither of us took the smallest harm, probably owing to the temporary absence of mosquitoes. The teeming hidden wild-life of the place appealed to us both irresistibly. The water-hog, or capincho, is a quaint beast, peculiar to South America. They are just like gigantic varnished glossy-black guinea pigs, with the most idiotically stupid expression on their faces. They are quite defenceless, and are the constant prey of alligators and jaguars. Consequently they are very timid. These creatures live in the water all day, but come out in the evenings to feed on the reeds and water-herbage. By concealing ourselves amongst the reeds, and keeping perfectly still, we were able to see these uncouth, shy things emerging from their day hiding-places and begin browsing on the marsh plants. To see a very wary animal at close quarters, knowing that he is unconscious of your presence, is perfectly fascinating. We never attempted to shoot or hurt these capinchos; the pleasure of seeing the clumsy gambols of one of the most timid animals living, in its fancied security, was quite enough. The capincho if caught very young makes a delightful pet, for he becomes quite tame, and, being an affectionate animal, trots everywhere after his master, with a sort of idiotic simper on his face.

One evening, on our return from the marsh, we were ill-advised enough to attempt a short cut home through the forest. The swift tropical night fell as we entered the forest, and in half an hour we were hopelessly lost, "fairly bushed," as Dick put it. There is a feeling of complete and utter helplessness in finding oneself on a pitch-dark night in a virgin tropical forest that is difficult to express in words. The impenetrable tangles of jungle; the great lianes hanging from the trees, which trip you up at every step; the masses of thorny and spiky things that hold you prisoner; and, as regards myself personally, the knowledge that the forest was full of snakes, all make one realise that electric-lighted Piccadilly has its distinct advantages. Dick had the true Australian's indifference to snakes. He never could understand my openly-avowed terror of these evil, death-dealing creatures, nor could he explain to himself the physical repugnance I have to these loathsome reptiles. This instinctive horror of snakes is, I think, born in some people. It can hardly be due to atavism, for the episode of the Garden of Eden is too remote to account of an inherited antipathy to these gliding, crawling abominations. We settled that we should have to sleep in the forest till daylight came, though, dripping wet as we both were from the swamp, it was a fairly direct invitation to malarial fever. The resourceful Dick got an inspiration, and dragging his interminable length (he was like Euclid's definition of a straight line) up a high tree, he took a good look at the familiar stars of his own Southern hemisphere. Getting his bearings from these, he also got our direction, and after a little more tree-climbing we reached our dilapidated temporary home in safety. I fear that I shall never really conquer my dislike to snakes, sharks, and earthquakes.

Jardine was a great and an omnivorous reader. Dick too was very fond of reading. Like the hero of "Mr. Sponge's Sporting Tour" he carried his own library with him. As in Mr. Sponge's case, it consisted of one book only, but in the place of being "Mogg's Cab Fares," it was a guide to the Australian Turf, a sort of Southern Cross "Ruff's Guide," with a number of pedigrees of Australian horses thrown in. Dick's great intellectual amusement was learning these pedigrees by heart. I used to hear them for him, and, having a naturally retentive memory, could in the " 'eighties " have passed a very creditable examination in the pedigrees of the luminaries of the Australian Turf.

Our evenings at Patiño Cué would have amused a spectator, had there been one. In the tumble-down, untidy apology for a room, Jardine, seated on a packing-case under the one wall light, was immersed in his favourite Herbert Spencer; looking, in his flowing ponchos, long grey beard, and bare legs, like a bespectacled apostle. He always seemed to me to require an eagle, or a lion or some other apostolic adjunct, in order to look complete. I, on another packing-case, was chuckling loudly over "Monsieur et Madame Cardinal," though Paris seemed remote from Paraguay. Dick, pulling at a green cigar, a far-off look in his young eyes, was improving his mind by learning some further pedigrees of Australian horses, at full length on the floor, where he found more room for his thin, endless legs; whilst the two "wasters" dozed placidly in their hammocks on the verandah. The "wasters," I should imagine, attended church but seldom. Otherwise they ought to have ejaculated "We have left undone those things which we ought to have done" with immense fervour, for they never did anything at all.

"Lotos-eaters" might be a more poetic name than "wasters," for if ever there was a land "in which it seemed always afternoon," that land is Paraguay. Could one conceive of the "wasters" displaying such unwonted energy, it is possible that—

> "And all at once they sang 'Our island home
> Is far beyond the wave; we will no longer roam'."

They had eaten of the Lotos-fruit abundantly, and in the golden sunshine of Paraguay, and amidst its waving green palms, they only wished—

> "In the hollow Lotos-land to live and lie reclined."

I should perhaps add that "caña," or sugar-cane spirit, is distilled in large quantities in Paraguay, and that one at least of the Lotos-eaters took a marked interest in this national product.

There were some beautiful nooks in the forest, more especially one deep blue rocky pool into which a foaming cascade pattered through a thick encircling fringe of wild orange trees. This little hollow was brimful of loveliness, with the golden balls of the fruit, and the brilliant purple tangles of some unknown creeper reflected in the blue pool. Dick and I spent hours there swimming, and basking *puris naturalibus* on the rocks, until the whole place was spoilt for me by a rustling in the grass, as a hateful ochre-coloured creature wriggled away in sinuous coils from my bare feet.

I accompanied Jardine once or twice to a little village some five miles away, where he got the few household stores he required. This tiny village was a piece of seventeenth-century Spain, dumped bodily down amid the riotous greenery of Paraguay. Round a tall white church in the florid Jesuit style, a few beautiful Spanish stone houses clustered, each with its tangle of tropical garden. There was not one single modern erection to spoil the place. Here foaming bowls of chocolate were to be had, and delicious mandioca bread. It was a picturesque, restful little spot, so utterly unexpected in the very heart of the South American Continent. I should like to put on the stage that tall white church tower cutting into the intense blue of the sky above, with the vivid green of the feathery palms reaching to its belfry, and the time-worn houses round it peeping out from thickets of scarlet poinsettias and hibiscus flowers. It would make a lovely setting for "Cavalleria Rusticana," for instance.

I never regretted my stay at Patiño Cué. It gave one a glimpse of life brought down to conditions of bed-rock simplicity, and of types of character I had never come across before.

We travelled back to Asuncion on the engine of the train; I seated in front on the cow-catcher, Dick, his coat off and his shirt-sleeves rolled back, on the footplate, officiating as amateur fireman.

This vigorous young Antipodean hurled logs into the fire-box of the venerable "Vesuvius" as fast as though he were pitching in balls when practising his bowling at the nets, with the result that the crazy old engine attained a speed that must have fairly amazed her. When we stopped at stations, "Vesuvius" had developed such a head of steam that she nearly blew her safety-valve off, and steam hissed from twenty places in her leaky joints. One ought never to be astonished at misplaced affections. I have seen old ladies lavish a wealth of tenderness on fat, asthmatical, and wholly repellent pugs, so I ought not to have been surprised at the immense pride the English driver took in his antique engine. I am bound to say that he kept her beautifully cleaned and burnished. His face beamed at her present performance, and he assured me that with a little coaxing he could knock sixty miles an hour out of "Vesuvius." I fear that this statement "werged on the poetical," as Mr. Weller senior remarked on another occasion. I should much like to have known this man's history, and to have learnt how he had drifted into driving an engine of this futile, forlorn little Paraguayan railway. I suspect, from certain expressions he used, that he was a deserter from the Royal Navy, probably an ex-naval stoker. As Dick had ridden ten miles that morning to say good-bye to a lady, to whom he imagined himself devotedly attached, he was still very smart in white polo-breeches, brown butcher-boots and spurs, an unusual garb for a railway fireman. For the first time in the memory of the oldest living inhabitant, the train reached Asuncion an hour before her time.

The river steamers' cargo in their downstream trip consisted of cigars, "yerba maté," and oranges. These last were shipped in bulk, and I should like a clever artist to have drawn our steamer, with tons and tons of fruit, golden, lemon-yellow, and green, piled on her decks. It made a glowing bit of colour. The oranges were the only things in that steamer that smelt pleasantly.

I can never understand why "Yerba maté," or Paraguayan tea, has never become popular in England. It is prepared from the leaves of the ilex, and is strongly aromatic and very stimulating. I am myself exceedingly fond of it. Its lack of popularity may be due to the fact that it cannot be drunk in a cup, but must be sucked from a gourd through a perforated tube. It can (like most other things) be bought in London, if you know where to go to.

At Buenos Ayres I was quite sorry to part with the laughing, lanky Australian lad who had been such a pleasant travelling companion, and who seemed able to do anything he liked with his arms and legs. I expect that he could have done most things with his brains too, had he ever given them a chance. Howard's great merit was that he took things as they came, and never grumbled at the discomforts and minor hardships one must expect in a primitive country like Paraguay. Our tastes as regards wild things (with the possible exception of snakes) rather seemed to coincide, and, neither of us being town-bred, we did not object to rather elementary conditions.

I will own that I was immensely gratified at receiving an overseas letter some eight years later from Dick, telling me that he was married and had a little daughter, and asking me to stand godfather to his first child. My blue satin bedroom looked more ridiculously incongruous than ever after the conditions to which I had been used at Patiño Cué.

The River Plate is over twenty miles broad at Buenos Ayres, and it is not easy to realise that this great expanse is all fresh water. The "Great Silver River" is, however, very shallow, except in mid-channel. Some twenty-five miles from the city it forms on its southern bank a great archipelago of wooded islands interspersed with hundreds of winding channels, some of them deep enough to carry ocean-going steamers. This is known as the Tigre, and its shady tree-lined waterways are a great resort during the sweltering heat of an Argentine summer. It is the most ideal place for boating, and boasts a very flourishing English Rowing Club, with a large fleet of light Thames-built boats. Here during the summer months I took the roughest of rough bungalows, with two English friends. The three-roomed shanty was raised on high piles, out of reach of floods, and looked exactly like the fishermen's houses one sees lining the rivers in native villages in the Malay States. During the intense heat of January the great delight of life at the Tigre was the midnight swim in the river before turning in. The Tigre is too far south for the alligators, biting-fish, electric rays (I allude to fish; not to beams of light), or other water-pests which Nature has lavished on the tropics in order to counteract their irresistible charm—and to prevent the whole world from settling down there. The water of the Tigre was so warm that one could remain in it over an hour. One mental picture I am always able to conjure up, and I can at will imagine myself at midnight paddling lazily down-stream on my back through the milk-warm water, in the scented dusk, looking up at the pattern formed by the leaves of the overhanging trees against the night sky; a pattern of black lace-work against the polished silver of the Southern moonlight, whilst the water lapped gently against the banks, and an immense joy at being alive filled one's heart.

I went straight from Buenos Ayres to Canada on a tramp steamer, and a month after leaving the Plate found myself in the backwoods of the Province of Quebec, on a short but very famous river running into the Bay of Chaleurs, probably the finest salmon river in the world, and I was fortunate enough to hook and to land a 28 lb. salmon before I had been there one hour. No greater contrast in surroundings can be imagined. In the place of the dead-flat, treeless levels of Southern Argentina, there were dense woods of spruce, cedar, and var, climbing the hills as far as the eye could see. Instead of the superficially courteous Argentine gaucho, with his air of half-concealed contempt for the "Gringo," and the ever-ready knife, prepared to leap from his waist-belt at the slightest provocation, there were the blunt, outspoken, hearty Canadian canoe-men, all of them lumbermen during the winter months. The fishing was ideal, and the fish ran uniformly large and fought like Trojans in the heavy water, but, unfortunately, every single winged insect on the North American Continent had arranged for a summer holiday on this same river at the same time. There they all were in their myriads; black-flies, sand-flies, and mosquitoes, all enjoying themselves tremendously. By day one was devoured by black-flies, who drew blood every time they bit. At nightfall the black-flies very considerately retired to rest, and the little sand-flies took their place. The mosquitoes took no rest whatever. These rollicking insects were always ready to turn night into day, or day into night, indiscriminately, provided there were some succulent humans to feed on. A net will baffle the mosquito, but for the sand-flies the only effective remedy was a " smudge " burning in an iron pail. A " smudge " is a fire of damp fir bark, which smoulders but does not blaze. It also emits huge volumes of smoke. We dined every night in an atmosphere denser than a thick London fog, and the coughing was such that a chance visitor would have imagined that he had strayed into a sanatorium for tuberculosis.

Things are done expeditiously in Canada. The ground had been cleared, the wooden house in which we lived erected, and the rough track through the forest made, all in eight weeks.

No one who has not tried it can have any idea of the intense cold of the water in these short Canadian rivers. Their course is so short, and they are so overhung with fir trees, that the fierce rays of a Canadian summer sun hardly touch them, so the water remains about ten degrees above freezing point. It would have been impossible to swim our river. Even a short dip of half a minute left one with gasping breath and chattering teeth.

I was surprised to find, too, that a Canadian forest is far more impenetrable than a tropical one. Here, the fallen trees and decay of countless centuries have formed a thick crust some two or three feet above the real soil. This moss-grown crust yields to the weight of a man and lets him through, so walking becomes infinitely difficult, and practically impossible. To extricate yourself at every step from three feet of decaying rubbish is very exhausting. In the tropics, that great forcing-house, this decaying vegetable matter would have given life to new and exuberant growths; but not so in Canada, frost-bound for four months of the twelve. Two-foot-wide tracks had been cut through the forest along the river, and the trees there were "blazed" (*i.e.*, notched, so as to show up white where the bark had been hacked off), to indicate the direction of the trails; otherwise it would have been impossible to make one's way through the *débris* of a thousand years for more than a few yards.

I never saw such a wealth of wild fruit as on the banks of this Canadian stream. Wild strawberries and raspberries grew in such profusion that a bucketful of each could be filled in half an hour.

There was plenty of animal life too. A certain pretty little black and white striped beast was quite disagreeably common. This attractive cat-like little creature was armed with stupendous offensive powers, as all who have experienced a skunk's unspeakably disgusting odour will acknowledge. Unless molested, they did not make use of the terrible possibilities they had at their command. There were also plenty of wandering black bears. These animals live for choice on grain and berries, and are not hostile to man without provocation, but they have enormous strength, and it is a good working rule to remember that it is unwise ever to vex a bear unnecessarily, even a mild-tempered black bear.

Our tumbling, roaring Canadian river cutting its way through rounded, densely-wooded hills was wonderfully pretty, and one could not but marvel at the infinitely varied beauty with which Providence has clothed this world of ours, wherever man has not defaced Nature's perfect craftsmanship.

The point of view of the country-bred differs widely from that of the town dweller in this respect.

Here is a splendid waterfall, churning itself into whirling cataracts of foam down the face of a jagged cliff. The townsman cries, "What tremendous power is running to waste here! Let us harness it quickly. We will divert the falls into hideous water-pipes, and bring them to our turbines. We will build a power-house cheaply of corrugated iron, and in time we shall so develop this sleepy countryside that no one will recognise it."

Here is a great forest; a joy to the eyes. "The price of timber is rising; let us quickly raze it to the ground."

"Our expert tells us that under this lovely valley there runs a thick seam of coal. We will sink shafts, and build blatantly hideous towns and factories, pollute this clear air with smoke and mephitic vapours, and then fall down and worship the great god Progress. We will also pocket fat dividends."

The stupid, unprogressive son of woods and green fields shudders at such things; the son of asphalte, stuffy streets, tramways, and arc lights glories in them.

Like many other things, it all depends on the point of view.

CHAPTER X

Former colleagues who have risen to eminence—Kiderlin-Waechter—Aehrenthal—Colonel Klepsch—The discomfiture of an inquisitive journalist—Origin of certain Russian scares—Tokyo—Dulness of Geisha dinners—Japanese culinary curiosities—" Musical Chairs "—Lack of colour in Japan—The Tokugawa dynasty—Japanese Gardens—The transplanted suburban Embassy house—Cherry-blossom—Japanese Politeness—An unfortunate incident in Rome—Eastern courtesy—The country in Japan—An Imperial duck catching party—An up-to-date Tokyo house—A Shinto Temple—Linguistic difficulties at a dinner-party—The economical colleague—Japan defaced by advertisements.

PETROGRAD was the only capital at which I was stationed in which there was a diplomatic *table d'hôte.* In one of the French restaurants there, a room was specially set apart for the diplomats, and here the " chers collègues " foregathered nightly, when they had no other engagements. When a Spaniard and a Dane, a Roumanian and a Dutchman, a Hungarian and an Englishman dine together frequently, it becomes a subject of thankfulness that the universal use of the French language as a means of international communication has mitigated the linguistic difficulties brought about by the ambitious tower-builders of Babel.

Two men whom I met frequently at that diplomatic *table d'hôte* rose afterwards to important positions in their own countries. They were Baron von Kiderlin-Waechter, the German, and Baron von Aehrenthal, the Austrian, both of whom became Ministers for Foreign Affairs in their respective countries, and both of whom are now dead. Kiderlin-Waechter arrived in Petrograd as quite a young man with the reputation of being Bismarck's favourite and most promising pupil. Though a South German by birth, Kiderlin-Waechter had acquired an overbearing and dictatorial manner of the most approved Prussian type. When a number of young men, all of whom are on very friendly terms with each other, constantly meet, there is naturally a good deal of fun and chaff passed to and fro between them. Diplomats are no exception to this rule, and the fact that the ten young men talking together may be of ten different nationalities is no bar to the interchange of humorous personalities, thanks to the convenient French language, which lends itself peculiarly to " persiflage."

Germans can never understand the form of friendly banter which we term chaff, and always resent it deeply. I have known German diplomats so offended at a harmless joke that they have threatened to challenge the author of it to a duel. I should like to pay a belated tribute to the memory of the late Count Lövendal, Danish Minister in Petrograd; peace to his ashes! This kindly, tactful, middle-aged man must during my time in Petrograd have stopped at least eight duels. People in trouble went straight to Count Lövendal, and this shrewd, kind-hearted, experienced man of the world heard them with infinite patience, and then always gave them sound advice. As years went on, Count Lövendal came to be a sort of recognised Court of Honour, to whom all knotty and delicate points were referred. He, if anyone, should have "Blessed are the peacemakers" inscribed on his tomb. At least four of the duels he averted were due to the inability of Germans to stand chaff. Kiderlin-Waechter, for instance, was for ever taking offence at harmless jokes, and threatening swords and pistols in answer to them. He was a very big, gross-looking, fair-haired man; with exactly the type of face that a caricaturist associates with the average Prussian.

His face was slashed with a generous allowance of the scars of which Germans are so proud, as testifying to their prowess in their student-duelling days. I think that it was the late Sir Wilfrid Lawson who, referring to the beer-drinking habits of German students and their passionate love of face-slashing, described them as living in a perpetual atmosphere of "scars and swipes." Though from South Germany, Kiderlin snapped out his words with true "Preussische Grobheit" in speaking German. Fortunately, it is impossible to obtain this bullying effect in the French language. It does not lend itself to it. I should be guilty of exaggeration were I to say that Kiderlin-Waechter was wildly adored by his foreign colleagues. He became Minister for Foreign Affairs of the German

Empire, but made the same mistake as some of his predecessors, notably Count Herbert Bismarck, had done. They attributed Bismarck's phenomenal success to his habitual dictatorial, bullying manner. This was easily copied; they forgot the genius behind the bully, which could not be copied, and did not realise that Bismarck's tremendous brain had not fallen to their portion. Kiderlin-Waechter's tenure of office was a short one; he died very suddenly in 1912. He was a violent Anglophobe.

Baron von Aehrenthal was a very different stamp of man. He was of Semitic origin, and in appearance was a good-looking, tall, slim, dark young fellow with very pleasing manners. Some people indeed thought his manners too pleasant, and termed them subservient. I knew Aehrenthal very well indeed, and liked him, but I never suspected that under that very quiet exterior there lay the most intense personal ambition. He became Austro-Hungarian Minister for Foreign Affairs in 1907, being raised to the rank of Count next year. This quiet, sleepy-mannered man began embarking on a recklessly bold foreign policy, and, to the surprise of those who fancied that they knew him well, exhibited a most domineering spirit. The old Emperor Francis Joseph's mental powers were failing, and it was Aehrenthal who persuaded him to put an end to the understanding with Russia under which the *status quo* in the Balkan States was guaranteed, and to astonish Europe in 1908 by proclaiming the annexation of Bosnia and Herzegovina to the Austrian Empire. This step, owing to the seething discontent it aroused in Bosnia, led directly to the catastrophe of Sarajevo on June 28, 1914, and plunged Europe into the most terrible war of history. Aehrenthal, whether intentionally or not, played directly into the hands of the Pan-Germanic party, and succeeded in tying his own country, a pliant vassal, to the chariot-wheels of Berlin. It was Aehrenthal who brought the immemorially old Hapsburg Monarchy crashing to the ground and by his foreign policy caused the proud Austrian Empire to collapse like a house of cards. He did not live to see the final results of his work, for he died in 1912.

Colonel Klepsch, the Austro-Hungarian Military Attaché at Petrograd, another *habitué* of the diplomatic *table d'hôte,* was a most remarkable man. He knew more of the real state of affairs in Russia, and of the inner workings and intentions of the Russian Government, than any other foreigner in the country, *and his information was invariably correct.* Nearly all the foreign Ambassadors consulted Colonel Klepsch as to the probable trend of affairs in Russia, and at times he called on them and volunteered pieces of information. It was well known that his source of intelligence was a feminine one, and experience had proved that it was always to be relied upon. To this day I do not know whether this mysterious, taciturn man was at times used as a convenient mouthpiece by the Russian Government, at the instigation of a certain person to whom he was devotedly attached; whether he acted on instructions from his own Ambassador, or if he took the steps he did on his own initiative. This tall, red-haired, silent man, with his uncanny knowledge of every detail of what was happening in the country, will always remain an enigma to me.

I mentioned earlier in these reminiscences that Lord Dufferin on one occasion accomplished the difficult feat of turning an English newspaper correspondent out of his house with the most charming courtesy.

After an interval of nearly forty years, I can without indiscretion say how this came about. The person in question, whom we will call Mr. Q., was an exceedingly enterprising journalist, the correspondent of a big London daily. He was also pretty unscrupulous as to the methods he employed in gathering information. It is quite obviously the duty of a newspaper correspondent to collect information for his paper. It is equally clearly the duty of those to whom official secrets are entrusted to prevent their becoming public property; so here we have conflicting interests. At times it happens that an "incident" arises between two Governments apparently trivial in itself, but capable of being fanned into such a fierce flame by popular opinion as to make it difficult for either Government to recede from the position they had originally taken up. The Press screams loudly on both sides, and every Government shrinks from incurring the unpopularity which a charge of betraying the national interests would bring upon it. Experience has shown that in these cases the difficulties can usually be smoothed down, provided the whole matter be kept secret, and that neither the public nor the Press of either of the two countries concerned have an inkling of the awkward situation that has arisen. An indiscreet or hysterical Press can blow a tiny spark into a roaring conflagration and work up popular feeling to fever-pitch. It may surprise people to learn that barely twenty years ago such a situation arose between our own country and another European Power (*not* Germany). Those in charge of the negotiations on both sides very wisely determined that the matter should be concealed absolutely from the public and the Press of both countries, and not one word about it was allowed to leak out. Otherwise the situation might have been one of extreme gravity, for it was again one of those cases where neither Government could give way without being accused of pusillanimity. As it was, the matter was settled amicably in a week, and to this day very few people know that this very serious difficulty ever occurred.

Nearly forty years ago, just such a situation had arisen between us and the Russian Government; but the Ambassador was convinced that he could smooth it away provided that the whole thing were kept secret.

Mr. Q. was a first-rate journalist, and his *flair*

as a newspaperman told him that *something* was wrong. From the Russians he could learn nothing; they were as close as wax; so Mr. Q. turned his attention to the Chancery of the British Embassy.

His methods were simple. He gained admission to the Chancery on some pretext or another, and then walking about the room, and talking most volubly, he cast a roving eye over any papers that might be lying about on the tables. In all Chanceries a book called the Register is kept in which every document received or sent out is entered, with, of course, its date, and a short summary of its contents. It is a large book, and reposes on its own high desk. Ours stood in a window overlooking the Neva. Mr. Q. was not troubled with false delicacy. Under pretence of admiring the view over the river, he attempted to throw a rapid eye over the Register. A colleague of mine, as a gentle hint, removed the Register from under Mr. Q.'s very nose, and locked it up in the archive press. Mr. Q., however, was not thin-skinned. He came back again and again, till the man became a positive nuisance. We always cleared away every paper before he was allowed admittance. I was only twenty-two or twenty-three then, and I devised a strictly private scheme of my own for Mr. Q.'s discomfiture. All despatches received from the Foreign Office in those days were kept folded in packets of ten, with a docket on each, giving a summary of its contents. I prepared two despatches for Mr. Q.'s private eye and, after much cogitation, settled that they should be about Afghanistan, which did not happen to be the particular point in dispute between the two Governments at that time. I also decided on a rhyming docket. It struck me as a pleasing novelty, and I thought the jingle would impress itself on Mr. Q.'s memory, for he was *meant* to see this bogus despatch. I took eight sheets of foolscap, virgin, spotless, unblackened, folded them in the orthodox fashion, and docketed them in a way I remember to this day. It ran: first the particular year, then "Foreign Office No. 3527. Secret and Confidential. Dated March 3. Received March 11." Then came the rhyming docket,

"General Kaufman's rumoured plan
To make Abdurrahman Khan
Ruler of Afghanistan."

Under that I wrote in red ink in a different hand, with a fine pen,

"*Urgent.* Instructions already acted on. See further instructions *re* Afghanistan in No. 3534.

I was only twenty-two then, and my sense of responsibility was not fully developed, or I should not have acted so flightily. It still strikes me though as an irresistibly attractive baited hook to offer to an inquisitive newspaperman. I grieve to say that I also wrote a "fake" decypher of a purely apocryphal code telegram purporting to have come from London. This was also on the subject of Afghanistan. It struck me at the time as a perfectly legitimate thing to do, in order to throw this Paul Pry off the scent, for the Ambassador had impressed on us all the vital importance of not disclosing the real matter in dispute. I put these flagrant forgeries in a drawer of my table and waited. I had not to wait long. My colleagues having all gone out to luncheon, I was alone in the Chancery one day, when Mr. Q.'s card was brought in to me. I kept him waiting until I had cleared every single despatch from the tables and had locked them up. I also locked up the Register, but put an eight-year-old one, exactly similar in appearance, in its place, opening it at a date two days earlier than the actual date, in order that Mr. Q. might not notice that the page (and "to-morrow's" page as well) was already filled up, and the bogus despatch and fake telegram from my drawer were duly laid on the centre table. At twenty-two I was a smooth-faced youth, in appearance, I believe, much younger than my real age. Mr. Q. came in. He had the "Well, old man" style, accompanied by a thump on the back, which I peculiarly detest. He must have blessed his luck in finding such a simple youth in sole charge of the Chancery. Mr. Q. pursued his usual tactics. He talked volubly in a loud voice, walking about the room meanwhile. The idiotic boy smoked cigarettes, and gaped inanely. Mr. Q. went as usual to the window where the Register lay in order to admire the view, and the pudding-brained youth noticed nothing, but lit a fresh cigarette. That young fool never saw that Mr. Paul Pry read unblushingly half a column of the eight-year-old Register (How it must have puzzled him!) under his very eyes. Mr. Q. then went to the centre table, where he had, of course, noticed the two papers lying, and proceeded to light a cigar. That cigar must have drawn very badly, for Mr. Q. had occasion to light it again and again, bending well over the table as he did so. He kept the unsuspicious youth engaged in incessant conversation meanwhile. So careless and stupid a boy ought never to have been left in charge of important documents. Finally Mr. Q., having gained all the information for which he had been thirsting so long, left in a jubilant frame of mind, perfectly unconscious that he had been subjected to the slightest crural tension.

When the Councillor of Embassy returned, I made a clean breast of what I had done, and showed him the bogus despatch and telegram I had contrived. Quite rightly, I received a very severe reprimand. I was warned against ever acting in such an irregular fashion again, under the direst penalties. In extenuation, I pointed out to the Councillor that the inquisitive Mr. Q. was now convinced that our difficulty with Russia was over Afghanistan.

I further added that should anyone be dishonourable enough to come into the Chancery and deliberately read confidential documents which he knew were not intended for his eye, I clearly could not be held responsible for any false impressions he might derive from reading them. That, I was told sharply, was no excuse for my conduct. After this "official wigging," the Councillor invited me to dine with him that night, when we laughed loudly over Mr. Q.'s discomfiture. That person became at length such a nuisance that "his name was put on the gate," and he was refused admission to the Embassy.

The great London daily which Mr. Q. represented at Petrograd published some strong articles on the grave menace to the Empire which a change of rulers in Afghanistan might bring about; coupled with Cassandra-like wails over the purblind British statesmen who were wilfully shutting their eyes to this impending danger, as well as to baneful Russian machinations on our Indian frontier. There were also some unflattering allusions to Abdurrahman Khan. I, knowing that the whole story had originated in my own brain, could not restrain a chuckle whilst perusing these jeremiads. After reading some particularly violent screed, the Councillor of Embassy would shake his head at me. "This is more of your work, you wretched boy!" After an interval of forty years this little episode can be recounted without harm.

Talking of newspaper enterprise, many years later, when the Emperor Alexander III died, the editor of a well-known London evening paper, a great friend of mine, told me in confidence of a journalistic "scoop" he was meditating. Alexander III had died at Livadia in the Crimea, and his body was to make a sort of triumphal progress through Russia. The editor (he is no longer with us, but when I term him "Harry" I shall be revealing his identity to the few) was sending out a Frenchman as special correspondent, armed with a goodly store of roubles, and instructions to get himself engaged as temporary assistant to the undertaker in charge of the Emperor's funeral. This cost, I believe, a considerable sum, but the Frenchman, having entered on his gruesome duties, was enabled to furnish the London evening paper with the fullest details of all the funeral ceremonies.

The reason the younger diplomats foregathered so in Petrograd was that, as I said before, Petrograd was to all intents and purposes extra-European. Apart from its charming society, the town, *qua* town, offered but few resources. The younger Continental diplomats felt the entire absence of cafés, of music-halls, and of places of light entertainment very acutely; so they were thrown on each other's society. In Far Eastern posts such as Pekin or Tokyo, the diplomats live entirely amongst themselves. For a European, there are practically no resources whatever in Tokyo. No one could possibly wish to frequent a Japanese theatre, or a Japanese restaurant, when once the novelty had worn off, and even Geisha entertainments are deadly dull to one who cannot understand a word of the language. Let us imagine a party of Europeans arriving at some fashionable

Japanese restaurant for a Geisha entertainment. They will, of course, remove their shoes before proceeding upstairs. I was always unfortunate enough to find on these occasions one or more holes in my socks gaping blatantly. In time one learns in Japan to subject one's socks to a close scrutiny in order to make sure that they are intact, for everyone must be prepared to remove his shoes at all hours of the day. We will follow the Europeans up to a room on the upper floor, tastefully arranged in Japanese fashion, and spotlessly neat and clean. The temperature in this room in the winter months would be Arctic, with three or four "fire-pots" containing a few specks of mildly-glowing charcoal waging a futile contest against the penetrating cold.

The room is apparently empty, but from behind the sliding-panels giggles and titters begin, gradually increasing in volume until the panels slide back, and a number of self-conscious overdressed children step into the room, one taking her place beside each guest. These are "Micos"; little girls being trained as professional Geishas. The European conception of a Geisha is a totally wrong one. They are simply entertainers; trained singers, dancers, and story-tellers. The guests seat themselves clumsily and uncomfortably on the floor and the dinner begins. Japanese dishes are meant to please the eye, which is fortunate, for they certainly do not appeal to the palate. I invariably drew one of the big pots of flowers which always decorate these places close up to me, and consigned to its kindly keeping all the delicacies of the Japaness *cuisine* which were beyond my assimilative powers, such as slices of raw fish sprinkled with sugar, and seasoned with salted ginger. The tiresome little Micos kept up an incessant chatter. Their stories were doubtless extraordinarily humorous to anyone understanding Japanese, but were apt to lose their point for those ignorant of the language. The abortive attempts of the Europeans to eat with chopsticks afforded endless amusement to these bedizened children; they shook with laughter at seeing all the food slide away from these unaccustomed table implements. Not till the dinner was over did the Geishas proper make their appearance. In Japan the amount of bright colour in a woman's dress varies in inverse ratio to her moral rectitude. As our Geishas were all habited in sober mouse-colour, or dull neutral-blue, I can only infer that they were ladies of the very highest respectability. They were certainly wonderfully attractive little people. They were not pretty according to our standards, but there was a vivacity and a sort of air of dainty grace about them that were very captivating. Their singing is frankly awful. I have heard four-footed musicians on the London tiles produce sweeter sounds, but their dancing is graceful to a degree. Unfortunately, one of the favourite amusements of these charming and vivacious little people is to play "Musical Chairs"—without any chairs! They made all the

European men follow them round and round the room whilst two Geishas thrummed on a sort of guitar. As soon as the music stopped everyone was expected to sit down with a bang on the floor. To these little Japs five feet high, the process was easy, and may have seemed good fun; to a middleaged gentleman, "vir pietate gravis," these violent shocks were more than painful, and I failed to derive the smallest amusement from them. No Japanese dinner would be complete without copious miniature cups of saké. This rice-spirit is always drunken hot; it is not disagreeable to the taste, being like warm sherry with a dash of methylated spirit thrown in, but the little saké bottles and cups are a joy to the eye. This innately artistic people delight to lavish loving care in fashioning minute objects; many English drawing-rooms contain saké bottles in enamel or porcelain ranged in cabinets as works of art. Their form would be more familiar to most people than their use.

Japanese always seem to look on a love of colour as showing rather vulgar tastes. The more refined the individual, the more will he adhere to sober black and white and neutral tints in his house and personal belongings. The Emperor's palace in Kyoto is decorated entirely in black and white, with unpainted, unlacquered woodwork, and no colour anywhere. The Kyoto palace of the great Tokugawa family, on the other hand, a place of astounding beauty, blazes with gilding, enamels, and lacquer, as do all the tombs and temples erected by this dynasty. The Tokugawas usurped power as

Shoguns in 1603, reducing the Mikado to a mere figure-head as spiritual Ruler, and the Shoguns ruled Japan absolutely until 1868, when they were overthrown, and Shogun and Mikado were merged into one under the title of Emperor. I fancy that the Japanese look upon the polychrome splendour of all the buildings erected by the Tokugawas as proof that they were very inferior to the ancient dynasty, who contented themselves with plain buildings severely decorated in black and white. The lack of colour in Japan is very noticeable on arriving from untidy, picturesque China. The beautiful neatness and cleanliness of Japan are very refreshing after slovenly China, but the endless rows of little brown, unpainted, tidy houses, looking like so many rabbit hutches, are depressing to a degree. The perpetual earthquakes are responsible for the low elevation of these houses and also for their being invariably built of wood, as is indeed everything else in the country. I was immensely disappointed at the sight of the first temples I visited in Japan. The forms were beautiful enough, but they were all of unpainted wood, without any colour whatever, and looked horribly neutral-tinted. All the famous temples of Kyoto are of plain, unpainted, unvarnished wood. The splendid group of temples at Nikko are the last word in Japanese art. They glow with colour; with scarlet and black lacquer, gilding, enamels, and bronzes, every detail finished like jewellers' work with exquisite craftmanship, and they are amongst the most beautiful things in the world; but they were all erected by the Tokugawa dynasty, as were the equally superb temples in the Shiba Park at Tokyo. This family seemed determined to leave Japan less colourless than they found it; in their great love for scarlet lacquer they must have been the first people who thought of painting a town red.

The same lack of colour is found in the gardens. I had pictured a Japanese garden as a dream of beauty, so when I was shown a heap of stones interspersed with little green shrubs and dwarf trees, without one single flower, I was naturally disappointed, nor had I sufficient imagination to picture a streak of whitewash daubed down a rock as a quivering cascade of foaming water. "Our gardens, sir," said my host, "are not intended to inspire hilarit . . ee, but rather to create a gentle melanchol . . ee." As regards myself, his certainly succeeded in its object.

A friend of mine, whose gardens, not a hundred miles from London, are justly famous, takes immense pride in her Japanese garden, as she fondly imagines it to be. At the time of King George's Coronation she invited the special Japanese Envoys to luncheon, for the express purpose of showing them her gardens afterwards. She kept the Japanese garden to the last as a *bonne-bouche,* half-expecting these children of the Land of the Rising Sun to burst into happy tears at this reminder of their distant island home. The special Envoys thanked her with true Japanese politeness, and loudly expressed their delight at seeing a real English garden. They added that they had never even imagined anything like this in Japan, and begged for a design of it, in order that they might create a real English garden in their native land on their return home.

As I have said, no Japanese woman can wear bright colours without sacrificing her moral reputation, but little girls may wear all the colours of the rainbow until they are eight years old or so. These little girls, with their hair cut straight across their forehead, are very attractive-looking creatures, whereas a Japanese boy, with his cropped head, round face, and projecting teeth, is the most comically hideous little object imaginable. These children's appearance is spoilt by an objectionable superstition which decrees it unlucky to use a pocket-handkerchief on a child until he, or she, is nine years old. The result is unspeakably deplorable.

The interior of our Embassy at Tokyo was rather a surprise. Owing to the constant earthquakes in Tokyo and Yokohama, all the buildings have to be of wood. The British Embassy was built in London (I believe by a very well-known firm in Tottenham Court Road), and was shipped out to Japan complete down to its last detail. The architect who designed it unhappily took a glorified suburban villa as his model. So the Tokyo Embassy house is an enlarged "Belmont," or "The Cedars," or "Tokyo Towers." Every familiar detail is there; the tiled hall, the glazed door into the garden, and the heavy mahogany chimneypieces and overmantels. In the library with its mahogany book-cases, green morocco chairs, and green plush curtains, it was difficult to realise that one was not in Hampstead or Upper Tooting. I always felt that I was quite out of the picture unless I sallied forth at 9 a.m. with a little black bag in my hand, and returned at 6 p.m. with some fish in a bass-basket. In spite of being commonplace, the house was undeniably comfortable. Everything Japanese was rigidly excluded from it. That in far-off lands is very natural. People do not care to be reminded perpetually of the distance they are away from home. In Calcutta the Maidan, the local Hyde Park, has nothing Eastern about it. Except in the Eden Gardens in one corner of it, where there is a splendid tangle of tropical vegetation, there is not one single palm tree on the Maidan. The broad sweeps of turf, clumps of trees, and winding roads make an excellent imitation of Hyde Park transferred to the banks of the Hooghly, and this is intentional. There is one spot in particular, where the tall Gothic spire of St. Paul's Cathedral rises out of a clump of trees beyond a great tank (it may be pointed out that "tank" in India does not refer to a clumsy, mobile engine of destruction, but is the word used for a pool or pond), which might be in Kensington Gardens but for the temperature. The average Briton likes to be reminded of his home, and generally manages to carry it about with him somehow. The Russian Embassy at Tokyo had been built in the same way in Paris and sent out, and was a perfect reproduction of a French Louis XV house. The garden of the British Embassy had one striking feature which I have seen nowhere else; hedges of clipped camellias, four feet high. When these blossomed in the spring, they looked like solid walls of pink, crimson, or white flowers, a really beautiful sight!

Some former British Minister had planted the public roads round the Embassy with avenues of the pink-flowering cherry, as a present to the city of Tokyo. The Japanese affect to look down on the pink cherry, when compared to their adored white cherry-blossom, I suppose because there is colour in it. Certainly the acres of white cherry-blossom in the Uyeno Park at Tokyo are one of the sights of Japan. In no other country in the world would the railways run special trains to enable the country-people to see the cherries in full bloom in this Uyeno Park. The blossom is only supposed to be at its best for three days. In no other country either would people flock by hundreds to a temple, as they did at Kyoto, to look at a locally-famed contrast of red plum-blossom against dark-brown maple leaves. I liked these Japanese country-people. The scrupulously neat old peasant women, with their grey hair combed carefully back, and their rosy faces, were quite attractive. Their intense ceremonious politeness to each other always amused me. Whole family parties would continue bowing to each other for ten minutes on end at railway stations, sucking their breath, and rubbing their knees. When they had finished, someone would recommence, and the whole process would have to be gone through again, the children sucking their breath louder even than their elders. Anybody who has lived in a warm climate must be familiar with the curious sound of thousands of frogs croaking at once in a pond or marsh at night-time. The sound of hundreds of Japanese wooden clogs clattering against the tiles of a railway platform is exactly like that. In the big Shimbashi station at Tokyo, as the clogs pattered over the tiles, by shutting my eyes I could imagine that I was listening to a frogs' orchestra in some large marsh.

Excessive politeness brings at times its own penalty. At the beginning of these reminiscences I have related how I went with a Special Embassy to Rome in my extreme youth. The day before our departure from Rome, King Humbert gave a farewell luncheon party at the Quirinal to the Special British Ambassador and his suite, including of course myself. At this luncheon a somewhat comical incident occurred.

When we took our leave, Queen Margherita, then still radiantly beautiful, offered her hand first to the Special British Ambassador. He, a courtly and gallant gentleman of the old school, at once dropped on one knee, in spite of his age, and kissed the Queen's hand " in the grand manner." The permanent British Ambassador, the late Sir Augustus

Paget, most courteous and genial of men, followed his temporary colleague's example, and also dropped on one knee. The Italian Ministers present could not do less than follow the lead of the foreigners, or show themselves less courteous than the *forestieri*, so they too had perforce to drop on one knee whilst kissing the Queen's hand. A hugely obese Minister, buttoned into the tightest of frockcoats, approached the Queen. With immense difficulty he lowered himself on to one knee, and kissed the Royal hand; but no power on earth seemed equal to raising him to his feet again. The corpulent Minister grew purple in the face; the most ominous sounds of the rending of cloth and linen re-echoed through the room; but still he could not manage to rise. The Queen held out her hand to assist her husband's adipose adviser to regain his feet, but he was too dignified, or too polite, to accept it. The rending of the statesman's most intimate garments became more audible than ever; the portly Minister seemed on the verge of an attack of apoplexy. It must be understood that the Queen was standing alone before the throne, with this unfortunate dignitary kneeling before her; the remainder of the guests were standing in a semicircle some twenty feet away. The Queen's mouth began to twitch ominously, until, in spite of her self-control, after a few preliminary splutters of involuntary merriment, she broke down, and absolutely shook with laughter. Sir Augustus Paget and a Roman Prince came up and saved the situation by raising, with infinite difficulty, the unfortunate

Italian statesman to his feet. As he resumed a standing position, a perfect Niagara of oddments of apparel, of tags and scraps of his most private under-garments, rained upon the floor, and we all experienced a feeling of intense relief when this capable, if corpulent, Cabinet Minister was enabled to regain the background with all his clothing outwardly intact.

And all this came about from an excess of politeness. The East has always been the land of flowery compliments, also the land of hyperbole. I once saw the answer the Viceroy of India had received from a certain tributary Prince, who had been reprimanded in the sharpest fashion by the Government of India. The native Prince had been warned in the bluntest of language that unless he mended his ways at once he would be forthwith deposed, and another ruler put in his place. A list of his recent enormities was added, in order to refresh his memory, and the warning as to the future was again emphasized. The Prince's answer, addressed direct to the Viceroy, began as follows:

"Your Excellency's gracious message has reached me. It was more precious to the eyes than a casket of rubies; sweeter to the taste than a honeycomb; more delightful to the ears than the song of ten thousand nightingales. I spread it out before me, and read it repeatedly: each time with renewed pleasure."

Considering the nature of the communication, that native Prince must have been of a touchingly grateful disposition.

The late Duke of Edinburgh was once presented with an address at Hong Kong from the Corporation of Chinese Merchants, in which he was told, amongst other things, that he "was more glorious than a phœnix sitting in a crimson nest with fourteen golden tails streaming behind him." Surely a charming flight of fancy!

True politeness in China demands that you should depreciate everything of your own and exalt everything belonging to your correspondent. Thus, should you be asking a friend to dinner, you would entreat him "to leave for one evening the silver and alabaster palace in which you habitually dwell, and to condescend to honour the tumble-down vermin-ridden hovel in which I drag out a wretched existence. Furthermore, could you forget for one evening the bird's-nest soup, the delicious sea-slugs, and the plump puppy-dogs on which you habitually feast, and deign to poke your head into my swill-trough, and there devour such loathsome garbage as a starving dog would reject, I shall feel unspeakably honoured." The answer will probably come in some such form as this: "With rapturous delight have I learnt that, thanks to your courtesy, I may escape from the pestilential shanty I inhabit, and pass one unworthy evening in a glorious palace of crystal and gold in your company. After starving for months on putrid offal, I shall at length banquet on unimagined delicacies, etc." Should it be a large dinner-party, it must tax the host's ingenuity to vary the self-depreciatory epithets sufficiently.

The mention of food reminds me that it is an acute difficulty to the stranger in Japan, should he wander off the beaten track and away from European hotels. Japanese use neither bread, butter, nor milk, and these things, as well as meat, are unprocurable in country districts. Europeans miss bread terribly, and the Japanese substitute of cold rice is frankly horrible. Instead of the snowy piles of smoking-hot, beautifully cooked rice of India, rice in Japan means a cold, clammy, gelatinous mass, hideously distasteful to a European interior. That, eggs, and tea like a decoction of hay constitute the standard menu of a Japanese country inn. I never saw either a sheep or cow in Japan, as there is no pasture. The universal bamboo-grass, with its sharp edges, pierces the intestines of any animal feeding on it, and so is worse than useless as fodder for cattle or sheep. All milk and butter are imported in a frozen state from Australia, but do not, of course, penetrate beyond Europe-fashion hotels, as the people of the country do not care for them.

The exquisite neatness of Japanese farm houses, with their black and white walls, thatched roofs, and trim little bamboo fences and gates, is a real joy to the eye of one who has grown accustomed to the slipshod untidy East, or even to the happy-go-lucky methods of the American Continent. I never remember a Japanese village unequipped with either electric light or telephones. I really think geographers must have placed the 180th degree in the wrong place, and that Japs are really the most Western of Westerns, instead of being the most Eastern of Easterns. Pretty and attractive as the Japanese country is, its charm was spoilt for me by the almost total absence of bird and animal life. There are hardly any wild flowers either, except deliciously fragrant wild violets. Being in Japan, it is hardly necessary to say that these violets, instead of being of the orthodox colour, are bright yellow. They would be in Japan. This quaint people who only like trees when they are contorted, who love flowerless gardens, whose grass kills cattle, who have evolved peach, plum and cherry trees which flower gloriously but never bear any fruit, would naturally have yellow violets. They are certainly a wonderfully hardy race. I was at beauful Nikko in the early spring when they were building a dam across the Nikko river. The stream has a tremendous current, and is ice-cold. Men were working at the dam up to their waists in the icy river, and little boys kept bringing them baskets of building stones, up to their necks in the swift current. Both men and boys issued from the river as scarlet as lobsters from the intense cold, and yet they stood about quite unconcernedly in their dripping thin cotton clothes in the keen wind. Had they been Europeans, they would all have died of pneumonia in two days' time. A race must have great powers of endurance that live in houses with paper walls without any heating appliances during the sharp cold of a Japanese winter, and that find thin cotton clothing sufficient for their wants.

The outlines and pleasing details of those black and white country dwellings with the graceful curves of their roofs are a relief to the eye after the endless miles of ugly little brown rabbit hutches of the towns. At Tokyo the enclosure and park of the Emperor's palace lay just outside the gates of our Embassy, surrounded by a moat so broad that it could be almost called a lake. It was curious in the heart of a town to see this moat covered with innumerable wild duck. Although I have been in the Imperial palace at Kyoto, I was never inside the one at Tokyo, so I cannot give any details about it. The glimpses one obtained from outside of its severe black and white outlines recalled a European mediæval castle, and had something strangely familiar about them. I was never fortunate enough either to be invited to an Imperial duck-catching party, which I would have given anything to witness. The idea of catching wild duck in butterfly nets would never occur to anyone but the Japanese. The place where this quaint amusement was indulged in was an extensive tract of flat ground intersected by countless reed-fringed little canals and waterways, much on the lines of a marsh in the Norfolk Broad district. I saw the Ambassador on his return from a duck-catching party. With superhuman efforts, and a vast amount of exercise, he had managed to capture three ducks, and he told me that he had had to run like a hare to achieve even this modest success. All the guests were expected to appear in high hats and frock-coats on these occasions, and I should have dearly loved to see the Ambassador arrayed in frock-coat and high hat bounding hot-foot over the marshes, his butterfly net poised aloft, in pursuit of his quacking quarry. The newspapers informed us the next day that the Crown Prince had headed the list as usual with a bag of twenty-seven ducks, and I always believe what I see in print. Really Europeans start heavily handicapped at this peculiar diversion. I have known many families in England where the sons of the house are instructed from a very early age in riding, and in the art of handling a gun and a trout rod, but even in the most sport-loving British families the science of catching wild duck in butterfly nets forms but seldom part of the sporting curriculum of the rising generation. Though the Imperial family are Shintoists, I expect that the Buddhist horror of taking animal life is at the bottom of this idea of duck-catching, for the ducks are, I believe, all set free again after their capture.

We always heard that the Emperor and his family lived entirely on rice and fish in the frugal Japanese fashion, and that they never tasted meat.

I had the opportunity of seeing a very fine house of sixty rooms, built in strict Japanese style, and just completed. Count Mitsu is one of the few very wealthy men in Japan ; he can also trace his pedigree back for three thousand years. He had built this house in Tokyo, and as it was supposed to be the last word in purity of style ("Itchi-Ban," or "Number One," as the Japanese express it), he very kindly invited the Ambassador and myself to go all over it with him. We had, of course, to remove our shoes on entering, and my pleasure was somewhat marred by the discovery of a large hole in one sock, on which I fancied the gaze of the entire Mitsu family was riveted. Nothing can equal the high-bred courtesy and politeness of Japanese of really ancient lineage. Countess Mitsu, of a family as old as her husband's, had a type of face which we do not usually associate with Japan, and is only found in ladies of the Imperial family and some others equally old. In place of the large head, full cheeks, and flat features of the ordinary Japanese woman, Countess Mitsu and her daughters had thin faces with high aquiline features, giving them an extraordinarily high-bred and distinguished appearance. This great house consisted of a vast number of perfectly empty rooms, destitute of one single scrap of furniture. There was fine matting on the floor, a niche with one kakemono hanging in it, one bronze or other work of art, and a vase with one single flower, and nothing else whatever. The Mitsus being a very high caste family, there was no colour anywhere. The decoration was confined to black and white and beautifully-finished, unpainted, unvarnished woodwork, except for the exquisitely chased bronze door-grips (door-handles would be an incorrect term for these grips to open and close the sliding panels). I must confess that I never saw a more supremely uncomfortable-looking dwelling in my life. The children's nurseries upstairs were a real joy. The panels had been painted by a Japanese artist with everything calculated to amuse a child. There were pictures of pink and blue rabbits, purple frogs, scarlet porcupines, and grass-green guinea-pigs, all with the most comical expressions imaginable on their faces. The lamps were of fish-skin shaped over thin strips of bamboo into the form of the living fish, then highly coloured, and fitted with electric globes inside them ; weird, luminous marine monsters ! Each child had a little Chinese dressing-table of mother-of-pearl eighteen inches high, and a tub of real Chinese "powder-blue" porcelain as a bath. The windows looked on to a fascinating dwarf garden ten feet square, with real waterfalls, tiny rivers of real water, miniature mountains and dwarf trees, all in perfect proportion. It was like looking at an extensive landscape through the wrong end of a telescope.

The polite infants who inhabited this child's paradise received us with immense courtesy, lying at full length on the floor on their little tummies, and wagging their little heads in salutation, till I really thought they would come off.

The most interesting thing in Count Mitsu's house was a beautiful little Shinto temple of bronze-gold lacquer, where all the names of his many ancestors were inscribed on gilt tablets. Here he and all his sons (women take no part in ancestor worship) came nightly, and made a full confession before the tablets of their ancestors of all they had done during the day ; craving for pardon should they have acted in a fashion unworthy of their family and of Japan. The Count and his sons then lighted the little red lamps before the tablets of their forebears to show that they were not forgotten, and placed the exquisitely carved little ivory "ghost-ship" two inches long in its place, should any of their ancestors wish to return that night from the Land of Spirits to their old home.

The underlying idea of undying family affection is rather a beautiful one.

That same evening I went to a very interesting dinner-party at the house of Prince Arisugawa, a son-in-law of the Emperor's. Both the dinner and the house were on European lines, but the main point of interest was that it was a gathering of all the Generals and Admirals who had taken a prominent part in the Russo-Japanese war. I was placed between an Admiral and a General, but found it difficult to communicate with them, Japanese being conspicuously bad linguists. The General could speak a little fairly unintelligible German; the Admiral could stutter a very little Russian. It was a pity that the roads of communication were so blocked for us, for I shall probably never again sit between two men who had had such thrilling experiences. I cursed the builders of the Tower of Babel for erecting this linguistic barrier between us.

I found that I was a full head taller than all the Japanese in the room. Princess Arisugawa appeared later. This tiny, dainty, graceful little lady had the same strongly aquiline type of features as Countess Mitsu, and the same high-bred look of distinction. She was beautifully dressed in European style, and had Rue de la Paix written all over her clothes and her jewels. I have seldom seen anyone with such taking graceful dignity as this daughter of the Imperial house, in spite of her diminutive stature.

The old families in Japan have a pretty custom of presenting every European guest with a little black-and-gold lacquer box, two inches high, full of sweetmeats, of the sort we called in my youth "hundreds and thousands." These little boxes bear on their tops in gold lacquer the badge or crest of the family, thus serving as permanent souvenirs.

In a small community such as the European diplomats formed at Tokyo, the peculiarities and foibles of the "chers collègues" formed naturally an unending topic of conversation. There was one foreign representative who was determined to avoid bankruptcy, could the most rigorously careful regulation of his expenditure avert such a catastrophe. His official position forced him to give occasional dinner-parties, much, I imagine, against his inclinations. He always, in the winter months, borrowed all the available oil-stoves from his colleagues and friends, when one of these festivities was contemplated, in order to warm his official residence without having to go to the expense of fires. He had in some mad fit of extravagance bought two dozen of a really fine claret some years before. The wine had long since been drunk; the bottles he still retained *with their labels.* It was his custom to buy the cheapest and roughest red wine he could find, and then enshrine it in these old bottles with their mendacious labels. At his dinner-parties these time-worn bottles were always ranged down the tables. The evidence of palate and eye was conflicting. The palate (as far as it could discriminate through the awful reek with which the oil-stoves filled the room), pronounced it sour, immature *vin ordinaire.* The label on the bottle proclaimed it Château Margaux of 1874, actually bottled at the Château itself. Politeness dictated that we should compliment our host on this exquisite vintage, which had, perhaps, begun to feel (as we all do) the effects of extreme old age. A cynical Dutch colleague might possibly hazard a few remarks, lamenting the effects of the Japanese climate on "les premiers crus de Bordeaux."

Life at any post would be dull were it not for the little failings of the "chers collègues," which always give one something to talk of.

The Japanese are ruining the beauty of their country by their insane mania for advertising. The railways are lined with advertisements; a beautiful hillside is desecrated by a giant advertisement, cut in the turf, and filled in with white concrete. Even the ugly little streets of brown packing-cases are plastered with advertisements. The fact that these advertisements are all in Chinese characters give them a rather pleasing exotic flavour at first; that soon wears off, and then one is only too thankful not to be able to read them. They remain a hideous disfigurement of a fair land.

One large Japanese-owned department store in Tokyo had a brass band playing in front of it all day, producing an ear-splitting din. The bandsmen were little Japanese boys dressed, of all things in the world, as Highlanders. No one who has not seen it can imagine the intensely grotesque effect of a little stumpy, bandy-legged Jap boy in a red tartan kilt, bare knees, and a Glengarry bonnet. No one who has not heard them can conceive the appalling sounds they produced from their brass instruments, or can form any conception of the Japanese idea of "rag-time."

We have in this country some very competent amateurs who, to judge from the picture papers, have reduced the gentle art of self-advertisement to a science.

I think these ladies would be repaid for the trouble of a voyage to Japan by the new ideas in advertisement they would pick up from that enterprising people. They need not blow their own trumpets, like the little Jap Highlander bandsmen; they can get it done for them as they know, by the Press.

CHAPTER XI

Petrograd through middle-aged eyes—Russians very constant friends—Russia an Empire of shams—Over-centralisation in administration—The system hopeless—A complete change of scene—The West Indies—Trinidad—Personal Character of Nicholas II—The weak point in an Autocracy—The Empress—An opportunity missed—The Great Collapse—Terrible stories—Love of human beings for ceremonial—Some personal apologies—Conclusion.

I RETURNED twice to Petrograd in later years, the last occasion being in 1912. A young man is generally content with the surface of things, and accepts them at their face value, without attempting to probe deeper. With advancing years comes the desire to test beneath the surface. To the eye, there is but little difference between electro-plate and solid silver, though one deep scratch on the burnished expanse of the former is sufficient to reveal the baser metal underlying it.

Things Russian have for some reason always had a strange attraction for me, and their glamour had not departed even after so many years. It was pleasant, too, to hear the soft, sibilant Russian tongue again. My first return visit was at midsummer, and seeing Peter's City wreathed in the tender vivid greenery of Northern foliage, and bathed in sunshine, I wondered how I could ever have mentally labelled it with the epithet "dreary." Rising from the clear swift-rushing waters of the many-channelled Neva, its stately pillared classical buildings outlined through the soft golden haze in half-tones of faintest cobalt and rose-madder, this Northern Venice appeared a dream-city, almost unreal in its setting of blue waters and golden domes, lightly veiled in opal mist.

Russians are not as a rule long-lived, and the great majority of my old friends had passed away. I could not help being affected by the manner in which the survivors amongst them welcomed me back. "Cher ami," said the bearer of a great Russian name to me, "thirty-three years ago we adopted you as a Russian. You were a mere boy then, you are now getting an old man, but as long as any of your friends of old days are alive, our houses are always open to you, and you will always find a place for you at our tables, without an invitation. We Russians do not change, and we never forget our old friends. We know that you like us and our country, and my husband and I offer you all we have." No one could fail to be touched by such steadfast friendship, so characteristic of these warm-hearted people.

The great charm of Russians with three or four hundred years of tradition behind them is their entire lack of pretence and their hatred of shams. They are absolutely natural. They often gave me as their reason for disliking foreigners the artificiality of non-Russians, though they expressly exempted our own nationality from this charge. That is, I think, the reason why most Englishmen get on so well with educated Russians.

Seeing Petrograd with the wearied eyes of experienced middle age, I quite realised that the imposing palaces that front the line of the quays and seem almost to float on the Neva, are every one of them built on piles, driven deep into the marshy subsoil. Every single house in the city rests on the same artificial base. Montferrand the Frenchman's great cathedral of St. Isaac has had its north front shored up by scaffolding for thirty years. Otherwise it would have collapsed, as the unstable subsoil is unable to bear so great a burden. On the Highest Authority we know that only a house built on the rock can endure. This city of Petrograd was built on a quagmire, and was typical, in that respect, of the vast Empire of which it was the capital: an Empire erected by Peter on shifting sand. The whole fabric of this Empire struck my maturer senses as being one gigantic piece of "camouflage."

For instance, a building close to St. Isaac's bears on its stately front the inscription "Governing Senate" (I may add that the terse, crisp Russian for this is "Pravitelsvouyuschui Senat"). To an ordinary individual the term would seem to indicate what it says; he would be surprised to learn that, so far from "governing," the Senate had neither legislative nor administrative powers of its own. It was merely a consultative body without any delegated initiative; only empowered to recommend steps for carrying into effect the orders it received.

And so with many other things. There were imposing façades, with awe-inspiring inscriptions, but I had a curious feeling that everything stopped at the façade, and there was nothing behind it.

Students of history will remember how, on the occasion of Catherine the Great's visit to the Crimea, her favourite, Potemkin, had "camouflage" villages erected along the line of her progress, so that wherever she went she found merry peasants (specially selected from the Imperial theatres) singing and dancing amidst flower-wreathed cottages. These villages were then taken down, and re-erected some fifty miles further along the Empress's way, with the same inhabitants. It was really a triumph of "camouflage," and did great credit to Potemkin's inventive faculty. Catherine returned North with most agreeable recollections of the teeming population of the Crimea; of its delightfully picturesque villages, and of the ideal conditions of life prevailing there.

The whole Russian Empire appeared to my middle-aged eyes to be like Potemkin's toy villages.

My second later visit to Petrograd was in 1912, in midwinter, when I came to the unmistakable conclusion that the epithet "dreary" was not misplaced. The vast open spaces and broad streets with their scanty traffic were unutterably depressing during the short hours of uncertain daylight, whilst the whirling snowflakes fell incessantly, and the low, leaden sky pressed like a heavy pall over this lifeless city of perpetual twilight.

The particular business on which I had gone to Petrograd took me daily to the various Ministries, and their gloomy interiors became very familiar to me.

I then saw that in these Ministries the impossible had been attempted in the way of centralisation. The principle of the Autocracy had been carried into the administrative domain, and every trivial detail affecting the government of an Empire stretching from the Pacific to the Baltic was in theory controlled by one man, the Minister of the Department concerned. Russians are conspicuously lacking in initiative and in organising power. The lack of initiative is perhaps the necessary corollary of an Autocracy, for under an Autocracy it would be unsafe for any private individual to show much original driving power: and organisation surely means successful delegation. A born organiser chooses his subordinates with great care; having chosen them, he delegates certain duties to them, and as long as they perform these duties to his satisfaction he does not interfere with them. The Russian system was just the reverse: everything was nominally concentrated in the hands of one man. A really able and zealous Minister might possibly have settled a hundredth part of the questions daily submitted for his personal decision. It required no great political foresight to understand that, were this administrative machine subjected to any unusual strain, it would collapse into hopeless confusion.

Being no longer young, I found the penetrating damp cold of Petrograd very trying. The airlessness too of the steam-heated and hermetically sealed houses affected me. I had, in any case, intended to proceed to the West Indies as soon as my task in Petrograd was concluded. As my business occupied a far longer time than I had anticipated, I determined to go direct to London from Petrograd, stay two nights there, and then join the mail steamer for the West Indies.

Thus it came about that I was drinking my morning coffee in a room of the British Embassy at Petrograd, looking through the double windows at the driving snowflakes falling on the Troitsky Square, at the frozen hummocks of the Neva, and at the sheepskin-clothed peasants plodding through the fresh-fallen snowdrifts, whilst the grey cotton-wool sky seemed to press down almost on to the roofs of the houses, and the golden needle of the Fortress Church gleamed dully through the murky atmosphere. Three weeks afterwards to a day, I was sitting in the early morning on a balcony on the upper floor of Government House, Trinidad, clad in the lightest of pyjamas, enjoying the only approach to coolness to be found in that sultry island. The balcony overlooked the famous Botanic Gardens which so enraptured Charles Kingsley. In front of me rose a gigantic Saman tree, larger than any oak, one mass of tenderest green, and of tassels of silky pink blossoms. At dawn, the dew still lay on those blossoms, and swarms of humming-birds, flashing living jewels of ruby, sapphire, and emerald, were darting to and fro taking their toll of the nectar. The nutmeg trees were in flower, perfuming the whole air, and the fragrance of a yellow tree-gardenia, an importation from West Africa, was almost overpowering. The chatter of the West Indian negroes, and of the East Indian coolies employed in the Botanic Gardens, replaced the soft, hissing Russian language, and over the gorgeous tropical tangle of the gardens the Venezulean mountains of the mainland rose mistily blue across the waters of the Gulf of Paria. I do not believe that in three short weeks it would be possible to find a greater change in climatic, geographical, or social conditions. From a temperature of 5° below zero to 94° in the shade; from the Gulf of Finland to the Spanish Main; from snow and ice to the exuberant tropical vegetation of one of the hottest islands in the world! The change, too, from the lifeless, snow-swept streets of Petrograd, monotonously grey in the sad-coloured Northern winter daylight, to the gaily painted bungalows of the white inhabitants of the Port-of-Spain, standing in gardens blazing with impossibly brilliant flowers of scarlet, orange, and vivid blue, quivering under the fierce rays of the sun, was sufficiently startling. The only flowers I have ever seen to rival the garish rainbow brilliance of the gardens of Port-of-Spain were the painted ones in the "Zauber-Garten" in the second act of "Parsifal," as given at Bayreuth.

It so happened that when Nicholas II visited India in 1890 as Heir-Apparent, I stayed in the same house with him for ten days, and consequently saw a great deal of him. He was, I am convinced, a most conscientious man, intensely anxious to fulfill his duty to the people he would one day rule; but he was inconstant of purpose, and his intellectual equipment was insufficient for his responsibilties. The fatal flaw in an Autocracy is that everything obviously hinges on the personal character of the Autocrat. It would be absurd to expect an unbroken series of rulers of first-class ability. It is, I suppose, for this reason that the succession to the Russian throne was, in theory at all events, not hereditary. The Tsars of old nominated their successors, and I think I am right in saying that the Emperors still claimed the privilege. In fact, to set any limitations to the power of an Autocrat would be a contradiction in terms.

Nicholas II was always influenced by those surrounding him, and it cannot be said that he chose his associates with much discretion. There was, in particular, one fatal influence very near indeed to him. From those well qualified to judge, I hear that it is unjust to accuse the Empress of being a Germanophil, or of being in any way a traitor to the interests of her adopted country. She was obsessed with one idea: to hand on the Autocracy intact to her idolised little son, and she had, in addition, a great love of power. When the love of power takes possession of a woman, it seems to change her whole character, and my own experience is that no woman will ever voluntarily surrender one scrap of that power, be the consequences what they may. When to a naturally imperious nature there is joined a neurotic, hysterical temperament, the consequences can be disastrous. The baneful influence of the obscene illiterate monk Rasputin over the Empress is a matter of common knowledge, and she, poor woman, paid dearly enough for her faults.

I always think that Nicholas II missed the great opportunity of his life on that fateful Sunday, January 22, 1905, when thousands of workmen, headed by Father Gapon (who subsequently proved to be an *agent provocateur* in the pay of the police), marched to the Winter Palace and clamoured for an interview with their Emperor. Had Nicholas II gone out entirely alone to meet the deputations, as I feel sure his father and grandfather would have done, I firmly believe that it would have changed the whole course of events; but his courage failed him. A timid Autocrat is self-condemned. Instead of meeting their Sovereign, the crowd were met by machine-guns. In 1912, Nicholas II had only slept *one night* in Petrograd since his accession, and the Empress had only made day visits. Not even the Ambassadresses had seen the Empress for six years, and there had been no Court entertainments at all.

The Imperial couple remained in perpetual seclusion at Tsarskoe Selo.

In my days, Alexander II was constantly to be seen driving in the streets of Petrograd entirely alone and unattended, without any escort whatever. The only things that marked out his sledge were the two splendid horses (the one in shafts, the loose "pristashka" galloping alongside in long traces), and the kaftan of his coachman, which was green instead of the universal blue of public and private carriages alike.

The low mutterings of the coming storm were very audible in 1912. Personally, I thought the change would take the form of a "Palace Revolution," so common in Russian history; *i.e.*, that the existing Sovereign would be dethroned and another installed in his place.

I cannot say how thankful I am that so few of my old friends lived to see the final collapse, and that they were spared the agonies of witnessing the subsequent orgies of murder, spoliation, and lust that overwhelmed the unhappy land and deluged it in blood.

Horrible stories have reached us of a kindly, white-headed old couple being imprisoned for months in a narrow cell of the Fortress, and then being taken out at dawn, and butchered without trial; of a highly cultivated old lady of seventy-six being driven from her bed by the mob, and thrust into the bitter cold of a Petrograd street in January, in her night-dress, and there clubbed to death in the snow. God grant that these stories may be untrue; the evidence, though, is terribly circumstantial, and from Russia comes only an ominous silence.

If I am asked what will be the eventual outcome in Russia, I hazard no prophecies. The strong vein of fatalism in the Russian character must be taken into consideration, also the curious lack of initiative. They are a people who revel in endless futile talk, and love to get drunk on words and phrases. Eighty per cent. of the population are grossly ignorant peasants, living in isolated communities, and I fail to see how they can take any combined action. It must be remembered that, with the exception of Lenin, the men who have grasped the reins of power are not Russians, but Jews, mainly of German or Polish origin. They do not, therefore, share the fatal inertness of the Russian temperament.

I started with the idea of giving some description of a state of things which has, perhaps, vanished for all time from what were five years ago the three great Empires of Eastern Europe.

There is, I think, inherent in all human beings a love of ceremonial. The great influence the Roman and Eastern Churches exercise over their adherents is due, I venture to say, in a great measure to their gorgeous ceremonial. In proof of this, I would instance lands where a severer form of religion prevails, and where this innate love of ceremonial finds its rest in the elaborate ritual of Masonic and kindred bodies, since it is denied it in ecclesiastical matters. The reason that Buddhism, imported from China into Japan in the sixth century, succeeded so largely in ousting Shintoism, the ancient national religion, was that there is neither ritual nor ceremonial in a Shinto temple, and the complicated ceremonies of Buddhism supplied this curious craving in human nature, until eventually Buddhism and Shintoism entered into a sort of ecclesiastical partnership together.

I have far exceeded the limits which I started by assigning to myself and, in extenuation, can only plead that old age is proverbially garrulous. I am also fully conscious that I have at times strayed far from my subject, but in excuse I can urge that but few people have seen, in five different continents, as much of the surface of this globe and of its inhabitants as it has fallen to my lot to do. Half-forgotten incidents, irrelevant it may be to the subject in hand, crowd back to the mind, and tempt one far afield. It is quite possible that these bypaths of reminiscence, though interesting to the writer, may prove wearisome to the reader, so for them I tender my apologies.

I have endeavoured to transfer to others pictures which remain very clear-cut and vivid in my own mind. I cannot tell whether I have succeeded in doing this, and I hazard no opinion as to whether the world is a gainer or a loser by the disappearance of the pomp and circumstance, the glitter and glamour of the three great Courts of Eastern Europe.

The curtain has been rung down, perhaps definitely, on the brave show. The play is played; the scenery set for the great spectacle is either ruined or else wantonly destroyed; the puppets who took part in the brilliant pageant are many of them (God help them!) broken beyond power of repair. —*Finita la commedia!*

INDEX

INDEX

L

M

N

O

P

Q

R

S

T

www.ingramcontent.com/pod-product-compliance
Lightning Source LLC
Chambersburg PA
CBHW051057311025
34804CB00027B/110
9781417922666